Nature's Suit

SERIES IN CONTINENTAL THOUGHT

Editorial Board

Ted Toadvine, Chairman, University of Oregon
Elizabeth A. Behnke, Study Project in Phenomenology of the Body
David Carr, Emory University
James Dodd, New School University
Lester Embree, Florida Atlantic University
José Huertas-Jourda, Wilfrid Laurier University†
Joseph J. Kockelmans, Pennsylvania State University
William R. McKenna, Miami University
Algis Mickunas, Ohio University
J. N. Mohanty, Temple University
Dermot Moran, University College Dublin
Thomas Nenon, University of Memphis
Rosemary Rizo-Patron de Lerner, Pontificia Universidad Católica del Perú, Lima
Thomas M. Seebohm, Johannes Gutenberg Universität, Mainz
Gail Soffer, Rome, Italy
Elizabeth Ströker, Universität Köln†
Nicolas de Warren, Wellesley College
Richard M. Zaner, Vanderbilt University

International Advisory Board

Suzanne Bachelard, Université de Paris†
Rudolf Boehm, Rijksuniversiteit Gent
Albert Borgmann, University of Montana
Amedeo Giorgi, Saybrook Institute
Richard Grathoff, Universität Bielefeld
Samuel Ijsseling, Husserl-Archief te Leuven
Alphonso Lingis, Pennsylvania State University
Werner Marx, Albert-Ludwigs Universität, Freiburg†
David Rasmussen, Boston College
John Sallis, Boston College
John Scanlon, Duquesne University
Hugh J. Silverman, State University of New York, Stony Brook
Carlo Sini, Università di Milano
Jacques Taminiaux, Louvain-la-Neuve
D. Lawrence Wieder†
Dallas Willard, University of Southern California†

Nature's Suit

Husserl's Phenomenological Philosophy of the Physical Sciences

LEE HARDY

OHIO UNIVERSITY PRESS / ATHENS

Ohio University Press, Athens, Ohio 45701
ohioswallow.com
© 2013 by Ohio University Press
All rights reserved

To obtain permission to quote, reprint, or otherwise reproduce or
distribute material from
Ohio University Press publications, please contact our rights and
permissions department at
(740) 593-1154 or (740) 593-4536 (fax).

Printed in the United States of America
Ohio University Press books are printed on acid-free paper.∞ ™

20 19 18 17 16 15 14 13   5 4 3 2 1

Library of Congress Cataloging-in-Publication Data

Hardy, Lee.
  Nature's suit : Husserl's phenomenological philosophy of the physical sciences / Lee Hardy.
    pages cm. — (Series in Continental thought ; No. 45)
  Includes bibliographical references and index.
  ISBN 978-0-8214-2065-2 (hc : alk. paper) — ISBN 978-0-8214-2066-9 (pb : alk. paper)
  — ISBN 978-0-8214-4470-2 (pdf)
  1. Husserl, Edmund, 1859–1938. 2. Phenomenology. 3. Physical sciences—Philosophy.
I. Title.
  B3279.H94H359 2014
  193—dc23
                                2013038522

> The rigor of science requires that we distinguish
> well the undraped figure of nature from the bright
> vesture with which we clothe it at our pleasure.
>
> —Heinrich Hertz

> Mathematics and mathematical science, as a garb of ideas
> ... encompasses everything which, for scientists and the
> educated generally, represents the lifeworld, dresses it up
> as "objectively actual and true" nature.
> It is through the garb of ideas that we take
> for true being what is actually a method.
>
> —Edmund Husserl

CONTENTS

Acknowledgments	ix
Abbreviations	xi
Introduction	1
1. Husserl: Realist or Instrumentalist?	1
2. Laws and Theories	5
3. The Plan of This Study	8

Part One: Husserl's Phenomenological Philosophy of Science

1 The Idea of Science in Husserl and the Tradition	13
1. The Classical Idea of Science	15
2. The Idea of Science in Husserl's Phenomenology	17
3. The Problem of Empirical Science: Locke	20
4. The Problem of Empirical Science: Husserl	26
5. The Unity of the Empirical Sciences	28
6. Explanation in the Empirical Sciences	31
7. The Laws of Empirical Science	34
8. Empirical Science as Science	35
9. The Idealization of the Idea of Science	36
10. Summary	38
2 Husserl's Phenomenology and the Foundations of Science	40
1. Pure Logic as a *Wissenschaftslehre*	45
2. Regional Ontology	57
3. Transcendental Consciousness as the Ground of the Sciences	61
4. Phenomenology as the All-Embracing Foundational Science	72

Part Two: Evidence and the Positing of Existence in Husserl's Phenomenology

3 Truth, Evidence, and Existence in Husserl's Phenomenology	77
1. Knowledge, Evidence, and Truth	83
2. Evidence as an Ideal Possibility	91
3. The Fallibility of Occurrent Cases of Evidence	93

4. Evidence and Justification	96
5. The Rational Indubitability of the Principle of Evidence	97
6. Summary and Transition	100
4 Evidence, Rationality, and Existence in Husserl's Phenomenology	102
1. Husserl's Theory of Rationality: *Ideas* I	103
2. The Strong Formulation and Philosophical Rationality	115
3. Rationality in Nontheoretical Contexts	118
4. Positive Scientific Rationality	121

Part Three: The Problem of Theoretical Existence in Husserl's Philosophy of the Physical Sciences

5 Physical Things, Idealized Objects, and Theoretical Entities	129
1. The Physical Thing	133
2. Geometry and the Physical Thing	146
3. Geometry and Physical Science	151
6 Consciousness, Perception, and Existence	163
1. Perceptions and Existence	166
2. Consciousness and Existence	168
3. The "Existence-Independence" of Intentional Relations	180
4. The Ontological Status of the Noema	186
5. Summary	191
Conclusion	195
1. Husserl's "Dogmatism"	195
2. The "Ambiguity" of Husserl's Philosophy of Science	197
3. Husserl's "Instrumentalism"	198
4. Husserl's "Provisional Instrumentalism"	201
5. Summary and Prospect	206
Notes	209
Bibliography	231
Index	245

ACKNOWLEDGMENTS

This book has been a long time coming, and so has accumulated a fair number of debts of gratitude along the way. Reaching back to the early period of my philosophical formation, I should like to thank a number of my former professors: Lester Embree, John Scanlon, Joseph Kockelmans, and Elisabeth Ströker, from whom I learned much about Husserl; and Larry Laudan, Carl Hempel, Wilfrid Sellars, and Kenneth Schaffner, from whom I learned much about the philosophy of science. I should also like to thank my colleagues at Calvin College. A number of the chapters of this work went through the dreaded Tuesday Colloquium of the philosophy department at Calvin College. The criticisms received there were to the point, usually helpful, and always delivered in a spirit of trust and friendship. I would be remiss if I did not pick out Del Ratzsch and Stephen Wykstra—both philosophers of science—for special thanks. John Van Dyke, of the physics department of the University of Illinois, reviewed the entire manuscript. I am grateful for his perceptive comments.

Thanks are also due to a number of colleagues across the Atlantic: to Ursala Panzer of the Husserl Archives at the University of Köln; to Elisabeth Ströker again, but this time as my host at the University of Köln during a sabbatical stay; to Ullrich Melle, present director of the Husserl Archives, for permission to make use of material from the unpublished manuscripts of Husserl; and to Rochus Sowa of the Husserl Archives, for his careful and thorough review of the unpublished material I incorporated into my text.

A couple of institutions are also on my thank-you list: Springer Science+Business Media B.V., for kind permission to publish a revised version of my article "The Idea of Science in Husserl and the Tradition," which appeared in *Phenomenology of Natural Science*, edited by Lee Hardy and Lester E. Embree (Dordrecht: Kluwer, 1992), 1–34. That piece appears as chapter 1 in this volume. My thanks also to the National Endowment for the Humanities for a Travel to Collections grant in support of my sabbatical work at the Husserl Archives in Köln, Germany; and to the Calvin College Alumni Association for a faculty research grant in support of the same endeavor.

ABBREVIATIONS

Simple citations of Husserl's works are included in the body of the text (e.g., C, 66 / H VI, 67). The English translation is given first, in the form of an abbreviation of its title followed by the page number. Where appropriate, the reference to the standard German edition of Husserl's works, *Husserliana*, is given after the slash with the letter *H*, followed by the volume number in roman numerals and the page number. For Husserl's *Logos* article of 1910, "Philosophie als Strenge Wissenschaft," the Berlinger edition is cited (*PSW*). The unpublished English translation by Dorion Cairns, "Philosophy as a Strict Science" (PSS), is used and cited for the English quotations of this work. But because the Cairns translation is not complete, the Quentin Lauer translation, "Philosophy as a Rigorous Science" (PRS), is sometimes used. The abbreviations for the English titles of Husserl's major works are as follows:

C	*The Crisis of the European Sciences and Transcendental Phenomenology*
CM	*Cartesian Meditations*
EJ	*Experience and Judgment*
FTL	*Formal and Transcendental Logic*
ID I	*Ideas Pertaining to a Pure Phenomenology and to a Phenomenological Philosophy*, volume I
ID II	*Ideas Pertaining to a Pure Phenomenology and to a Phenomenological Philosophy*, volume II
ID III	*Ideas Pertaining to a Pure Phenomenology and to a Phenomenological Philosophy*, volume III
IP	*The Idea of Phenomenology*
LI I	*Logical Investigations*, book I
LI II	*Logical Investigations*, book II

POA	*Philosophy of Arithmetic*
PP	*Phenomenological Psychology*
PRS	"Philosophy as a Rigorous Science"
PSS	"Philosophy as a Strict Science"
PSW	*Philosophie als Strenge Wissenschaft*

I have also made in-text citations of a number of classic works from the philosophical tradition, for instance, Plato's *Republic* and John Locke's *An Essay Concerning Human Understanding*. Because so many editions of these works are now available, I could not assume that my readers use the same edition I use, and therefore I could not assume that my page numbers align with theirs. References are made to book, chapter, and section in most cases; for Plato and Aristotle I use the page numbers of the canonical Greek texts, which appear in the margins of most English translations of their works. The following abbreviations are also used in the text:

Enquiry	*An Enquiry Concerning Human Understanding* (Hume)
Essay	*An Essay Concerning Human Understanding* (Locke)
PA	*Posterior Analytics* (Aristotle)
Republic	*The Republic* (Plato)

INTRODUCTION

In an article titled "Husserl's Phenomenology and Scientific Realism" Joseph Rouse notes that "those philosophers of science at all familiar with Husserl tend to associate him with views akin to instrumentalism, which has been largely discredited today; he is therefore thought to be of historical interest at best."[1] It is not difficult to find evidence in support of this statement. In his comments on a paper by John Compton, for instance, Ernan McMullin refers to Husserl's orientation in the philosophy of science as "broadly instrumentalist."[2] This orientation was due, McMullin surmises, to the fact that "Husserl shared the generally positivist understanding of natural science in the middle Europe of his day."[3] Gary G. Gutting, in his article titled "Husserl and Scientific Realism," holds that Husserl's position on science in the Galileo analysis of the *Crisis* is "anti-realist." Furthermore, he takes Husserl's antirealism to be based upon certain theses about the nature of empirical science often associated with positivism.[4] In his article "Husserl's Later Philosophy of Natural Science" Patrick A. Heelan also claims that Husserl was an antirealist with respect to scientific theories.[5] In his contribution to *The Cambridge Companion to Husserl*, Herman Philipse takes it that Husserl's philosophy of science, following Bishop Berkeley and Ernst Mach, was clearly instrumentalist.[6]

1. HUSSERL: REALIST OR INSTRUMENTALIST?

Indeed, there seems to be a consensus in the secondary literature that Husserl's understanding of science was deeply indebted to the positivism of his day and thus inclined toward an instrumentalist interpretation of scientific theories. "Husserl's approach to the sciences of nature," remarks Aurelio Rizzacasa, "with its idea of the objectivity of principles and its insistence on induction and verification, is very close to positivism in spite of the fact that he has rejected its philosophical consequences."[7] In his comparison of Husserl's and Heidegger's philosophies of science, Theodore J. Kisiel claims that "the favorite theses of logical positivism in its nadir of instrumentalism and operationalism still seem to lurk behind Husserl's formulations of his own phenomenological positivism: the empty language of mathematics is applied to the invariant mass of the lifeworld merely in order to acquire a measure of predictive control over it. Physical theories are thus reduced to merely an abstract interlude and useful complication in our practical concerns, and therefore can be suppressed at any time without the loss of any real knowledge."[8]

Such interpretations of Husserl's philosophy of science are not without foundation in the Husserlian corpus. One of the major theses of the positivist philosophy of science is that scientific theories do not aim at giving us a literally true account of the unobservable deep structure of nature, but rather sophisticated symbolic machinery for generating useful predictions about observable phenomena within nature. It would seem that Husserl agrees. In the "Prolegomena" to the *Logical Investigations*, he claims that those involved in the empirical sciences are "more concerned with practical results and mastery than with essential insight" (*LI* I, 245 / *H* XVIII, B 253). In *Ideas* I he points out that the utility of physics consists in the fact that "any cognition in physics serves as an index to the course of possible experiences with the things pertaining to the senses and their occurrences found in those experiences. It serves, therefore, to orient us in the world of current experience in which we all live and act" (*ID* I, 85 / *H* III 1, 83; translation modified). In the laws of the physical sciences, "the functional co-variation of empirical phenomena are generalized and fixed with exact, mathematical precision.... Thus one can outline the empirical regularities of the practical life-world which are to be expected. In other words, if one has the formula [i.e., the law], one already possesses, in advance, the practically desired prediction of what is to be expected with empirical certainty in the intuitively given world of concretely actual life, in which mathematics is merely a special praxis" (*C*, 43 / *H* VI, 43).

Furthermore, in the *Crisis*, Husserl claims that the objective correlates of the mathematical laws of the physical sciences do not really exist. For the proper objects of such laws are idealized, mathematical objects, not real physical things. The "essential principle" behind Galilean physics, indeed, behind modern mathematical physics in general, is that nature is, in itself, mathematical (*C*, 53 / *H* VI, 53). In the science of Galileo, we can already detect, Husserl claims, the "surreptitious substitution of the mathematically substructed world of idealities for the only real world, the one that is actually given through perception, that is ever experienced and experienceable—our everyday life-world" (C, 48–49 / H VI, 48–49). Here, however, the practitioners of modern science have been "misled into taking these formulae and their formula meaning for the true being of nature itself" (C, 43–44 / H VI, 43). In this way nature as it appears to us in sensuous intuition gets demoted to the status of "mere appearance," while nature as it is projected in the physical sciences is dignified by such honorific titles as "objective world," "true being," and "nature in itself" (C, 29 / H VI, 27). They fail to realize that

> the "objective" world is a mere ideal construct, developed for the sake of making exact laws possible. Mathematics and mathematical science, as a garb of ideas . . . encompasses everything which, for scientists and the educated generally, represents the life-world, dresses it up as "objectively actual and true" nature. It is through the garb of ideas that we take for true being what is actually a method—a method which is designed for the purpose of progressively improving, *in infinitum*, through "scientific" predictions the rough predictions which are the only ones originally possible within the sphere of what is actually experienced and experienceable in the life-world. (C, 51–52 / H VI, 52)

The phenomenological critique of modern mathematical physics, then, is to expose the objective physical world for the construct it is by recourse to the mental processes of abstraction and idealization by which it was constituted. "What Husserl criticized about science," Heelan points out, "was not that it used mathematical models but that, (generally) led by a false metaphysics, it (generally) mistook them for reality."[9]

In light of the above, there would seem to be at least strong prima facie evidence for the position that Husserl's philosophy of science is committed to some form of instrumentalism. Husserl characterizes the laws of the physical sciences as nothing more than sophisticated instruments of prediction; and he claims that the proper objects of the laws of those sciences enjoy, at best, an ideal, mathematical existence, not a real, physical existence. In some important sense the physical sciences do not describe the real world.

Nonetheless, there are a number of Husserl interpreters who would claim that Husserl's phenomenology is consistent with a realistic construal of the physical sciences. Francis J. Zucker states that the phenomenological method takes a "basically realist stance" on science and thus rejects all forms of instrumentalism.[10] Joseph Rouse maintains that Husserl "would not use his account of idealization as an argument for anti-realism about theoretical entities."[11] Furthermore, Husserl's phenomenology on the whole is "consistent" with the implicit realism of the practicing physical scientist.[12] In line with these views, Gail Soffer claims that "a consistent development of Husserl's thought does not lead to instrumentalism, but to an epistemically sophisticated version of realism."[13]

A middle position has been developed by Charles W. Harvey. He admits that "there is a definite strain in his [Husserl's] thinking toward an instrumentalistic position in the philosophy of science."[14] But, he claims, Husserl's instrumentalism is "moderate" and only "provisional."[15] This is because Husserl denies real physical existence only to those entities that are imperceptible in principle. But many of the entities that now pass for theoretical entities because they are currently imperceptible may become perceptible in the future with the technological advance of scientific instrumentation. They are imperceptible only in fact, not in principle. In section 52 of *Ideas* I, it appears that Husserl classifies such theoretical entities as atoms and ions among those things that are imperceptible in principle. Here, however, Husserl "was victim to the historical contingencies surrounding the vision of egos."[16] With the invention of the cloud chamber, it is now possible to perceive ions, Harvey claims. Thus what was formerly posited as a theoretical entity is no longer such. Many of the entities posited as theoretical at one point in time may at some later point in time become perceptible by means of the appropriate instruments. Since Husserl allows for the real physical existence of entities that may at this point be imperceptible—but are not in principle imperceptible—his instrumentalism is only provisional.

Clearly the question of Husserl's instrumentalism remains largely unsettled in the secondary literature. There is little agreement on the question of whether the Husserl philosophy of science is committed to instrumentalism or realism, or in what sense it is committed to instrumentalism or realism. In addition to providing a general orientation to Husserl's philosophy of science, the chief aim of this study is to make a contribution to the resolution of this issue by taking up in depth the problem of theoretical existence in Husserl's philosophy of the physical sciences. My primary thesis will be that Husserl was indeed an instrumentalist, but that his instrumentalism is restricted to an interpretation of scientific laws, not theories. His phenomenolgy is in fact consistent with a realistic construal of scientific theories.

2. LAWS AND THEORIES

In his introductory essay to *The Structure of Scientific Theories*, Frederick Suppe claims that within the philosophy of science, the problem of the "nature and structure of scientific theories" has preeminence, since "theories are the vehicle of scientific knowledge."[17] "It is only a slight exaggeration," he continues, "to claim that a philosophy of science is little more than an analysis of theories and their roles in the scientific enterprise."[18] The overriding concern within the Anglo-American secondary literature on Husserl's philosophy of science about the question of Husserl's instrumentalism reflects Suppe's conviction that the theory of scientific theory is central to the philosophy of science. Thus the question of whether Husserl's philosophy of science is committed to a realist or an instrumentalist interpretation of scientific theories is quite understandably the first question that will be addressed to Husserl within anglophone circles. My intention in this study to give an answer to this question that is both intelligible within the contemporary Anglo-American discussion of science and faithful to Husserl's phenomenological approach to science.

Because my thesis hangs upon the distinction between laws and theories, it would be prudent at the outset to indicate in a rough and preliminary way what I have in mind by this distinction. Scientific laws specify the functional interdependence of quantified physical variables. As such, their intent is to capture lawlike regularities in the behavior of empirical phenomena.[19] Galileo's law of free-falling bodies, which determines the velocity of free-falling bodies as a function of lapse time, and Boyle's law, which specifies the pressure of a gas as a function of temperature and volume, are examples of such laws. They state *how* empirical objects behave. Free-falling bodies accelerate at a rate proportional to the square of the elasped time of their fall; the pressure of a gas within a given container is inversely proportional to the volume of that container. But laws do not explain *why* empirical objects behave the way they in fact do. Scientific theories are developed and proposed in order to provide just such an explanation. Typically, theories explain by postulating unobservable entities that causally interact in such a way as to produce the regular behavior of empirical objects captured in scientific laws. For the law of free-falling bodies there is the theory of gravitational force; for the gas laws there is kinetic theory. As Bas C. van Fraassen characterizes the "generally accepted" account of theories, "theories account for the phenomena (which means, the observable processes and structures) by postulating other processes and structures not directly accessible to observation."[20] Others agree. The causal interaction of the entities postulated by the theory, writes Richard N. Boyd, are to "explain the predicted regularities in the behavior of observable phenomena."[21] Peter Kosso counts as a theory "any description of the unexperienced world that is part of what accounts for and helps us understand the experienced world."[22] Stathis Psillos, in his defense of scientific realism, states that theories "explain and predict observable phenomena by reference to unobserved phenomena."[23] This is the received view of the nature and role of scientific theories.

Realist and instrumentalist interpretations of scientific theories differ with respect to the semantic value they assign to theories and the ontological status they accord their corresponding objects. A realist account of scientific theories claims that scientific theories are intended to be true, and that theoretical terms are intended to refer to physical realities. Thus the evidence we have for the truth of a theory will at the same time move us to accept the existence of the entities as postulated by that theory. As Suppe puts it, scientific theories, if true, refer to "real but nonobservable physical entities or their attributes. For example, 'electron jump' as a term in VT [the theoretical vocabulary] refers to a behavioral characteristic of a nonobservable object, an electron, which really exists."[24]

On the other hand, an instrumentalist will claim that the acceptance of a theory for scientific purposes does not at the same time commit one to believing that the theory is true.[25] A scientific theory is not the kind of thing that is true or false.[26] It is nothing more than a rule for generating conditional statements, laws, or predictions about empirical phenomena. The virtue of a theory is not its truth, but its "empirical adequacy" (i.e., its track record in generating true statements about observable states of affairs). Theories, if accepted, will be accepted on the basis of their empirical adequacy, their simplicity, their comprehensiveness, and the like. But the acceptance of a theory, on the instrumentalist account, does not at the same time commit one to the belief that the theory itself is true, that its theoretical terms refer, or that the entities it postulates exist.[27] Here scientific theories have no semantic punch.

The logical positivist philosophy of science generally holds to an instrumentalist account of scientific theories.[28] Theories are nothing but "axiomatic calculi," which can be provided with a partial interpretation in an observational vocabulary by way of correspondence rules. As purely syntactical machinery, they serve only to enrich the scope and predictive power of those empirical generalizations known as scientific laws. The subsequent reaction against logical positivism followed upon the stunning developments in theoretical physics ever since the early twentieth century. It seemed that the only plausible explanation of such developments would have to provide scientific theories with a semantics of their own.

The distinction between laws and theories depends, accordingly, upon a bi-level analysis of science. Laws state in the language of mathematics the regular functional interdependencies between observable physical phenomena; theories seek to explain why such regularities hold by postulating unobservable entities and specifying their causal capacities. Laws make predictions possible; theories provide explanations. The realist-instrumentalist dispute within contemporary Anglo-American philosophy of science is to a large degree predicated upon the bi-level analysis of science. It is a dispute over the nature of theories, not laws. The key question is how best to construe the nature of theories, which go beyond what is observable in order to explain it. The instrumentalist insists that science ultimately refers only to that which is observable. Science does so in its laws, which are empirical generalizations over the behavior of observable phenomena. Theories are merely instruments that enhance the unity and the reach of these empirical generalizations. The realist holds that science refers not only to observable phenomena and processes, but also, in its theories, to unobservable entities and processes. The empirical adequacy of a theory provides grounds for believing that it is true and that the entities it postulates exist, not just that it is useful in making empirical predictions.

My interpretation of Husserl trades on this generally accepted distinction between scientific laws and scientific theories. I will claim that Husserl's "instrumentalism" is in fact an interpretation of scientific laws, not theories. For that reason Husserl's phenomenological critique of science does not speak directly to the contemporary debate within Anglo-American circles over the nature of scientific theories. Much of the confusion surrounding the interpretation of Husserl's philosophy of science in the English secondary literature is in large part due to the assumption that in the *Crisis*, Husserl is addressing himself to the same set of issues that are being currently discussed by Anglo-American philosophers of science. Due to this hermeneutical indiscretion, the true import of Husserl's claims about the nature of the physical sciences are subjected to not a little distortion and, in some cases, rendered thoroughly implausible. Part of the purpose of this study is to place Husserl's phenomenological critique of science in its proper setting, and to demonstrate that, understood within this setting, it is entirely compatible with the theoretical dimensions of contemporary science.

What I will argue, in effect, is that Husserl's phenomenology is consistent with a realistic construal of scientific theories. I will not, by way of addition, argue as a biographical fact that Husserl himself was inclined, or would have been inclined, to give a realistic construal of scientific theories; nor will I claim that Husserl made a clear distinction between laws and theories; nor will I claim that Husserl developed or even projected a phenomenology of theoretical entities as such. My thesis is more modest, more strictly conceptual in nature, and more concerned with the contemporary prospects of Husserlian phenomenology within the philosophy of science than with certain biographical facts surrounding the person of Husserl. I will argue only that, given the distinction between scientific theories and laws, Husserl's stated phenomenological critique of modern mathematical physics is entirely compatible with a realistic interpretation of scientific theories. In the conclusion to this study, I will briefly indicate what resources are to be found in Husserl's thought for a phenomenology of theoretical entities.

3. THE PLAN OF THIS STUDY

Like Gaul, this study of the problem of theoretical existence in Husserl's philosophy of science is divided into three parts. Part 1, consisting of the first two chapters, provides a general overview of Husserl's phenomenological philosophy of science. The first chapter identifies and situates Husserl's idea of the basic structure of scientific knowledge within the tradition of philosophical reflection on the nature of science. It then proceeds to indicate how this idea was "idealized" in Husserl's later theory of evidence. The second chapter follows Husserl in his attempt to gain phenomenological access to the ultimate foundation of the sciences. Part 2 anticipates certain initial objections that might be made against the thesis that Husserl's phenomenology is consistent with a realistic construal of scientific theories. The first objection is based upon a certain interpretation of Husserl's theory of truth (chapter 3). If Husserl holds to an evidence theory of truth, and the existence of theoretical entities could never become evident in the required sense, then it could never be true that theoretical entities exist. The second objection is drawn from Husserl's theory of rationality (chapter 4). If Husserl holds that we are justified in believing only that which is evident, and the existence of theoretical entities could never become evident, then we could never be justified in believing that theoretical entities exist. The third part argues directly for the main thesis of the study. In chapter 5 I maintain that Husserl's "instrumentalism" is restricted to an interpretation of scientific laws, not theories, and that the things he denies exist in any physical sense are not theoretical entities but rather idealized objects. The last chapter, chapter 6, takes up the question of the possibility of the real existence of things that are imperceptible. More general questions pertaining to the compatibility of Husserl's phenomenology with any form of realism are also raised and discussed.

Such are the conceptual parameters of this study. But there are, in addition, two material limitations. First, this study is largely confined to a reading of and reaction to the Anglo-American secondary literature on Husserl's philosophy of science spanning the last fifty years. Second, this study is primarily based upon an analysis and interpretation of Husserl's major published works. The second material limitation is based upon the first. Given the general unavailability of Husserl's unpublished research manuscripts, the discussion of Husserl's philosophy of science in the secondary literature is based almost exclusively upon Husserl's major published works, most of which are available in English editions. Hence the as yet untranslated works of Husserl will play a secondary role in the discussion; the unpublished manuscripts, a tertiary role—they will appear, in German, in the notes.

PART ONE

Husserl's Phenomenological Philosophy of Science

CHAPTER ONE

•••••••••••••••••••••••••••••••

THE IDEA OF SCIENCE IN HUSSERL AND THE TRADITION

My chief task in this chapter will be to outline the contours of Husserl's conception of the basic structure and defining characteristics of scientific knowledge. In doing so, I will first attempt to locate this conception within the tradition of philosophical reflection on the nature of science, taking Aristotle and Locke as key representatives of this tradition. I will then indicate the main features of Husserl's understanding of empirical science. Finally, I will take into consideration certain passages from Husserl's later works in which the traditional conception of science is explicitly converted into a regulative Idea, together with the implications of such a conversion for the epistemic status of the foundations of the eidetic disciplines, including phenomenology itself.[1]

The central thesis of this chapter is that Husserl takes over from the classical philosophical tradition the strong foundationalist account of scientific knowledge as a unified system of deductively interconnected necessary truths derived from self-evident universal and generic principles. In response to some of the standard objections to Husserl's philosophy of science, however, it will be noted that he neither applies this account *tout court* to the empirical sciences in general nor to the physical sciences in particular.

The term "strong foundationalism" is taken from the literature of contemporary meta-epistemological research within Anglo-American philosophical circles. Most generally, it denotes a conception of the structure and properties a specified body of beliefs must have if it is to count as science, knowledge, or, at least, a body of justified beliefs. The guiding intuition of foundationalist epistemologies is that within a given cognitive structure, a distinction is to be drawn between beliefs that are based upon other beliefs, and beliefs that are not based upon other beliefs but are themselves basic. Some beliefs are founded; others will serve as the foundations. In the context of a theory of justified belief, a foundationalist will hold that while we are justified in holding some beliefs only on the basis of other beliefs, we are justified in holding basic beliefs without further ado. If we were not to recognize some beliefs as properly basic and held that for every belief we would be justified in holding it only on the basis of other beliefs, the process of justification could never be brought to proper closure. For any belief that served as the basis for another belief would in turn be based upon another belief and so on ad infinitum. Any point at which the process of justification was brought to a halt would be, strictly speaking, arbitrary, and no belief would be ultimately justified.

This foundationalist intuition is given clear expression by Husserl himself in the opening sections of the *Cartesian Meditations*, where he makes a distinction between mediate judgments and immediate judgments in connection with the idea of science. Mediate judgments are grounded on other judgments, whereas immediate judgments are grounded not upon other judgments, but upon the direct intuitive experience of the state of affairs judged (*CM*, 10 / *H* I, 51). Likewise, in *Ideas* I, Husserl speaks of "immediately evident judgments," to which all other judgments ultimately refer back in the process of "mediate grounding" (*ID* I, 13 / *H* III 1, 18; see also *ID* I, 338 / *H* III 1, 326).

Strong foundationalism, as opposed to various forms of weak foundationalism, holds that only those beliefs that are certain, evident in the strongest sense, can count as properly basic. In Husserl's understanding of the structure of scientific knowledge, this requirement of strong foundationalism represents an essential component of the idea of genuine science. For "genuine science and its own genuine freedom from prejudice require at the foundation of all proofs," as Husserl has it in *Ideas* I, "immediately valid judgments which derive their validity [directly] from originally presentive intuitions" (*ID* I, 36 / *H* III 1, 42). In the introduction to *Formal and Transcendental Logic*, he asserts that the sciences, if they are to be genuine, must be grounded on a foundation that is "absolute" (*FTL*, 7 / *H* XVII, 6). In the First Meditation of the *Cartesian Meditations*, Husserl insists that the question of the beginning of science, the foundation, is the question of "those cognitions that are first in themselves and can support the whole storied edifice of universal knowledge" (*CM*, 14 / *H* I, 54). As such, these cognitions "must carry with them an absolute certainty, if advancing from them and constructing on their basis a science governed by the idea of a definitive system of knowledge . . . is to be capable of having any sense" (*CM*, 14 / *H* I, 55). For what the scientist demands of all principles is "absolute indubitability" (*CM*, 15 / *H* I, 55).[2] As we will see in chapter 2 of this study, it is the specific task and overarching aim of phenomenology, as a transcendental first philosophy, to provide the sciences with a foundation that meets this requirement. Our concern here will be restricted to the strong foundationalist account of science, although there are many instances one could cite of strong foundationalism as, more generally, an account of knowledge or justified belief.

1. THE CLASSICAL IDEA OF SCIENCE

The use of the architectural metaphor of foundations in connection with the structure of science received its initial effective-historical impetus in the first of Descartes's *Meditations on First Philosophy*. There the metaphor was employed to suggest that the edifice of scientific knowledge rests upon certain basic principles or foundations. If those foundations turned out to be weak, improperly laid, or in some important respect substandard, then any cognitive structure built upon them would inevitably collapse of its own accord. The task of the *Meditations*, then, was to secure the foundations of the sciences so that anything established within them would be both stable and lasting. In the Second and Fifth Meditations, Descartes located the first principle of the sciences in the clear and distinct perceptions of necessary truths, a principle that was established in the certitude of the cogito experience and guaranteed in the proof of the existence of a wholly good and all-powerful creator God. As such, the principle of rational insight into necessary truths was to supplant that of sense perception, which is obscure, sometimes unreliable, and, according to the argument of the Sixth Meditation, primarily fitted for the nonepistemic purposes of practical life.

But the formal structure of the strong foundationalist account of science had already been decisively articulated long before by Aristotle in the *Posterior Analytics*. I will refer to the core content of this early formulation of the conception of the structure of scientific knowledge as the "classical idea of science." It was destined to become the dominant way of understanding the nature of science and displays a remarkable degree of conceptual tenacity to this day. Ensconced in the Scholastic concept of *scientia*, it managed to survive the flood of philosophical criticism directed against the Aristotelian-Scholastic tradition by the early modern philosophers, and immediately resurfaced within the new setting of the Cartesian philosophy of the cogito. Not until 1899, with the "axiomatic turn" accomplished in David Hilbert's formalism, did the classical idea meet a worthy contender within the circle of the formal disciplines, where it traditionally held sway.

According to Aristotle, a fact may be known, but it is not known scientifically unless and until it has been demonstrated from premises that are more general and better known. When such a demonstration has been carried out, we will know not only that a certain fact is the case, but *why* it is the case, the conclusion being related to the premises as effect to cause (*PA*, 71b20–22). But if the premises from which the initial demonstration proceeded are themselves to be known scientifically, they must in turn be demonstrated from other premises that are still more general and better known. Thus, at each level of discursive reasoning, the demand for a demonstration of the premises can be reiterated. But if the process of demonstration is not to become involved in an infinite regress, it must eventually terminate in premises that are themselves "indemonstrable" (72b19–22). These propositions will serve as the "axioms" of the system of demonstrative knowledge that is to be derived from them. They themselves are not demonstrable in terms of propositions that are more basic. Rather, they are grounded in an immediate rational insight (*nous*) into their truth. Propositions that serve as axioms are not known on the basis of other propositions that provide evidence for them. We hold these truths to be "self-evident."

What holds for the order of propositions also holds for the order of concepts. Some concepts are defined on the basis of other concepts. The latter concepts can, in turn, be defined by other concepts. But if the process of definition is to come to an end, some concepts must themselves be basic and indefinable. The primitive concepts within a cognitive structure cannot be further defined, but are derived from an immediate rational insight into the generic essences of the object domain under consideration.

According to the Aristotelian conception, then, scientific knowledge is demonstrative knowledge. By virtue of its logical structure, all demonstrative knowledge ultimately rests upon a basis of indemonstrable first principles. If demonstrative knowledge is to count as knowledge, however, the first principles upon which it rests are not to be established on the basis of purely methodological desiderata; nor are they to be hypothetically postulated for subsequent testing. For then they would be uncertain and ultimately no better than mere opinion. Rather, the foundations of genuine science must be absolute. The first principles of a science are to possess the certainty that is achieved through the clear apprehension of the necessity of their truth. The science constructed on those first principles through the systematic derivation of all and only that which is entailed by the first principles will then be certain throughout. For the entire science will be exclusively composed of necessary truths about that which "cannot be otherwise." And such is Aristotle's position: "Scientific knowledge and its object differ from opinion and the object of opinion in that scientific knowledge is commensurately universal and proceeds by necessary connections, and that which is necessary cannot be otherwise. So though there are things which are true and real and yet can be otherwise, scientific knowledge clearly does not concern them . . . it is opinion that is concerned with that which may be true or false, and can be otherwise" (PA, 88b30–89a2).

In sum, the classical idea of science, as initially formulated by Aristotle, can be characterized in the following way: Science is a unified system of necessary truths deductively derived from self-evident first principles. The first principles of any science will be composed of universal principles that necessarily hold for all beings, generic principles that necessarily hold for all beings within the relevant genus, and the first principles of logic, presupposed by all demonstration.

2. THE IDEA OF SCIENCE IN HUSSERL'S PHENOMENOLOGY

It is clear from Husserl's comments on the structure of science in both his earlier and later works that his position is in many respects in agreement with the classical tradition. In the "Prolegomena to Pure Logic," Husserl states that to know something in the scientific sense is to know the grounds from which it is necessarily determined in the manner in question (LI I, 227 / H XVIII, B 231). That is, scientific knowledge is a matter of seeing how a certain state of affairs follows from certain laws and antecedent conditions. This, in fact, is what scientific explanation amounts to. To be able to say how something follows from certain laws and antecedent conditions is to be able to explain it. "Every explanatory interconnection is deductive" (LI I, 229 / H XVIII, B 233).

Scientific knowledge, then, according to Husserl, is grounded knowledge. It is achieved through a demonstration in which the fact to be scientifically known is deduced from antecedent conditions. For any state of affairs that we would claim to know scientifically, we must be in a position to show how it necessarily follows from other states of affairs. If, in turn, we are to claim to know these antecedent states of affairs scientifically, we must also be in a position to show how they follow from other states of affairs. The process of grounding knowledge is reiterable (CM, 10 / H I, 51). But it must eventually terminate in certain principles if it is to avoid either an infinite regress or a circularity (*LI* I, 116 / *H* XVIII, B 84). Such principles must be immediately known if they are to function as the first principles of science wherein all other propositions of the science are grounded. They themselves are groundless, if by "groundless" we simply mean that their truth is not apprehended on the basis of other propositions (*LI* I, 152 / *H* XVIII, B 134). Thus the very idea of science contains within itself the distinction between mediate and immediate judgments. Mediate judgments are ultimately grounded in a deductive fashion in immediate judgments. The immediate judgments are grounded not in other judgments, but in the direct intuitive experience of the states of affairs corresponding to them (*CM*, 10 / *H* I, 51).[3]

Although Husserl admits that the methods of science include much more than deductive thought sequences, he nonetheless holds the latter to be of central significance. All other methods employed in science, he maintains, are either substitutes for such arguments or "auxiliary devices" that "prepare, facilitate, ensure or render possible" subsequent thought sequences by which certain propositions are deductively grounded (*LI* I, 68 / *H* XVIII, B 23). Examples of the first class would be certain "algorithmic methods," "whose peculiar function is to save as much genuine deductive mental work as possible by artificially arranged mechanical operations on sensible signs" (*LI* I, 69 / *H* XVIII, B 24). Also included here would be certain procedures by which objectively valid empirical judgments are obtained. Examples of the second class would include the disambiguation of terms, the development of a symbolic vocabulary, and classification. All such methods are pertinent to science only insofar as they ultimately relate to the deductive grounding of propositions, for "each actual advance in science is performed in an act of grounding [*Begründung*]" (*LI* I, 69 / *H* XVIII, B 24; translation modified).

A representative example of Husserl's understanding of the basic structure of science can be found in connection with his comments on the problem of grounding the logical principles of deduction in the science of pure logic:

> If, however, all proof rests on principles governing its procedure, and if its final justification involves an appeal to such principles, then we should either be involved in a circle or in an infinite regress if the principles of proof themselves required further proof, in a circle if the principles of proof used to justify the principles of proof were the same as the latter, in a regress if both sets of principles were repeatedly different. Plainly, therefore the demand for a fundamental

> justification of all mediate knowledge can only have a sense if we can both see and know certain ultimate principles on which all proof in the last instance rests. All principles which justify possible proofs must therefore be deductively inferable from certain last, immediately evident principles, so that even the principles of the deduction in question all themselves occur among such principles. (*LI* I, 116 / *H* XVIII, B 85)

All structures require an ultimate ground on which to stand.

It should be clear from the above that, for Husserl, an isolated bit of knowledge, no matter how evident, does not count as scientific knowledge. To be scientific, it must be incorporated into a unified system of grounds (*LI* I, 62 / *H* XVIII, B 14–15). "No truth," Husserl maintains, "is . . . isolated in science: it occurs in combination with other truths in theoretical connections bound by relations of ground and consequent" (*LI* I, 173 / *H* XVIII, B 162). Any judgment that is to count as scientific must have its place in the order of grounds that pertain to a specific discipline (*LI* I, 63 / *H* XVIII, B 15). "The essence of science," Husserl writes, "involves unity in the whole system of grounded validation: not only isolated pieces of knowledge, but their grounded validations themselves . . . must achieve systematic unity" (*LI* I, 62 / *H* XVIII, B 15). The type of systematic unity that is displayed in the structure of science is the "unity of demonstration" (*LI* I, 227, 229 / *H* XVIII, B 231, 233). And what constitutes this unity is the one basic proposition, or homogeneous set of propositions, from which all other propositions belonging to that science can be deduced. What makes science science, then, is an "ideal interconnection" (*LI* I, 225 / *H* XVIII, B 228) that is established through the systematic derivation of a body of propositions from one and the same proposition, or set of propositions (*LI*I, 228 / *H* XVIII, B 232).[4]

Again, it must be emphasized that for Husserl, as well as Aristotle, these basic propositions are not to be accepted as hypotheses for subsequent testing, or postulated on the basis of purely methodological considerations. Rather, their truth must be self-evident. They must be certain, if the foundations of the sciences are to be secure. And the certainty that is located in the foundations must be relayed throughout the entire system by relations of entailment if that which is established within the sciences is to be lasting and stable. This is the fundamental requirement of the strong foundationalist conception of scientific knowledge. "Propositions that are immediate objects of insight lead, in evident elementary arguments, to propositions that become evident therewith as consequent truths" (*FTL*, 42 / *H* XVII, 37). A genuine scientific theory, that is, a deductively ordered one, is a complex built entirely with "steps of insight," thus making up a "unity of truth" (*FTL*, 42–43 / *H* XVII, 37).

3. THE PROBLEM OF EMPIRICAL SCIENCE: LOCKE

Aristotle claimed, and Husserl would surely concur, that scientific knowledge concerns "necessities" (*PA*, 89a10). It is insight into these necessities, either immediate or mediate, that gives certainty to scientific knowledge: "When a man thinks a truth incapable of being otherwise he always thinks that he knows it" (89a6–7). Thus the proper object of science will never be a contingent states of affairs: "There are things which are true and real and yet can be otherwise, scientific knowledge clearly does not concern them.... It is opinion that is concerned with that which may be true or false, and can be otherwise" (88b30–89a2). For this reason, in *Ideas* I, Husserl expressly reserves the classical idea of science for the sciences of eidetic necessities, the sciences of essence, as opposed to the sciences of matters of fact. Geometry, as a regional eidetic science of space, does not deal with what is actually the case in the world of shapes, but with "ideal possibilities" (*ID* I, 16 / *H* III 1, 21). Thus the mental act in which geometry is founded is not the experiencing of a factual state of affairs, but the "seeing" of essences (*ID* I, 16 / *H* III 1, 21). So it is, Husserl claims, with all eidetic sciences:

> Grounded on the predicatively formed eidetic states of affairs [*Wesensverhalte*] (or the eidetic axioms), seized upon in immediate insight, are the mediate, predicatively formed eidetic states of affairs which become given in a thinking with mediated insight—a thinking according to principles, all of which are objects of immediate insight. Consequently each step in a mediate grounding is apodictically and eidetically necessary. The essence of purely eidetic science thus consists of proceeding in an exclusively eidetic way; from the start and subsequently, the only predicatively formed states of affairs are such as have eidetic validity and can therefore be either made originarily given immediately (as grounded immediately in essences originarily seen) or else can become "inferred" from such "axiomatic"

predicatively formed states of affairs by pure deduction. (*ID* I, 16–17 / *H* III 1, 21–22; translation modified)

The classical idea of science as a system of propositions derived from self-evident first principles is thus duly restricted in its application to the formal and material eidetic sciences (the sciences of logic and geometry, for example). For the laws—even the basic laws—of the sciences of matters of fact are not true by necessity. It is logically possible that the physical universe run according to laws that are wholly different from the ones that in fact hold. For that reason the truth of such laws, being contingent, cannot be established through "immediate insight." The high probability of the truth of such laws may be established through certain inductive procedures, but their truth will never in this way become certain. The empirical sciences are not about that which "cannot be otherwise." They do not concern self-evident necessities. But if scientific knowledge is to be distinguished by the certainty of its claims, in what sense can the empirical sciences count as science? Are they really nothing more than well-organized bodies of opinion?

It was precisely these questions, precipitated by the classical idea of science, that John Locke took up in book IV of his *Essay Concerning Human Understanding*. His treatment of them, together with his position on the epistemic status of the empirical sciences, is especially instructive given our present systematic concerns.

In line with the Western philosophical tradition since Plato, Locke consistently expresses his theory of knowledge in the metaphor of vision. We know that, and only that, which we can see. All else is a matter of surmise and presumption—or faith. In line with the modern philosophical tradition since Descartes, Locke maintains that what we see are "ideas" in our own mind, the immanent contents of consciousness, which function as "images" or "signs" of realities external to our minds. Presumably these realities exert a causal influence on our minds in such a way that they give rise to ideas that resemble them to some degree. But what gives rise to knowledge in the propositional sense is our ability to see the way in which our ideas agree or disagree with one another. Thus knowledge, according to Locke, is the perception of the relations between our ideas (*Essay* IV, i, 2).

But this definition of knowledge, although true to Locke's initial formulation in the opening sections of book IV, needs to be qualified in the light of his subsequent exposition together with his insistence that knowledge be attended by certainty. Knowledge, it turns out, is not just the perception of connections between ideas, but the perception of necessary connections between abstract ideas. For necessity is the objective correlate of certainty, as Aristotle already pointed out in book I of the *Posterior Analytics*. I see that certain ideas are related thus; and if I can also see that they cannot be related otherwise, then I am certain that they are thus related. I can then claim to know that they are thus related. But if the relations in question are contingent, I can never be sure that they might not be related otherwise. Hence the relations that form the proper object of genuine knowledge are necessary relations. And since necessary relations can obtain only between abstract ideas, the range of ideas that can give rise to genuine knowledge must be restricted to those that are abstract. There are no necessary relations that obtain either between or within concrete, complex ideas other than those that are merely nominal. The only exception to this restriction of knowledge to necessary relations between abstract ideas is our knowledge of the existence of ourselves, God, and external things—all of which, Locke assures us, we can be certain.

Knowledge, then, for Locke, is a matter of perception. As such it admits of two degrees, as perception is either immediate or mediate. Immediate perception is simply the direct intuition of relations between our ideas. It is the immediate grasp of what lies directly before our minds. This "intuitive knowledge," as Locke calls it, "is certain, beyond all doubt, and needs no probation" (*Essay* IV, xvii, 14). Furthermore, "it is upon this intuition that depends all the certainty and evidence of all our knowledge" (IV, ii, 1).

Although all knowledge ultimately depends upon the immediate perception of the relations between ideas, it does not follow that all relations between ideas are immediately perceived. In some, indeed, in many cases, the perception of the relation between ideas will be mediated by the perception of the relation between other ideas. The relation between two ideas will be established only through the "intervention" of other ideas. For most human beings, for instance, the relation of equality between the idea of two right angles and the idea of the interior angles of a triangle is not immediately apparent. Such a relation must be demonstrated in order to be seen; that is, the interior angles of a triangle must be perceived to be equal to other angles that are in turn perceived to be equal to two right angles. Thus the relation is mediated by relations to other ideas—although each step of the demonstration takes place on the basis of an immediate perception of some relation between ideas. And so, by an unbroken chain of inference, each link forged in direct intuition, the relation of ideas asserted in the conclusion becomes evident (*Essay* IV, ii, 1). Such knowledge, gained through mediate perception, Locke calls "demonstrative knowledge."

Although knowledge in its first degree represents a stronger form of evidence, and is epistemically preferable for a number of reasons, Locke admits that the circle of ideas the relations of which admit of direct intuition is very small indeed. Thus the extension and establishment of human knowledge will depend upon the exercise of human reason in its discursive capacities—the discovery and deductive ordering of intermediate ideas (*Essay* IV, iii, 3). Locke equates the body of demonstrative knowledge so constructed with scientific knowledge, as evidenced by his interchangeable use of the modifiers "scientifical" and "demonstrative." The curious implication of this position for the epistemic status of the "natural sciences" will be pointed out presently. But here it should be noted that, thus far, Locke and Husserl are in agreement with respect to the formal structure of scientific knowledge. Both subscribe to the main tenets of the classical idea of science, even if they disagree with respect to what science is about—for Locke, necessary relations between abstract ideas; for Husserl, eidetic states of affairs.

Locke's description of scientific knowledge rounds out the core of his theory of knowledge in general. For science and knowledge are, in Locke, coextensive: "These two, viz. intuition and demonstration, are the degrees of our knowledge; whatever comes short of one of these, with what assurance soever embraced, is but faith, or opinion, but not knowledge" (*Essay* IV, ii, 14). Yet, out of consideration for the temporal limitations of the human understanding, Locke is compelled to widen the concept of knowledge by allowing for "habitual" as well as "actual" knowledge. Actual knowledge consists in the present perception of the relations of ideas, as described above; whereas habitual knowledge consists of all those propositions once perceived but now "lodged in the memory" and available for recall (IV, i, 8). Thus we may say that a person knows that $7 + 5 = 12$, even if that person is not presently perceiving the relation of equality between the constituent ideas of the proposition. This departure from the principle of intuition strictly conceived is motivated by the fact that "our finite understandings are able to think clearly and distinctly but on one thing at once" (IV, i, 8). Hence, "if men have no knowledge of any more than what they actually thought on, they would all be very ignorant: and he that knew most would know but one truth, that being all that he was able to think on at one time" (IV, i, 8). We come by our ideas in succession, not all at once. It is possible, of course, that there exist forms of propositional consciousness that contemplate many true propositions at once. Such possible forms of consciousness may be arrayed in a hierarchy of intellectual power culminating in a consciousness that thinks all true propositions at once, that is, God as the philosophers are wont to conceive of him (II, x, 9). Only God, then, would know all things in the strict sense. That Locke allows for a nonintuitive form of knowledge represents a concession on his part to the temporal structure and finite capacities of the human mind. Although it must be acknowledged here that the nonintuitive form of knowledge is nonetheless conditioned by an act of intuition, since it comprises only those propositions lodged in the memory that have once been perceived.

Locke then proceeds to draw a distinction between two degrees of habitual knowledge: first, those cases where, upon recall, the mind actually perceives the relation between the ideas in question; and second, where the mind no longer perceives the relation, but remembers that it did, at one time, perceive that relation. Presumably, in all those cases of intuitive knowledge where the relation between ideas is to be perceived immediately, habitual knowledge will be of the first sort. However, in what Locke calls demonstrative knowledge, where the perception of the relation between ideas depends upon the perception of the relations between other ideas in a proof, it may be that one remembers the conclusion, and remembers that one proved the conclusion, but cannot remember the details of the proof itself—especially if the proof was long and complicated. Such cases, Locke maintains, are still to count as knowledge, not out of undue sympathy for those with deficient memories or who lack the requisite sagacity, but rather because a new proof can be constructed taking the memory that one had proved the conclusion as a premise: Necessary relations between abstract ideas are immutable; if I had proved a certain relation to hold at one time, it follows that this relation still holds. Hence, if I have proved a proposition to be true, where that proposition represents a necessary relation between two abstract ideas, then I can know that that proposition is still true (*Essay* IV, i, 8). The truth of the proposition in question has been proved again, though not in the original manner.

Intuitive knowledge and demonstrative knowledge, in both their actual and habitual forms, then, constitute the whole of Locke's theory of knowledge. But we have yet to touch upon his theory of belief and the rationality of belief. For although human knowledge can be extended by way of deduction, the domain of the possible extension of knowledge in this fashion is considerably smaller than the domain of ideas in general. Deduction will be restricted to the set of necessary relations between abstract ideas. But the bulk of our lives as human beings is spent in commerce with concrete substances—complex ideas—whose constituent simple ideas are, as far as we can tell, only contingently related. The exigencies of human life and our practical circumstances often demand that we act on the basis of something decidedly less than knowledge in its intuitive or demonstrative form (*Essay* IV, xiv, 2). Hence we must act on what we take to be the probable relations between ideas, "for the state we are at present in, not being that of vision, we must in many things content ourselves with faith and probability" (IV, ii, 6). Locke does not recommend that we entirely flee the world of sense and opinion to live only for the intelligible world of intellectual insight and genuine knowledge. Such a calling is too wonderful for us mortals. Indeed, as Locke states, man "would be at a great loss if he had nothing to direct him but what has the certainty of knowledge" (IV, xiv, 1). We must live to a large degree on the basis of opinion, where intuitive insight into necessary relations is lacking.

But this is not to excuse us, in this regard, from the claims of reason. It is not the case that in matters of opinion "anything goes." There are rational guidelines for the governance of one's beliefs and opinions, which can be summarized in the following general rule: one ought to apportion one's assent to a proposition in accordance with the probability of that proposition's being true. "The Mind, if it is to proceed rationally, ought to examine of the grounds of probability, and see how they make more or less for or against any proposition, before it assents to or dissents from it; and upon a due balancing of the whole, reject or receive it with a more or less firm assent proportionably to the preponderancy of the greater grounds of probability on one side or the other" (*Essay* IV, xv, 5). Hence, on the Lockean view, one ought to believe a particular proposition only if, on all the available evidence, it is more probable than not.

As mentioned earlier, Locke's definition of scientific knowledge as a body of propositions demonstrated on the basis of the intuitive apprehension of the necessary relations between abstract ideas has at least one striking implication for the epistemic status of the so-called "sciences of nature." We are now in a position to see what that implication is: given the current limitations on the intuitive powers of the human mind, the sciences of nature can never become genuinely scientific. They will never count as bodies of knowledge in the strict sense, although, as bodies of belief, they may be perfectly rational.

The main reason why the natural sciences fall short of knowledge is that natural bodies are, for Locke, collocations of simple ideas between which we can intuit no necessary relations. This is because the simple ideas of which the complex idea of a natural substance is composed—secondary qualities for the most part—are dependent upon the primary qualities of the imperceptible material parts of the natural substance in question. In addition to this, the mechanism by which the primary qualities produce secondary qualities is hidden to us. Hence, Locke concludes that "natural philosophy is not capable of being made a science" (*Essay* IV, xii, 10). In fact, Locke writes, we are "so far from being capable of such a thing [a perfect science of natural bodies] that I conclude that it is lost labour to seek after it" (IV, iii, 29).

Because of Locke's restriction of knowledge and science to the domain of certainty that can be achieved only through insight into that which cannot be otherwise, it turns out, on his view, that there can be no natural science in the strict sense, only more or less justified bodies of opinion concerning the natural world. Furthermore, "our knowledge concerning corporeal substances will be very little advanced by any of them [such opinions] till we are made to see what qualities and powers of bodies have a necessary connexion or repugnancy one with another" (*Essay* IV, iii, 16). But such insight is denied to us.

4. THE PROBLEM OF EMPIRICAL SCIENCE: HUSSERL

The extended review of Locke's general theory of "scientific knowledge" is motivated by more than purely systematic questions concerning the epistemic status of the empirical sciences. It may also throw some light on the text-historical background of Husserl's *Logical Investigations* (1900–1901). The order of the exposition of Husserl's own theory of knowledge and science in section 6 of the "Prolegomena to Pure Logic" bears a striking resemblance to Locke's treatment of the same issues in the *Essay Concerning Human Understanding*. Husserl begins with intuitive knowledge, which is then extended through demonstration (*LI* I, 63 / *H* XVIII, B 16). He proceeds to broaden the concept of knowledge to include what is remembered ("habitual knowledge"), making reference to the argument from memory in elliptical form (*LI* I, 61 / *H* XVIII, B 13). Finally, he takes up probable knowledge (*LI* I, 61–62 / *H* XVIII, B 13–14). Such a resemblance is not entirely fortuitous. At the beginning of his work on the *Logical Investigations* around 1890, Husserl made an intensive study of Locke's, Berkeley's, and Hume's epistemologies.[5] In the winter semester of 1891–92, Husserl conducted a seminar on Locke's *Essay Concerning Human Understanding* as a *Privatdozent* at the University of Halle.[6] This seminar was repeated in the winter semester of 1898–99, a year before the publication of the *Logical Investigations*. It is entirely likely, then, that Husserl formed his position on epistemological matters in dialogue with Locke.

But to whatever degree a similarity exists between the order of exposition in Locke's and Husserl's theories of science, there is not an agreement on all points of substance. While Locke's commitment to the classical idea of science compels him to discount the scientific pretensions of "natural science," Husserl claims that "empirical science is also a science" (*LI* I, 246 / *H* XVIII, B 255). Yet Husserl was fully cognizant of the contingent character of the objects of empirical science and the implications this has for the epistemic status of its claims. The sciences of nature are sciences of matters of fact. They deal with real individuals that, in certain respects, could have been otherwise. "Individual existence of every sort is, quite universally speaking, 'contingent.' It is thus; in respect of its essence it could be otherwise" (*ID* I, 7 / *H* III 1, 12). Furthermore, it is not only individuals within nature that are contingent. So are the laws of nature. "Even though definite laws of Nature obtain according to which if such and such real circumstances exist in fact then such and such definite circumstances must exist in fact, such laws express only *de facto* rules which themselves could read quite otherwise" (*ID* I, 7 / *H* III 1, 12). Given, then, that the empirical sciences do not deal with necessities, and, for precisely this reason, cannot achieve certainty in their foundations through direct insight, to what degree can they count as science? Must Husserl, like Locke, banish the natural sciences from the domain of science; or will he make it lie down on a Procrustean bed built to the specifications of the classical idea of science?

In his work on Husserl's philosophy of science, Christopher Prendergast claims that Husserl took the latter route: Husserl's conception of the structure of scientific theory—both eidetic and empirical—is decisively and exclusively shaped by the classical idea of science.[7] This interpretation of Husserl in turn serves as the basis for Prendergast's major criticism: in maintaining that all science is ultimately founded on the intuitive apprehension of essences, Husserl betrays his reactionary and dogmatic inclinations, shoring up the status quo and protecting the established sciences from the major conceptual revisions that are often demanded on empirical and methodological grounds if any genuine theoretical progress is to be made. A similar criticism is made by the Dutch philosopher Cornelius van Peursen: "His [Husserl's] analysis of the rectilinear process of critical methodology cannot cope with the new shift in the philosophy of science that stresses the fundamentally transformative character of methodological renewal."[8]

In essential agreement with Karl Popper and the critical rationalist school, Prendergast claims that what makes science scientific is not the certainty of its foundations, secured once and for all through direct intuition of essence or insight into supposedly self-evident propositions. Rather, what makes science scientific is its openness to testing and empirical falsification at all levels.[9] Theories are one and all of a hypothetical nature, to be evaluated on primarily logical and methodological grounds.[10] Definitions are not established once and for all on the basis of the intuition of essences, but represent linguistic proposals that can be abandoned or revised if they yield theoretically undesirable results. In effect, Husserl's philosophy of science, rooted in the classical idea of science, has been rendered untenable by recent work in the philosophy of science, which has shown that, as Wilfrid Sellars puts it, science "is rational, not because it has a foundation but because it is a self-correcting enterprise which can put any claim in jeopardy though not all at once."[11]

In what follows I will attempt to show that the Husserl whom Prendergast, van Peursen, and others attack is but a flimsily constructed straw person. The "real" Husserl made a sharp distinction between the sciences of the ideal and the sciences of the real and restricted the classical idea of science to the former. There is a residual sense in which empirical science is founded upon essential intuition, but only in the sense that the empirical sciences are constrained by the a priori framework established by the relevant formal and material eidetic sciences (*ID* I, 18 / *H* III 1, 24). In themselves, however, the empirical concepts and theories of the sciences of nature are tentative and revisable, grounded not in intuition but in such methodological criteria as empirical adequacy, consistency, simplicity, and the like. Thus, unlike phenomenology and other eidetic disciplines, the methods of the empirical sciences are "indirect" (PRS, 147 / *PSW*, 71); they are not deductive, but hypothetical-deductive. Moreover, in his later work, Husserl holds that "evidence" had by way of direct insight is never to count simply as a fait accompli but rather as an ideal standard for ongoing criticism of existing science. This is so even for the eidetic disciplines.

5. THE UNITY OF THE EMPIRICAL SCIENCES

The "Prolegomena to Pure Logic" could easily give the impression that the classical idea of science as a system of deductively interconnected necessary truths derived from self-evident axioms comprises Husserl's general theory of science. But such is not the case. The "Prolegomena" is, after all, about pure logic, which, as a formal eidetic discipline, is not only itself a deductively ordered eidetic science but a theory of any deductively ordered eidetic science. It is not until the very end of the "Prolegomena," in section 72, that Husserl turns his attention to the empirical sciences as such. There he explicitly limits the competence of pure logic as a theory of science to those sciences that are of a purely deductive character, sciences whose unity is a "deductive unity" (*LI* I, 246 / *H* XVIII, B 255).

Now any science, insofar as it involves explanation, will display a deductive order. For, as we noted earlier, Husserl subscribes to something like the hypothetical-deductive model of scientific explanation (*LI* I, 229 / *H* XVIII, B 233). In that respect, every explanatory empirical science will fall under the province of pure logic as a theory of deductive systems. Nonetheless, "logic so regarded does not include, as a special case, the ideal conditions of empirical science in general" (*LI* I, 246 / *H* XVIII, B 255). But lest we draw any Lockean conclusions about the nonscientific character of the empirical sciences, Husserl immediately proceeds in the next sentence to assert that "empirical science is also science, and naturally falls, in regard to its theories, under the laws of the sphere delimited above [the sphere of pure logic]" (*LI* I, 246 / *H* XVIII, B 255). There is, then, some respect in which empirical science falls under the classical idea of science, and some respect in which it does not. With respect to its theories, it falls under this idea. But, Husserl claims, "empirical science cannot be reduced to its theories" (*LI* I, 246 / *H* XVIII, B 255). What is it, then, that belongs to the empirical sciences in addition to their theoretical content that distinguishes them in principle from the purely deductively ordered eidetic sciences?

Husserl's answer: their method. The key to Husserl's answer to this question lies in the epistemic status of the basic laws or propositions of the empirical sciences. Because these laws are contingent, their truth cannot be established through direct insight. Their truth is only probable, and must therefore be established in a different manner. Rather than being set up once and for all on the basis of their self-evidence, they must be formulated as hypotheses, have their empirical consequences deduced from them, and be submitted to a process of testing, modification, and verification (*Umänderung und Verifikation*) (*LI* I, 246 / *H* XVIII, B 255). In the standard terms of contemporary philosophy of science, the empirical sciences are not deductive but "hypothetical-deductive." For in purely deductive systems, the axioms are not only more general but better known than the theorems. Truth and certainty are communicated downward through the process of deduction. But in the empirical sciences the reverse is generally the case. The "axioms" are but theoretical proposals. They are in question. What is "better known" are the experimental reports that correspond to the "theorems," the observable implications of the axioms under consideration. If the implications clash with what in fact is observed, then, assuming that the antecedent is not complex and that all the relevant variables are accounted for, the theory is falsified, *modus tollens* (see *IP*, 14 / *H* II, 17–18). If, on the other hand, the implications are consistent with what is observed, then the theory has been in some sense and to some degree confirmed. It has not, of course, by that token been "verified" in the deductive sense. To think so would be to commit the fallacy of affirming the consequent, as has been pointed out in the logical criticism leveled against the verificationist school of scientific methodology.

What this state of affairs signifies for Husserl is that the "whole complex apparatus of knowledge-processes in which the theories of the empirical sciences arise" are subject to ideal laws and norms that are not contained in or to be derived from the "Idea of Theory" germane to pure logic (*LI* I, 247 / *H* XVIII, B 257). Rather, they are to be located under the "Idea of the Empirical Unity of Explanation" or the "Idea of Probability" (*LI* I, 247 / *H* XVIII, 257). It follows, then, that the unity of the empirical sciences is different from the unity of the eidetic sciences. The unity of the eidetic sciences is purely logical. Everything follows from the axioms, which are themselves self-evident. But the unity of the empirical sciences is methodological. The laws and theories of the empirical sciences are established through the methodical procedures of empirical testing. With regard to their theoretical content, statically conceived, the empirical sciences are indeed deductively ordered. But the basic laws are established not by virtue of their inherent epistemic merit, but through the "indirect" methods of the science in question. Over time, the basic concepts and laws of the empirical sciences are changed, modified, and sometimes replaced wholesale. For "inductive science can never construct an adequate world-picture [*Weltvorstellung*], however far it may carry us" (*LI* II, 831 / *H* XIX 2, B2 200). What, if anything, remains constant and provides an enduring unity to a science is the set of methodical procedures by which the laws and theories are evaluated. Furthermore, these procedures stand under ideal norms specified by the Idea of the Empirical Unity of Explanation. What this means, Husserl maintains (somewhat optimistically), is that for theories of a certain type there is but one proper methodical procedure for evaluating them; and on any given body of evidence, the proper methodical procedure will justify only one theory (*LI* I, 247 / *H* XVIII, B 256–57). Insofar as the empirical sciences are scientific, many of the theoretical difficulties that arise within them can be resolved through purely logical criticism—the detection of equivocations, fallacious inferences, and so forth. But insofar as the empirical sciences are empirical, many of the theoretical issues must be resolved through an appeal to the facts (*IP*, 15–16 / *H* II, 18).

It should be pointed out in this connection, however, that in espousing something like the hypothetical-deductive model of empirical scientific rationality, Husserl is not under the naive impression that the base of observed facts against which theories are to be tested is itself theory-neutral. As theories change, Husserl notes, "the facts themselves do not remain quite unchanged; they too change as the process of knowledge progresses" (*LI* I, 246 / *H* XVIII, B 255). It is not as if our understanding of the "true nature" of sensuously perceived facts remains a constant while the theoretical hypotheses are gradually adjusted to them through the process of empirical testing. Rather, within this very process the theories that we come to accept change our original understanding of the facts. In this brief passage Husserl clearly anticipates by some sixty years the critique waged against the logical empiricist philosophy of science by the likes of Norwood Russell Hanson, Thomas S. Kuhn, and Paul K. Feyerabend.

6. EXPLANATION IN THE EMPIRICAL SCIENCES

The hypothetical character of the empirical sciences with respect to the epistemic status of laws and theories in the context of justification carries over into Husserl's concept of empirical scientific explanation as well. We recall that, for Husserl, to explain a given fact is to deduce it from general laws and antecedent conditions: "Every explanatory interconnection is deductive" (*LI* I, 229 / *H* XVIII, B 233). Now the *explanandum*, according to Husserl, may be of two sorts. It may be an individual proposition, which pertains to the "actual existence of singular individuals," or it may be a general proposition stating a law that itself holds for individual existence (*LI* I, 228 / *H* XVIII, B 232). Individual propositions—and general propositions, if they state laws discovered a posteriori—are, however, contingent. But to "explain" them is to show how they are necessary (*LI* I, 227 / *H* XVIII, B 231). How can such propositions be explained? How can contingent propositions be shown to be necessary? Only by presupposing certain antecedent conditions from which the proposition in question necessarily follows. For "if the interconnection of one fact with others is one of law, then its existence, resting on the laws which govern interconnections of the sort in question, and on the assumption of the pertinent circumstances, is determined as a necessary existence" (*LI* I, 228 / *H* XVIII, B 231).

But the question naturally arises here: In what sense can that which exists contingently exist necessarily after it has been explained? Or, to give the question a *de dicto* formulation: In what sense can a proposition that is only contingently true become necessarily true once it has been deduced? Is the contingency of the natural world merely an appearance, which science dispels once it has explained everything? Do the empirical sciences, by virtue of their deductive structure, deal only in necessary truths after all?

The most plausible—and most charitable—construal of Husserl's claim here is, to use a Scholastic distinction, to maintain that the necessity referred to is one of the "consequence" and not of the "consequent." That is, to explain a contingent fact is to show that it necessarily follows from certain "presupposed circumstances." It is not to show that the fact itself is necessary, but only that it necessarily follows from certain antecedently given conditions. What is necessary is not the consequent, but the consequence. The diagonal between the opposite corners of my desk just happens to be of a certain length. It could have been otherwise. Its being that length is a wholly contingent matter. But, given that the corners of my desk are right angles together with the length of its sides, it necessarily follows that the length of the diagonal is precisely what it happens to be. It does not follow, however, that the diagonal is necessarily that length. To draw that conclusion would be to misconstrue the scope of the necessity operator. Thus, even though the deductive inferences in a scientific explanation are necessary, the *explanandum* retains its contingent status. The laws together with the antecedent conditions of the *explanans* are hypothetically assumed.

In any case, to explain an individual proposition, a contingent matter of fact, is to show how it necessarily follows from certain laws and antecedent conditions. But in addition to individual propositions there are also general propositions (*LI* I, 228 / *H* XVIII, B 231). These general propositions have the character of laws in that they apply to all facts that fall under them. Such laws, if they are not basic, must also fit into the deductive scheme of the science of which they are a part, not as an individual falls under a law, but rather as a special case of a more general law (*LI* I, 228 / *H* XVIII, B 232). In this way the laws that govern a certain range of facts can themselves be explained by recourse to more general laws under which they are subsumed. This process of explanation is to be reiterated until one arrives at those laws that are basic to the entire science and at the same time most general. They are by their own nature—not due to any incapacity on the part of human nature—indemonstrable. They are the first principles, the axioms, of the science. These laws, Husserl writes, "are called the basic laws. The systematic unity of the ideally closed sum total of laws resting on one basic lawfulness as their final ground, and arising out of it thorough systematic deduction, is the unity of a systematically complete theory" (*LI* I, 228 / *H* XVIII, B 232).

Basic laws, as explanatory principles, comprise the unity of the sciences insofar as they are theoretical. In the abstract, theoretical, nomological sciences, interest is focused upon the construction of a science as a deductive order of grounds resting upon such laws. Although such sciences are capable of explaining empirical states of affairs, such is not their overarching aim. In a strictly theoretical context, empirical states of affairs function only as instances or examples of laws and concepts (*LI* I, 231 / *H* XVIII, B 236). But there is another group of sciences whose unity is constituted not by the theoretical order of the *explanans*, but by the empirical character of the *explanandum*. Such a unity is "extra-essential"; it is external to the sciences as sciences. Nonetheless, it provides the unity for the so-called concrete or descriptive sciences like geology, astronomy, and anatomy. These sciences achieve their focus by virtue of being directed toward "one and the same individual object, or to one and the same empirical genus" (*LI* I, 230 / *H* XVIII, B 234). As such they are free to draw upon a number of the theoretical sciences for the sake of explanation. Furthermore, their aim, unlike the theoretical sciences, is not the construction of a science unified on the basis of law, but rather the explanation of the actual features of an empirical object or range of empirical objects within the same genus or species (e.g., the topological characteristics of the floor of the Atlantic Ocean, or the mating habits of the scissor-tailed flycatcher). Their aim is not to contribute to the building up of a theoretical structure that could in turn be used for the explanation of empirical matters, but the actual employment of the relevant theoretical structures for the explanation of empirical matters.

In addition to the unities that can be established on the basis of law or object, there is the unity a science can achieve by virtue of being directed to one and the same value (*LI* I, 231 / *H* XVIII, B 236). Such is the case with the normative disciplines, as Husserl understands them. Ethics, for instance, organizes itself around the value of the good, deriving its basic norm from the definition of the good and arranging all other ethical norms under that basic norm by way of derivation or specification. Again, such unity is considered to be extra-essential to science conceived as a deductive system of laws; and the science constituted on the basis of such a unity will again be dependent upon the theoretical sciences for its specifically theoretical content.

7. THE LAWS OF EMPIRICAL SCIENCE

As we have seen, the basic difference between the sciences of the ideal and the sciences of the real is based upon the difference in the epistemic status of their respective laws: ideal laws are necessarily true; real laws are only contingently true. Thus the former can be known and justified a priori on the basis of direct insight; the latter can be known only a posteriori on the basis of "induction from the singular facts of experience" (*LI* I, 99 / *H* XVIII, B 62). Strictly speaking, what can be known of the laws of the natural sciences is not their truth or validity in the straightforward sense, but only the probability of their truth. "Instead of absolute knowledge which is denied us, we use our insight on individual and general facts of experience, and from these first work out those apodictic probabilities (so to speak) in which all attainable knowledge of the real is comprehended" (*LI* I, 106 / *H* XVIII, B 72). In the domain of the natural sciences, then, knowledge in the strict sense is available only on the level of second-order propositions pertaining to the probabilities of laws. "The probability, and not the law, is justified by insight" (*LI* I, 99 / *H* XVIII, B 62). Newton's law of gravitation, for instance, has itself never been proved in the demonstrative sense; "what has been proved is a proposition of the form: our knowledge up to date serves to found a probability of the highest theoretical dignity to the effect that, insofar as experience yields to the instruments at hand, either Newton's law, or one of the endlessly many conceivable mathematical laws within the limits of unavoidable experimental error is true" (*LI* I, 106 / *H* XVIII, B 72). However, in a "wider, modified sense," Husserl is prepared to allow for beliefs in laws that have acquired a high probability also to count as knowledge (*LI* I, 62 / *H* XVIII, B 14). In this respect he is more generous than Locke, who reserves the title of knowledge only for those beliefs that are certain. Probable beliefs may be more or less rational, but for Locke they will never count as knowledge.

Within the domain of the laws of nature Husserl distinguishes between exact and inexact laws. An inexact law is a roughly stated correlation of succession and coexistence. Its extension is vague and indefinite. It states general patterns of regularity without precision. By contrast, an exact law, expressed in the language of mathematics, has a precise extension. But for this very reason exact laws must be viewed, from an epistemological standpoint, as "idealizing fictions" (*LI* I, 106 / *H* XVIII, B 72). Newton's law of gravitation can again be taken as an example. Although it is well grounded in fact, in its exact form it represents nothing more than an "ideal possibility," since many other mathematical formulations of that law can be given that fit well within the limits of experimental error. Exact laws make such disciplines as theoretical mechanics, acoustics, and optics possible, but they do not exclude other possible systems of laws. They are mere "approximations" of genuinely valid laws that are, for us, unattainable (*LI* I, 100 / *H* XVIII, B 63). All available inductive evidence does not serve to uniquely justify one particular formulation of the law, but rather a range of formulations from which one will be selected. Newton's law of gravitation, then, cannot be taken as "absolutely valid," for (using a somewhat outdated example) "Weber's basic law for electrical phenomena could quite well function as the basic law of gravity. The differentiating factor in both formulae conditions differences in calculated values not exceeding the field of unavoidable observational error . . . hence we know *a priori* that endlessly many laws could and must do the same work as the Newtonian law of gravitation" (*LI* I, 100 / *H* XVIII, B 63). In the light of the fact that the empirical evidence will never force the selection of a unique formulation of an exact law, Husserl recognizes that the final choice of a law will be based on other methodological criteria, such as simplicity (*LI* I, 100 / *H* XVIII, B 63).

8. EMPIRICAL SCIENCE AS SCIENCE

Due to the contingent character of the laws of empirical science, the open-ended character of the inductive process by which they are confirmed, and the ineluctable margin of error in all observation, the laws of the empirical sciences are not only tentative, but approximate. The kind of knowledge they afford, when compared to knowledge in the strict sense defined by the classical idea of science, is knowledge only in a "wider, modified sense" (*LI* I, 62 / *H* XVIII, B 14). But is it not a piece of equivocation to call the empirical sciences "sciences" when they lack the distinguishing characteristics of scientific knowledge? In precisely what respect do the empirical sciences count as sciences? According to Husserl's account, there are at least two respects in which they do. One, as we already noted, is that they consist of a deductively ordered unified system of laws (*LI* I, 65 / *H* XVIII, B 18–19). In their formal structure, statically conceived, they are like the eidetic disciplines. Second, although their laws will never be more than probable, yielding knowledge in the wide but not the strict sense, knowledge in the strict sense is the ideal goal toward which they strive. "Knowledge in the precise sense—its being quite evident that S is P—then counts as the absolutely fixed, ideal limit which the graded probabilities for the being-P of S approach asymptotically" (*LI* I, 62 / *H* XVIII, B 14). The laws are never more than probable, but there is a constant attempt on the part of the empirical sciences to raise the probability to 1 through further induction, experimentation, and adjustment. There is a constant attempt to improve instrumentation by which the margin of observational error can be reduced. In this way the empirical sciences are ever converging on the idea of science in the classical sense. They prove themselves to be sciences not so much by what they are as by what they aim to be. Hence Husserl's concept of science remains univocal, in spite of the difference in the epistemic status of the sciences of the ideal and the sciences of the real.

9. THE IDEALIZATION OF THE IDEA OF SCIENCE

It should be pointed out, however, in bringing this chapter to a close, that the difference in epistemic status between the eidetic and empirical sciences was significantly diminished as a result of Husserl's further inquiry into the nature of evidence given the temporal structure of experience. In fact, the whole sense of Husserl's foundationalist account of science was significantly altered in his later works. In his earlier works, Husserl often gave the impression through his use of the term "intuition" (*Anschauung*) in connection with the apprehension of essences that the certainty of the foundation of the eidetic disciplines could be secured once and for all through some momentary vision (*ID* I, 8 / *H* III 1, 13). But as the intuition of essence was later developed into a method of eidetic variation, it became clear that the apprehension of eidetic states of affairs is not achieved in an instant; rather, it is an open-ended process involving the imaginative variation of endless possibilities (*PP*, 53–65 / *H* IX, 72–87). The method of eidetic variation is in principle inductive. It is an induction not over individual facts, but over imagined possibilities. For this reason, as Elisabeth Ströker has pointed out, the method of eidetic variation can never establish eidetic claims once and for all. For the actual number of variations carried out will always be finite.[12] Thus the claims of the eidetic sciences, like the claims of the empirical sciences, will acquire a measure of tentativity, and necessarily remain open to future modifications in the light of new evidence. In addition to this, Ströker contends that Husserl's eventual discovery of the horizontal structure of all experience "convinces Husserl that even evidence first conceived of as adequate can still implicitly contain unfulfilled intentions, indeed, must contain them, so that adequate evidence and its objective correlate, truth, become an idea lying in infinity. . . . Husserl thereby established that all evidence—far from offering absolute certainty and security against deception and error—has an irrevocably *presumptive* character."[13] This position on the relativity of all evidence becomes explicit in *Formal and Transcendental Logic*, where Husserl openly admits that "the possibility of deception is inherent in the evidence of experience. . . . This too holds for every evidence, for every 'experience' in the amplified sense. Even an ostensibly apodictic evidence can become disclosed as deception and, in that event, presupposes a similar evidence by which it is 'shattered' " (*FTL*, 156 / *H* XVII, 139–40).

Thus, with the idealization of the strong foundationalist idea of science, the "absolute" foundations of even the eidetic sciences are delivered from the lingering spirit of dogmatism. For at no time and in no discipline can one claim with certainty to be in final possession of the truth. The strong foundationalist requirement of absolute certainty and, correlatively, perfectly adequate evidence, to be located at the foundations of all genuine science is no longer a statement of accomplished fact on the part of some sciences, but postulated as the enduring aim and final goal of all the sciences (*CM*, 8 / *H* I, 49). According to Husserl's position in *Formal and Transcendental Logic*, it is but an unvarnished piece of naïveté to suppose that there is such a thing as "truth-in-itself" that can be grasped once and for all on the basis of evidence. Such truth would then be "possessed" when seen with "evidence," evidence here being construed as a quality or characteristic of a mental act.[14] But, Husserl maintains, truth is an "Idea" in the Kantian sense, lying at infinity (*FTL*, 250–51 / *H* XVII, 221; see also *C*, 111 / *H* VI, 113). Thus every truth-claim in practical as well as scientific life is relativized to truth as an ideal. It is always exposed to the future course of experience and subsequent evidence.[15]

This does not mean that all truth is relative, in the sense that one truth-claim is just as good as any other. For although all truth-claims necessarily fall short of the ideal of adequate evidence, the ideal of adequate evidence remains as criterion for the criticism of extant truth-claims. At every level of inquiry there is a question of evidence, of what is actually given. And this question can and ought to be pursued in keeping with the "spirit of self-responsibility" (*FTL*, 279 / *H* XVII, 246):

> The peculiar formal stamp of the intentionality ruling throughout the unity of scientific living and the formations it produces determines the peculiar stamp of scientific reason, as a reason that actualizes "genuine" cognition by an unremittingly concomitant criticism of cognition. Accordingly the systematic product of scientific reason—science, as a theory to be further developed *ad infinitum*—has the peculiar sense of being a system of judgments that, while undergoing an incessant criticism, are consciously made adequate to an evidential giving of the categorial objects themselves and that are, in this sense, truths: originally correct judgments, adjusted to the truly and actually existent itself, ideally embracing and (with their "complete" system) exhausting all the true being of the province. (*FTL*, 128–29 / *H* XVII, 114)

Adequate evidence, whether actual possession or infinite goal, remains the criterion.

In Husserl's later view, what is characteristic of scientific knowledge is not so much the security and finality of its cognitions as the openness of its cognitions to criticism in the light of further evidence. Ever falling short of an "actualization of a system of absolute truths" science must, in following the idea of absolute truth, surpass itself ad infinitum (*CM*, 12 / *HI*, 53). This holds not only for the formal and material eidetic sciences, but even for phenomenology itself, which, as a transcendental material eidetic science of pure consciousness, would provide an absolute foundation for all the other sciences. Thus, the "inherently first critique of knowledge" would be, Husserl writes, "the transcendental self-critique of phenomenological knowledge itself" (*FTL*, 288 / *H* XVII, 294; emphasis deleted).

10. SUMMARY

Husserl's philosophy of science has often been faulted as dogmatic, unduly informed by a foundationalist epistemology. I have argued that such charges are unjustified on two counts. First, although Husserl was throughout his philosophical career an adherent of the strong foundationalist account of science, he limited the validity of that account to the purely eidetic sciences. Such sciences display a deductive unity derived from their axioms. Being both self-evident and indemonstrable, axioms form their "foundations." But in section 72 of the "Prolegomena to Pure Logic," Husserl clearly states that the empirical sciences, including the physical sciences, do not find their unity in their deductive structure. Nor are they founded, once and for all, upon certain self-evident axioms and concepts. Rather, their unity is to be located in the idea of empirical explanation. Their laws are not certain, but only more or less probable on a given body of empirical evidence. The theories of the empirical sciences are thus "frequently modified in the course of scientific progress"; as the "process of knowledge progresses," we "progressively correct our conceptions" (*LI* I, 246 / *H* XVIII, B 256).

Second, the strong foundationalist idea of science was itself idealized as a direct consequence of Husserl's later theory of evidence. Even the eidetic sciences could now no longer claim to have final insight into necessary states of affairs. For once the method of the eidetic sciences was developed as a form of induction over imagined possibilities, all de facto eidetic claims were relativized to future evidence. Furthermore, due to the ineluctably temporal structure of experience, even the reflective apprehension of mental processes within consciousness could no longer claim to lay hold of adequate evidence. Phenomenological claims as well were relativized to the course of future evidence.

Husserl's foundationalism—if one can still speak of such—is thus functional rather than substantial. While priority relations in the order of cognitions are still recognized, at each level the achievement of certainty through adequate evidence is referred to as an Idea in the Kantian sense—something approached but never acquired. The cognitions of the eidetic sciences still lie at the foundations of the empirical sciences; but this is not to say that such cognitions have been secured, or can be secured, once and for all. Similarly, the cognitions of phenomenology are intrinsically prior to those of the positive sciences; but this is not to say that they have been, or could be, secured once and for all.

CHAPTER TWO

••••••••••••••••••••••••••••••

HUSSERL'S PHENOMENOLOGY AND THE FOUNDATIONS OF SCIENCE

In the preceding chapter I argued that Husserl appropriated the classical idea of science from the tradition and that he retained this idea throughout the course of his philosophical development. We noted, however, that in the course of that development Husserl converted the idea of science from a universal in the traditional sense to an Idea in the Kantian sense. The former would admit of genuine instantiation on the part of some sciences; the latter can only be approximated sub specie aeternitatis by any science.

To locate Husserl's conception of scientific knowledge within the classical tradition of reflection on the nature of science is not to challenge Husserl's self-understanding of the matter. Nor is it to posit a hidden conceptual dependence upon the tradition where Husserl claimed originality. In *Formal and Transcendental Logic*, Husserl explicitly takes up "the old Platonic idea" of science, "the idea of genuine science as science grounded on an absolute foundation," as the guiding idea of philosophy (*FTL*, 7 / *H* XVII, 6). Similarly, in the *Crisis* Husserl represents phenomenology as the fulfillment of the ancient ideal of philosophy as a universal science, initiated by Plato and renewed by Descartes (*C*, 7–16 / *H* VI, 5–14). As such, phenomenology is to fulfill the sense of philosophy's "primal establishment as the universal and grounding science" (*C*, 112 / *H* VI, 114–15). Thus Husserl holds that beneath the modern conflict of interpretations over the proper aim and method of philosophy lies a deep teleological unity that was fixed in the founding of philosophy during the ancient period (*C*, 113 / *H* VI, 115). The originality of phenomenology lies not in the proposal of a new idea of genuine science, but in the provision of the methodological prerequisites by which the traditional idea can be properly approached for the first time. The discipline of phenomenology is to make good on "what was originally and always sought in philosophy" (*C*, 17 / *H* VI, 16).

Although Husserl makes no reference to specific passages from Plato's dialogues in *Formal and Transcendental Logic* or the *Crisis*, it is quite natural to assume that he had in mind the classic treatment of the relation between the sciences of hypothetically based discursive reasoning (*dianoia*) and dialectically achieved philosophical insight (*noesis*) in the image of the divided line at the end of book VI of the *Republic*. In the lower section of the intelligible segment of the line, the soul "is compelled to investigate from hypotheses, proceeding from these not to a first principle but to a conclusion" (*Republic*, 510b). For the deductive sciences that belong to this section of the line—geometry and the like—the hypotheses function as unexamined assumptions. The practitioners of such sciences "do not deem it necessary to give any account of them either to themselves or to others as if they were clear to all" (510c). Thus, "because they do not go back to a first principle but proceed from hypotheses," they do not have any "clear understanding of their subjects" (511c).

The sciences, then, by virtue of their deductive structure, are based upon theoretical foundations that remain, in practice, obscure. This lack of clarity means that they do not have a complete and perfect understanding of their own subjects. They stand in need of a thoroughgoing examination of their foundations. Such an examination cannot, however, proceed deductively. For the process of deduction always begins with a set of hypotheses that it assumes to be valid and perspicuous. Rather, the examination of the foundations must be carried out, according to Plato, dialectically—the dialectic being precisely that method whereby previously unexamined assumptions are made thematic and subjected to criticism. Thus we have the initial division of intellectual labor between philosophy and the sciences, and at the same time a specification of the method and task of philosophy: utilizing the dialectic, it is to make its way to "the first principle of all that exists" (*Republic*, 511b), in terms of which the subject matter of the sciences is to be rendered completely intelligible (511c).

This theme is echoed in Husserl's repeated emphasis on the theoretical "naiveté" of the sciences and their need of completion through a philosophical clarification of their foundations. In the "Prolegomena to Pure Logic" of the *Logical Investigations*, for instance, Husserl claims that the sciences are theoretically "incomplete" in that "they cannot claim to have demonstrated all the last premises in their syllogisms, nor to have explored the principles on which the success of their method reposes" (*LI* I, 58 / *H* XVIII, B 10). What Husserl means by the "incompleteness" of the sciences is not that they stand in need of additional truths produced according to their standard operating procedures, but that they lack an "inner clarity and rationality" that is independent of their lateral expansion (*LI* I, 58 / *H* XVIII, B 10). Although the sciences have provided us with a "formerly undreamt of mastery over nature, they cannot satisfy us theoretically. They are, as theories, not crystal-clear: the function of all their concepts and propositions is not fully intelligible, not all of their presuppositions have been exactly analyzed, they are not in their entirety raised above all theoretical doubt" (*LI* I, 59 / *H* XVIII, B 10). That the sciences stand in need of such a clarification is amply demonstrated by the fact, Husserl later claims, that in every science there is a controversy about "the true sense of its fundamental concepts" (*FTL*, 16 / *H* XVII, 15).

The final clarification of the foundations of the sciences is not, however, to be carried out by the sciences themselves. The basic concepts and principles of the sciences will always function as the assumptions, not the objects, of their research. Rather, the investigation of the ultimate sense of their basic concepts is the exclusive task of philosophy, or, in this case, phenomenology as the fundamental philosophical discipline. Carrying out such investigations, Husserl writes in the *Cartesian Meditations*, "would have to lead to all the concepts which, as unexplored, function as fundamental in all positive sciences, but which accrue in phenomenology with all-round clarity and distinctness that leaves no further room for any conceivable questioning" (*CM*, 154 / *H* I, 180–81; translation modified). In his article "The Method of Clarification," Husserl states that "the first work to be undertaken is obviously concerned with the conceptual material with which science operates, and first of all, the primitive concepts."[1]

As we noted in the last chapter, however, concepts that are primitive or basic to a science are those that can no longer be defined by recourse to other concepts. They are "logically simple" and hence "indefinable." Clarification will not take place through definition. "What one can do in such cases," Husserl indicates in the *Philosophy of Arithmetic*, "consists only in pointing to the concrete phenomena from or through which the concepts are abstracted, and laying clear the nature of the abstraction process involved" (*POA*, 125 / *H* XII, 119). Here Husserl follows the empiricist strategy of clarifying concepts by tracing them back to the concrete experiences from which they were drawn (compare Hume, *Enquiry*, section 2). In the phenomenological clarification of the foundations of the sciences, then, "the point is to lead the sciences back to their origin, which demands insight and rigorous validity, and to transform them into systems of intuitive knowledge through work which clarifies, makes distinct, and grounds ultimately, and to reduce the concepts and statements of the sciences to conceptual essences (themselves apprehended in intuition) and objective data themselves, to which they give appropriate expression insofar as they are actually true."[2] Phenomenology is to keep the entire superstructure of the sciences in touch with its generative base in experience.

In thus specifying the structure of science, the foundationalist conception of scientific knowledge at the same time marks out the peculiar task of the philosophy: scientific knowledge is ultimately founded upon certain primitive concepts; philosophy is to clarify those primitive concepts. Science is founded research; philosophy is foundational research. The philosophical approach to the clarification of basic concepts will, of course, vary from one philosophy to the next. The phenomenological clarification of primitive concepts of the sciences, as evidenced from the quotations above, is not a matter of dialectical examination, purely logical analysis, or stipulative definition, but rather of bringing the referents of those concepts, the things themselves, to intuitive givenness. As Theodore De Boer points out, the phenomenological clarification of a concept takes place through a description of the phenomena from which the concept has been abstracted.[3] Thus, "proceeding from the existing sciences, Husserl proposes to go back to the sources, the phenomena from which the very first concepts arise."[4]

This, at least, was the initial working concept of what it would mean to carry out a phenomenological clarification of the sciences. But it is commonly recognized that Husserl's concept of the ultimate foundations of the sciences, and what would count as an appropriate phenomenological clarification of those foundations, underwent a radicalization with the invocation of the transcendental reduction and the subsequent exploration of its methodological implications.[5] In this chapter I will argue that in Husserl's phenomenology there are in fact two distinct dimensions to the problem of the foundations of the sciences. The first dimension has already been indicated. It concerns the "conceptual foundations" of the sciences, to be secured through the phenomenological clarification of concepts. This dimension is "first" both in the sense that it represents Husserl's initial idea of the foundations of the sciences and what would count as their clarification, and in the sense that it represents the first level of problems encountered in foundational research. But as we will see, it was precisely the pursuit of a phenomenological clarification of such basic concepts as "knowledge," and the "objectivity" of knowledge, that led Husserl to novel methodological moves, which in turn disclosed the ultimate foundation of all knowledge: transcendental consciousness. For the purposes of this chapter, I will call this more basic dimension the "transcendental ground" of the sciences, to be clarified through the self-explication of transcendental subjectivity, in which the world constantly presupposed by the sciences and all the objectivities found in it are actively or passively constituted. To follow the metaphor of foundation, I will maintain that Husserl eventually came to see that the ultimate clarification of the sciences would have to take into account the transcendental ground (*Boden*) on which their conceptual foundation (*Unterlage*) is laid.

The systematic basis for the division and stratification of the problem of the foundation of scientific knowledge is provided by an ontological distinction Husserl makes in the *Logical Investigations* between three different orders of connections that pertain to scientific knowledge. First are the psychological connections between the cognitive experiences in which knowledge is realized in the mind of the knower; second, the material connections between the matters known; and third, the logical connections between those judgments in which the unity of scientific knowledge is constituted. "In the case, e.g., of physics we distinguish between the pattern of connections of the mental states of the physical thinker from that of the physical nature that he knows, and both from ideal patterns of connection of the truths in physical theory" (*LI* I, 186 / *H* XVIII, B 179). Three separate but related domains: the mental, the material, and the logical; the knower, the known, and knowledge.

The logical and material connections make up the two sides of the conceptual foundations of the sciences. Taking physics again as an example, Husserl states that the basic material concepts used and presupposed by such a science—like existence, space, time, causality—need to be clarified by investigations of a "metaphysical" sort (*LI* I, 59–60 / *H* XVIII, B 11). These "metaphysical investigations," as Husserl calls them in the *Logical Investigations*, are destined to become the regional ontologies of the *Ideas* I and II. In the *Crisis*, such regional ontologies are set within an all-embracing ontology of the lifeworld, the given practical world of perceptual experience from which all scientific activity takes its point of departure. On the other hand, as ideal systems of propositions connected by the relations of ground and consequent, the sciences require certain "epistemological investigations" into the basic logical concepts of truth, proposition, concept, and the like. These epistemological investigations are carried out in the pure logic of Husserl's *Logical Investigations*, *Formal and Transcendental Logic*, and *Experience and Judgment*.

The "psychological connections" mentioned in this passage of the *Logical Investigations* contain the mundane correlate of what was to become, under the aegis of the transcendental *epoché*, the transcendental subjectivity of Husserl's later period. Insofar as they belong to a mundane subjectivity, however, psychological connections can in no way be construed as the basis of the sciences. Ever wary of the problem of psychologism after Gottlob Frege's stinging review of his *Philosophy of Arithmetic*, Husserl points out that the propositional content of the sciences "is quite independent of the scientist's subjectivity" (*LI* I, 173 / *H* XVIII, B 162). Nonetheless, the psychological connections of the *Logical Investigations* represent a placeholder for Husserl's later concept of the transcendental ground of the sciences.

The initial tripartite ontological distinction between the ideal realm of concepts and propositions, the world of nature, and the sphere of consciousness also provides the systematic framework in which the thematic progression of Husserl reflections on the foundations of the sciences takes place. First, the pure logic of the *Logical Investigations* as a *Wissenschaftslehre*; then the regional and lifeworld ontologies of the *Ideas* and the *Crisis*, establishing the formal and material a priori conceptual foundations of the sciences; and finally, transcendental subjectivity as the hidden ground of the sciences in *Formal and Transcendental Logic* and the *Crisis*.[6]

1. PURE LOGIC AS A *WISSENSCHAFTSLEHRE*

In the introduction to *Formal and Transcendental Logic*, Husserl claims that not just any activity guided by a theoretical interest automatically qualifies as genuine science. Rather, only the theoretical activity that is accompanied by a reflective justification of its own method with reference to pure principles derived from insight into the idea of genuine science can count as science in the precise sense. Science in this sense had its start with "Plato's grounding of logic, as a place for exploring the essential requirements of 'genuine' knowledge and 'genuine' science and thus for setting forth norms, in conformity with which a science consciously aiming at thoroughgoing justification, a science consciously justifying its methods and theory, might be built" (*FTL*, 1 / *H* XVII, 1; translation modified). A genuine science must be so constructed that it is able to justify every step it takes according to principles (*FTL*, 1 / *H* XVII, 1). For that reason, a necessary condition of the possibility of genuine science is the insight into those principles by which the method and results of a science might be ordered and justified (*FTL*, 1 / *H* XVII, 1). Science must measure up to norms that are derived from an insight into the essence of science. The discipline, then, which is conceptually prior to science and makes genuine science possible, is logic, which Husserl takes to be equivalent to a "theory of science" (*Wissenschaftstheorie*) (*FTL*, 2 / *H* XVII, 2).[7] By working out in detail the essence of genuine science, logic as a theory of science gives to existing science "its norm and guidance" (*FTL*, 4 / *H* XVII 4). Logic, then, will have a purely theoretical component (*reine Logik*) and a practical component (*Kunstlehre*), insofar as it involves not only insight into the essence of scientific knowledge elaborated in pure principles, but also the specification of norms for the actualization of scientific knowledge within specifically human theoretical activity.

In recent times, however, a lamentable reversal in the priority relation between the existing sciences and the theory of science has taken place. According to Husserl, this event occurred in the nineteenth century when the proliferating special sciences became ostensibly "self-sufficient," "no longer caring about logic—indeed, thrusting logic aside almost scornfully" (*FTL*, 3 / *H* XVII, 3). Logic qua theory of science was then construed as an a posteriori discipline, taking the existing sciences, especially the natural sciences, to be normative in themselves. Insofar as logic was guilty of complicity in this reassignment of its theoretical status, it abdicated its normative role, its true "historical vocation" (*FTL*, 4 / *H* XVII, 4). Instead of a leader, it became a follower. "Instead of seeking out the pure essential norms of science in all its essential formations in order to give the sciences fundamental guidance and to make it possible for them to be genuine sciences in shaping their methods and in rendering an account of every step, logic has been pleased to let itself be guided by the *de facto* sciences, particularly the much-admired natural sciences, in conceiving its ideal of science and in setting its own problems" (*FTL*, 3 / *H* XVII 3; translation modified).

But logic, Husserl maintains, it not an a posteriori science, generalizing over past and current practices of scientists. Rather, it is an a priori science, with an irrevocably normative component. It establishes criteria by which good and bad arguments, methods, and theories may be distinguished. In *Formal and Transcendental Logic*, Husserl makes clear his understanding of the task and research domain of logic:

> As a theory of science concerned with principles, logic intends to bring out "pure" universalities, "apriori" universalities . . . it does not intend to conduct an empirical investigation into so-called sciences that are given beforehand—cultural formations that have in

fact come into existence and go by that name—and abstract their empirical types; on the contrary, free from every restriction of the factual (which supplies it only with points of departure for a criticism of examples), it intends to make completely clear the final ideas that hover dimly before us whenever we are actuated by a purely theoretical interest. Constantly investigating the pure possibilities of a cognitive life, as such, and those of the cognitional formations, as such, attained therein, logic intends to bring to light the essential forms of genuine cognition and genuine science in all their fundamental types, as well as the essential presuppositions by which genuine cognition and genuine science are restricted and the essential forms of the true methods, the ones that lead to genuine cognition and genuine science. (*FTL*, 28 / H XVII, 25; translation modified)

The research domain of logic is not nature and human psychology, nor culture and human history, but the ideal realm of concepts, propositions, and their relations.

Those who insist upon the relevance of the history of science for the philosophy of science, however, might raise the following objection: If logic does not take its point of departure from the de facto sciences, how can it posit evaluative criteria for the sciences without being arbitrary? In the *Logical Investigations*, Husserl answers this question in the following way: Logic, as a theory of science, takes its point of departure not from what the sciences are in fact, but from what they in fact aim to be. That is, the sciences are to be evaluated in terms of the goal that they set for themselves, in terms of what Husserl calls the "Idea of science." For "sciences are mental creations which are directed to a certain end, and which are for that reason to be judged in accordance with that end" (*LI* I, 70–71 / H XVIII, B 26). In other words, the standards for the evaluation of science are internally generated by the scientific project itself. Although they have an a priori basis (the aim is an Idea in the ideal sense), they are not imported outside of actual scientific practice. "Whether a science is truly a science, or a method a method, depends on whether it accords with the aims that it strives for. Logic seeks to search into what pertains to genuine, valid science as such, what constitutes the Idea of science, so as to be able to use the latter to measure the empirically given sciences as to their agreement with their Idea, the degree to which they approach it, and where they offend against it" (*LI* I, 71 / H XVIII, B 26). Rather than simply comparing the existing sciences to find out what is typical of them, or attempting to explain them by reference to the cultural and scientific context from which they arose, logic as a normative discipline will seek to formulate general propositions that capture those characteristics a science, theory, or method must possess if it is to measure up to the standards implied in the goal to which it is directed. "Its [logic's] formal cognitions are the standards for measuring the extent to which ostensible science conforms to the idea of genuine science" (*FTL*, 31 / *H* XVII, 27).

The evaluative criteria set forth by logic, however, must never be merely general, but always specific. For what is being evaluated are the methods and theories put forth by human beings. Thus logic, in its normative application, must take into account the actual constitution of the human mind (*LI* I, 71 / *H* XVIII, B 27). The science being evaluated is a human endeavor; the Idea of science is being pursued by beings with a specific set of mental capacities and limitations. Nevertheless, the criteria of evaluation must be rooted in the a prirori principles that follow from the Idea of science itself.

In Husserl's estimation, part of the "tragedy of modern scientific culture" is the direct result of a widespread scorn for the question of "first principles." This tragedy is not to be located in the fact that it is no longer possible for any one person to assimilate and appreciate the vast domain of scientific knowledge as it spreads rapidly out in all directions with the development of the special sciences, but rather in the fact that the special sciences themselves are not unified according to the pure principles that flow from the essence of science as such (*FTL*, 3 / *H* XVII, 3). Uprooted in this way, the sciences have become much more a matter of technique, picked up through practical experience in the actual conduct of science, than a matter of genuine insight. In this sense, modern science has abandoned the "ideal of genuine science" and the "radicalness of scientific self-responsibility" (*FTL*, 3–4 / *H* XVII, 3). "No longer," Husserl writes, "is its inmost driving force that radicalness which unremittingly imposes on itself the demand to accept no knowledge that cannot be accounted for by originary first principles, which are at the same time matters of perfect insight" (*FTL*, 4 / *H* XVII, 3–4).

Such, then, are what might be called the "existential" motivations behind Husserl's interest in pure logic as a theory of science. The turn away from the question of first principles and the project of rigorous grounding through evidence signals for Husserl nothing less than a weakening of the will to science on the part of Western humanity. "At bottom," Husserl laments, "these sciences have lost their great belief in themselves, in their absolute significance," for the possibility of "a truly satisfying life, an individual and social life of practical reason" (*FTL*, 5 / HXVII, 4). The overarching Enlightenment project of providing a rational basis for human life hangs in the balance.

It should be clear at this point that Husserl considered the development of a pure logic to be essential for the actualization of the sciences. In this section I will indicate the task and structure of logic as a theory of science, as a *Wissenschaftslehre*, especially as it was set forth by Husserl in the *Logical Investigations*.

Since the aims of science are realized only by way of theories, the theory of science will be a theory of theory (i.e., a theory of the conditions of the possibility of theory in general). In Husserl's book, theories are, by definition, bodies of deductively interconnected truths (*LII*, 232 / H XVIII, B 236–37). Thus, an account of the conditions of the possibility of theory will necessarily be an account of the conditions of the possibility of truth and deductive unity (*FTL*, 5 / H XVII, 4).

The question pertaining to the possibility of science in this sense can, Husserl points out, be understood in two ways: subjectively or objectively. Subjectively, the question pertains to the possibility of knowledge on the part of a knowing subject, human or otherwise. It would require an answer that would specify those conditions that must be satisfied if there are to be genuine cases of knowing. Those conditions are of two sorts, real and ideal. With respect to human beings, the real conditions are the causal psychological conditions upon which our thinking depends (*FTL*, 5 / H XVII, 4). The ideal conditions, in turn, are of two kinds, noetic and logical. The noetic conditions are derived from an analysis of the Idea of knowledge itself. From such an analysis would flow the requirement, for instance, that the knowing subject must be able to perform those acts in which knowledge is realized. Thus, to know that q follows from p, the subject must be able to see that q follows from p. An internalist when it comes to the theory of epistemic justification, Husserl holds that knowledge just is evident true judgment. To know that q follows from p, it is not enough to judge that q follows from p when q in fact follows from p. One must also be able to *see* that q follows from p. The judgment, if it is to count as knowledge, must be accompanied by evidence understood as *seeing* that something is the case.

Although the simple fact that q follows from p is not a sufficient condition for the knowledge-status of any judgment that asserts that q follows from p, it is a necessary condition. Thus the inquiry into the noetic conditions of knowledge leads directly to the logical conditions of knowledge. Such conditions comprise the logical relations that obtain between propositions—in this case, the logical relation of entailment. The move from the noetic to the logical conditions of knowledge, however, represents at the same time a move from the subjective to the objective conditions of the possibility of theory. For "it is also evident that truths are what they are, and that, in particular, laws, grounds, principles, are what they are, whether we have insight into them or not. Since they do not hold insofar as we have insight into them, but we can have insight into them only insofar as they hold, they must be regarded as objective or ideal conditions of the possibility of our knowledge of them" (*LI* I, 233 / *H* XVIII, B 237).

Thus a second group of conditions can be specified on the basis of the analysis of concepts that pertain to the ideal contents of knowledge—the concepts of truth, proposition, entailment, and the like. Furthermore, Husserl maintains, this analysis can take place wholly without reference or relation to the Idea of subjectivity. "The laws in question have a meaning-content which is quite free from such a relation, they do not talk, even in ideal fashion, of knowing, judging, inferring, representing, proving, etc., but of truth, concept, proposition, syllogism, ground and consequent, etc." (*LI* I, 233 / *H* XVIII, B 238–39). These conditions pertain not to the possibility of acts of knowledge on the part of the knowing subject, but to the possibility of the objective ideal content of knowledge. By "objective content," Husserl means what is known in the act of knowledge, a content that stands as an ideal unity over and against that particular act and all other possible acts in which that knowledge is realized in a knowing subject. A theory is the objective ideal content of possible acts of scientific knowledge (*LI* I, 234 / *H* XVIII, B 240). More specifically, a theory consists of true propositions (the ideal elements) bound together in the relation of ground and consequent (the ideal form) (*LI* I, 234 / *H* XVIII, B 240).

In what sense will an analysis of concepts establish the conditions of the possibility of theory? The concepts in question are those that are essential to the concept of a theory—assuming that the concept of theory is complex and can be broken down into primitive concepts. If it is the case that a theory is a body of deductively interconnected truths, then the concepts that bear analysis will be, among others, "truth" and "proposition," together with the concepts that are relevant to deductive logical relations. On the basis of this conceptual analysis, certain laws, certain a priori analytic judgments, will follow. If a theory is to count as a genuine theory, it must "accord" with these laws (*LI* I, 235 / *H* XVIII, B 241). To evaluate a theory, to see if it does in fact accord with the laws that constitute the conditions of theories in general, is what Husserl calls the "logical justification" of the theory (*LI* I, 235 / *H* XVIII, B 241).

In the "Prolegomena to Pure Logic" of the *Logical Investigations*, Husserl distinguished three tasks that together define the proper province of pure logic. The first is the identification and clarification of those "primitive concepts" that serve as the necessary conditions of theories as deductively interconnected systems of true propositions. As we have seen, such concepts would include the concept of truth, proposition, concept, and various forms of logical relations between propositions—hypothetical, disjunctive, conjunctive, and the like. These concepts fall under the general category of meaning. Correlated with them are concepts falling under objective categories, such as object, property, state of affairs, number, and relation. These concepts, too, must be identified and clarified. Thus a pure logic will include not only a formal logic, but a formal ontology (cf. *FTL*, 72–148 / *H* XVII, 63–132).

By the "clarification" of concepts, Husserl has in mind an insight achieved into their corresponding essences through an ideational abstraction (that is, the isolation of an essence) performed on the basis of an adequate presentation of one or more of their instances, and the fixation of an unambiguous terminology by which the concepts in question are expressed (*LI* I, 238 / *H* XVIII, B 244–45). If the concept is complex, then it must be broken down to its constituent concepts so that the essence of each can be grasped together with the form of their combination (*LI* I, 238 / *H* XVIII, B 244). The goal here is to establish clear and distinct concepts and a univocal theoretical vocabulary.

The second task of logic as a theory of science is the formulation of laws, grounded in the clarified primitive concepts, which regulate both the complication of concepts, propositions, and theories, and, on the objective side, objects, states of affairs, and fields of research. These laws will themselves constitute what could be called a "metatheory," a theory of the forms of theories, and, on the objective side, a theory of the forms of research domains. The laws that comprise the metatheory are to have their foundation in basic laws that are in turn rooted in the relevant primitive categorical concepts (*LI* I, 239 / *H* XVIII, B 246). By virtue of their formal universality, these laws will embrace the content and objects of all scientific knowledge and thus lie at the basis of all the particular sciences. All sciences, if they are to count as sciences, must conform to these laws (*LI* I, 239 / *H* XVIII, B 246).

The theory of science, then, is to be derived from the basic, categorial concepts pertaining to the structure of the ideal content of science. As such, this theory is adequate for an account of theories in general. But the task remains to specify the different logically possible types or forms of theories.

This is the third task of the theory of science as articulated by Husserl. On the basis of the formal logical laws developed in accordance with the second task, a truly comprehensive theory of science will then proceed to lay out the full range of possible forms of theories. In other words, it will internally differentiate the Idea of Theory (*LI* I, 239–40 / *H* XVIII, B 247). The objective correlate of the theory of possible theories is, according to Husserl, the mathematical theory of manifolds, where a manifold is understood to be "a field which is uniquely and solely determined by falling under a theory of such a form, whose objects are such as to permit certain associations which fall under certain basic laws of this or that determinate form (here the only determining feature)" (*LI* I, 241 / *H* XVIII, B 248–49). A field of objects is here characterized in a purely formal manner, without regard to the material genus under which its objects might fall.

As it turns out, the great proportion of the work in pure logic as described by Husserl will be carried out not by the philosopher, but by the mathematician. For "the construction of theories, the strict, methodical solution of all formal problems, will always remain the home domain of the mathematician" (*LI* I, 244 / *H* XVIII, B 252). Those who object to the "takeover" of pure logic by the mathematicians do so on the basis of the prejudice that the essence of mathematics has to do with number and quantity in particular. On the contrary, Husserl maintains that mathematics is actually a theory of formal relations in general. Number and quantity are not the only matters that admit of formal treatment. For this reason the "mathematical form of treatment" of formal logical problems is "the only scientific one, the only one that offers us systematic closure and completeness, and a survey of all possible questions together with the possible forms of their answers" (*LI* I, 244 / *H* XVIII, B 253).

At this point we might well wonder whether Husserl, after having outlined the tasks of a pure logic, has not proceeded forthright to hand over the entire discipline to the mathematicians. Indeed, at this point Husserl himself asks, "What is left over for philosophers, if the development of all true theories falls in the mathematician's field?" (*LI* I, 244 / *H* XVIII, B 253). As it turns out, there is a division of theoretical labor reserved for the philosopher. But what it is exactly, and how it is to be distinguished from that of the mathematician, is not entirely clear in the *Logical Investigations*.

That there is something left over for the philosopher in the domain of pure logic follows immediately from the fact that the mathematicians are primarily engaged in the construction of theories. Husserl likens their activity to that of mechanics, who build machines without insight into the theoretical principles upon which machines operate. Husserl then makes two points on the basis of this analogy: one, that practicing mathematicians have practical rather than theoretical interests at heart; and two, that practicing mathematicians are unreflective with respect to the basic concepts and laws upon which their own theory is founded. Although, as mathematicians, they have the distinction of working on a general theory of science, as special scientists they fail to thematize the fundamental ideas pertaining to their own discipline (*LI* I, 245 / *H* XVIII, B 254).

Let us examine these two claims in turn. First, that the interests of the mathematician are not primarily theoretical. Presumably, a discipline is of a practical sort if its primary focus is not the truth about the nature of things, but the empirical results that follow from the application of a theory. If the theory yields the desired results, then it is considered useful and worthy of acceptance. The theory in question may be imperfectly understood, but that is of no concern to the one who uses it, as long as it "works" and thereby facilitates a greater measure of control over a certain segment of empirical reality. Now the "special sciences," Husserl maintains, are all characterized by this attitude, for they are "more concerned with practical results and mastery than with essential insight" (*LI* I, 245 / *H* XVIII, B 253).

Leaving aside for the moment the question of whether the special sciences are more practically than theoretically motivated, it is not clear that mathematics is itself a special science. For earlier Husserl had stated that the theory of deductive forms ranges over all the special sciences, since it deals with that which makes science science. If mathematics is itself a special science, it is a peculiar one in that it is also a general theory of science. If the general theory of deductive systems is itself a deductive system, then it includes itself within its own domain.

Furthermore, since mathematics deals with laws and complications of laws that derive from concepts alone, it is not clear to what degree or in what sense it is directed toward practical results in the empirical world of real events, objects, and processes. Its primary interest would seem to be directed toward the ideal world, or worlds, of possibility and necessity. From the possibility of utilizing metaphors drawn from the practical arts in the characterization of what mathematicians do—"constructing" theories—it does not follow that their activity is or can be straightforwardly characterized as practical. Presumably those with purely theoretical interests will also engage in the "construction" of theories. But that does not mean their activity is on par with and has essentially the same goals as the activity of a mechanic. Without a more detailed and explicit definition of what it means to be a "practical" discipline, and without an argument for including mathematics under the rubric of the special sciences, it is not clear in what respect the work of the mathematician can be cordoned off from that of the philosopher in connection with the development of a pure logic.

To find out what Husserl himself might mean by a "practical discipline" in this connection we must turn to a later text, the *Cartesian Meditations*. In section 38 of that work, Husserl claims that even the "logical" or theoretical disciplines can be seen as works of practical reason insofar as they actively constitute their objects on the basis of the material ultimately supplied in passive constitution (that is, roughly, perception). Here "practical reason" does not mean the branch of philosophy that ascertains and grounds the principles of human action, nor does it mean the "applied" sciences, but rather those sciences within the theoretical disciplines that are constructive, which constitute new objectivities on the basis of the old. In this figurative sense only is mathematics a practical discipline.

Second, is it the case that the practicing mathematician is unreflective, that "the mathematician constructs theories of number, quantities, syllogisms, manifolds, without needing to have ultimate insight into the essence of theory in general, and that of the concepts and laws which are its conditions" (*LI* I, 245 / *H* XVIII, B 253)? It would seem that this is not necessarily the case. A theory, on Husserl's own account, is a deductively organized system of laws ultimately derived from certain primitive concepts. The theory of number, for instance, is based upon the concept of number. Now it is entirely possible that a mathematician could develop a theory of number without having inquired into the nature and essence of theory itself. And the same could be said for any mathematical theory that is based upon concepts of the objective sort—the first, second, and fourth examples of mathematical theories in the passage quoted above. But the third example, the theory of syllogisms, the theory of deductive forms of inference, is quite different. It is based upon a concept that pertains to the form of the ideal content of any theory, including itself. It is a concept that belongs to the category of meaning. Here mathematicians are dealing with those very laws that constitute the conditions of theory as such. It is difficult to see how, in this case, they are oblivious to the conditions of theory, since these conditions are the subject matter of their own theory.

But perhaps a closer reading of the above quotation and some attention to Husserl's positive description of the specific interests and tasks of the philosopher will give us a more precise idea of where the division between the labor of the philosopher and that of the mathematician lies. Strictly speaking, it is not that mathematicians fail to deal with the concepts and laws that serve as the condition of the possibility of theory, but that they lack final insight into the essence of such concepts and laws. As the physicist Hermann Weyl put it, "inasmuch as the mathematician operates with concepts in a strict and formal fashion in constructing science, he must be reminded from time to time that origins in their dim and distant depths refuse to be grasped by his methods."[8] Even if it is the case, then, that mathematicians are busy constructing a theory of deductive inference, which in turn counts as a general theory of theory, they can do so qua mathematicians without insight into the essence of those concepts from which the laws of deductive inference are derived and upon which they are ultimately based. Since these concepts lie at the very basis of the discipline, to the degree that they remain unclear the entire discipline is not entirely transparent to itself. It is not theoretically complete in the sense described above.

It is precisely here that the philosopher comes into the picture. Taking his example from the natural sciences, Husserl says that the scientist is content to have established laws on the basis of which we can predict the future course of real events, or reconstruct the course of real events in the past. But the philosopher "wants to clarify the essence of a thing, an event, a cause, an effect, of space, of time, etc." (*LI* I, 245 / *H* XVIII, B 254). If it is the case that the natural scientist is interested, or primarily interested, only in prediction, then it may be that his interests are practical rather than theoretical. But the difference that is relevant here also covers the difference between the mathematician and the philosopher, even if both of them maintain primarily theoretical interests. The natural scientist constructs a deductively organized nomological system, while the philosopher investigates the concepts presupposed by the natural scientist in the construction of that system. Likewise, while the mathematician is busy with the construction of formal systems, the philosopher is in the business of clarifying the concepts presupposed in the construction of those systems. Hence, in terms of the three tasks of pure logic as delineated by Husserl, the work of the philosopher is largely limited to the first: the clarification of primitive concepts. As such, "philosophical research so supplements the scientific achievements of the natural sciences and the mathematician, as for the first time to perfect pure, genuine, theoretical knowledge. The *ars inventiva* of the special investigator and the philosopher's critique of knowledge, are mutually complimentary scientific activities, through which complete theoretical insight, comprehending all relations of essence, first comes into being" (*LI* I, 245 / *H* XVIII, B 254).

Earlier I mentioned that logic as a theory of science has both a strictly theoretical and a normative component. The normative component, however, admits of a further differentiation. In the "Prolegomena to Pure Logic," Husserl draws a methodological distinction between norms and rules (*LI* I, 171 / *H* XVIII, B 158–59; see also *C*, 92 / *H* VI, 94–95). This distinction coincides with, and is in fact based upon, the ontological distinction between the ideal and the real domains of being. Purely logical norms for human thought are not based upon empirical research into the real patterns of human thinking. Rather, they are "normative transformations" of theoretical laws that are rooted in the concepts of truth, proposition, entailment, and the like (*LI* I, 172 / *H* XVIII, B 160). Such laws, then, are a priori, analytic, and self-evident once the meaning of the relevant concepts has been clearly grasped. But these laws are, in themselves, not of a normative character. They simply state ideal logical relations that obtain between propositions (e.g., that q is entailed by the conjunction of p and p→q). But they do have normative implications, such as: it would be valid for an intelligent being to conclude q given p and p→q; or, given p and p→q, an intelligent being should conclude q. Thus the theoretical laws of pure logic can be normatively transformed into forms of valid inference (i.e., "purely logical norms"). Such norms have their roots in the objective side of science. Again, "objective" signifies the ideal propositional content of a science. "Purely logical" refers to the ideal form of such content.

In addition to these norms, there are also technical rules for human thought. Such rules pertain to the "production and criticism of scientific knowledge" and are developed with an eye to the specific real constitution of the human mind (*LI* I, 171 / *H* XVIII, B 162). Based upon empirical considerations germane to psychology, they consist of a collection of "human devices" for acquiring, defining, and elaborating a particular theoretical domain. All of these devices, or "methods," are "adapted to the human constitution as it at present normally is" (*LI* I, 173 / *H*XVIII, B 162). If our sensory apparatus were differently organized, our empirical methods of data collection might also be different, just as our methods of mathematical calculation might be different if our mental capacities were much stronger, or significantly weaker. The majority of humans cannot immediately see what 1,411 divided by 17 is. So we have invented the method of long division. If we could immediately see that 1,411 divided by 17 is 83 (as a few savants can), we wouldn't need the method of long division in that case. If we could immediately see the solution to all problems in division, we wouldn't need the method at all. Thus logic "can also be included in a logico-practical technology and perhaps combined with an empirical anthropological component" (*FTL*, 31 / *H* XVII, 27).

Science, then, admits of two kinds of treatment. One takes its point of departure from the array of methods by which human beings produce and criticize scientific knowledge; the other takes its point of departure from the ideal propositional content of science. The former pertains to the "subjective" side of science, the latter to the "objective" side. In *Formal and Transcendental Logic*, Husserl speaks of a logic "whose two-sided theme is all possible forms of the actions productive of and cognitive of scientific cognitional formations; on the Objective side, these formations themselves" (*FTL*, 108 / *H* XVII, 96). This thematic two-sidedness will be reflected in the normative domain, as he already noted in *Logical Investigations*. "Norms accordingly fall into two classes. One class of norms regulates all proof and all apodictic connection *a priori*; it is purely ideal, and only relates to our human knowledge by way of self-evident application. The other is empirical [corresponding to "rules"], and relates essentially to the specifically human side of the science. It has its roots in our general human constitution" (*LI* I, 174 / *H* XVIII, B 167).

On Husserl's taxonomy of the tasks of the discipline of logic as a theory of science, the bulk of contemporary Anglo-American philosophy of science falls within the category of the "subjective normative," insofar as the center of recent discussion has been the question of scientific rationality (i.e., the rules by which scientific knowledge is to be generated and appraised, given the structure of scientific theories together with psychological, social, and historical constitution of human beings). By way of contrast, the older, logical empiricist philosophy of science was "objective normative" insofar as it focused upon the logical structure of the propositional content of finished scientific theories to the exclusion of the question of how they are actually produced and criticized within their own historical context. Husserl's position is that both sides of the normative question must be developed in tandem if a full account of science is to be given.

2. REGIONAL ONTOLOGY

As we have seen, pure logic consists of both a formal logic and a formal ontology. Formal logic is a theory of the formal structure of the ideal propositional content of scientific theories. As such, it is a strictly theoretical discipline. But it also admits of a normative transformation, whereby the laws of formal logic are converted into criteria governing the realization of scientific knowledge on the part of a knowing subject. Given these normative criteria, the rules for scientific practice on the part of a particular kind of knowing subject (e.g., the human knowing subject) can be specified. Understood both as a human practice and as a deductively unified system of true propositions, science will thus exhibit a conceptual dependence upon formal logic. Furthermore, insofar as science is about something, it will also be subject to the conceptual constraints of a formal ontology. A formal ontology is a theory of the formal structure of any object whatever.

A special science, however, will not be about any object whatever, but about objects of a particular kind. A special science is specialized by virtue of the fact that it restricts its investigation to a certain domain, or region, of objects within the world. The basic regions of the world, Husserl contends, are delimited by a unified nexus of generic essences. Insight into these essences will generate a fund of material a priori truths that hold unconditionally for all objects within the region defined by those essences. These truths will, in turn, constitute an eidetic science of a generically defined region of being, or, what Husserl will call a "regional ontology." "Any concrete empirical objectivity finds its place within a highest material genus, a 'region,' of empirical objects. To the pure regional essence, then, there corresponds a regional eidetic science, or, as we can also say, a regional ontology" (*ID* I, 18 / *H* III, 23–24). Every empirical science, then, will fall under the province of some regional ontology. "Any sciences of matters of fact (any experiential science) has essential theoretical foundations in eidetic ontologies. For . . . it is quite obvious that the abundant stock of cognitions relating in a pure, an unconditionally valid manner to all possible objects of the region—in so far as these cognitions belong partly to the empty form of any objectivity whatsoever and partly to the regional *Eidos* which, as it were, exhibits a necessary material form of all objects in the region—cannot lack significance for the exploration of empirical facts" (*ID* I, 18 / *H* III, 24; emphasis deleted). For this reason, the "empirical sciences must be grounded on the regional ontologies which are relevant to them and not merely on the pure logic common to all sciences" (*ID* I, 32 / *H* III, 39; emphasis deleted).

In this section I will briefly outline the task and structure of regional ontology as set out in part 1 of Husserl's *Ideas* I. But I will not endeavor to examine the actual content of the regional ontologies of the natural and the historical worlds as executed by Husserl in *Ideas* II. Such would take us beyond the introductory scope of this chapter.

The "experiential sciences" (*Erfahrungswissenschaften*), or empirical sciences, are sciences of matters of fact. They are founded upon acts that posit real individual existence in space and time. Individual existence—with the possible exception of God—is contingent. For any existing individual object, it is true that it could have been otherwise than it happens to be (*ID* I, 7 / *H* III, 12). But the contingency of existing things is correlated to a necessity, a necessity rooted in their essence, or *Eidos*. Every individual object has its essence, and every essence has its possible individual instantiations (*ID* I, 15 / *H* III, 21). Thus, for any contingently existing thing, there is a stock of truths that necessarily hold for it, truths that are stratified according to different levels of generic universality (*ID* I, 8 / *H* III, 12–13).

The ontological relation between individual objects and their essences serves as the ground of the conceptual relation between the empirical and eidetic sciences (*ID* I, 15 / *H* III, 21). This relation is characterized by a one-sided dependence. While the eidetic sciences are independent of the factual findings of the empirical sciences, being based not on the experience of individuals but rather on the seeing of essences (*Wesensanschauung*), the empirical sciences are dependent upon the eidetic sciences (*ID* I, 17 / *H* III, 23). This dependency manifests itself in three respects, the first two of which have already been discussed in the preceding section:

1. Insofar as empirical science engages in acts of mediate grounding, it "must proceed according to the formal principles treated by formal logic" (*ID* I, 18 / *H* III, 23).

2. Insofar as empirical science deals with objects, "it must be universally bound by the laws that belong to the essence of anything objective whatever. It thereby enters into a relation with the complex of formal-logical disciplines " (*ID* I, 18 / *H* III, 23).

3. Insofar as any object belongs to a material genus, "any eidetic truth belonging to the pure essences comprised in that [materially essential] composition must yield a law by which the given factual singularity, like any other possible singularity, is bound" (*ID* I, 18 / *H* III, 23).

Every regional ontology will have its own generic-specific structure. For every material essence has its place within a hierarchy of essences, ranging from the most general to the most specific. The hierarchy will be bounded by the highest genus at the top and the *infirmae species*—or "eidetic singularities"—at the bottom. The highest genus is such that there are no genera above it; the eidetic singularities are such that there are no essential particularities below them. Within this hierarchy Husserl distinguishes between self-sufficient and non-self-sufficient essences. A non-self-sufficient essence is one that is essentially related to another essence such that together they constitute the unity of an essence. For example, the non-self-sufficient essence visible "sensuous quality" is essentially bound up with the essence "extension." This means that any object instantiating visible "sensuous quality" will necessarily co-instantiate "extension." Any sensuously appearing visible quality must have some extension. Any essence where this is not the case is self-sufficient. A non-self-sufficient essence is called an *"abstratum"*; a self-sufficient essence is called a *"concretum."* An individual object falling under a *concretum* is called an *"individuum"* (ID I, 29 / H III, 35–36). A region is then defined as the highest generic unity belonging to a *concretum* (ID I, 18 / H III, 23).

The development of a regional ontology is a necessary condition for the complete "rationalization" of an empirical science. A science is rational when every particular appearing within that science is completely determined with respect to the hierarchy of eidetic universalities ranging over it (ID I, 19 / H III, 24). Such a rationalization took place, in part, with the application of geometry at the inception of the modern physical sciences. For it was at that point the "people made clear to themselves that the material thing is essentially *res extensa* and that geometry is therefore the ontological discipline relating to an essential moment of material thinghood, namely the spatial form" (ID I, 19 / H III, 24; emphasis deleted).

The sorting of objects into their appropriate ontological regions, and the development of the eidetic disciplines of the various *abstracta* within those regions, will have an impact upon not only the content of the corresponding empirical sciences, but their conduct as well. This point is brought out most clearly in *Ideas* III. There Husserl claims that the norms for the methods of the empirical sciences must be drawn from regional ontology. For in all science, methodical grounding and ultimate justification lead back to certain experiences in which the objects ostensibly known are given in intuition (ID III, 20 / H V, 23). But as there are essentially different types of objects, so there are different ways in which objects are given. Hence, "the method of every science must be determined by the sort of originarily bestowing intuition, or the basic sort of originary apprehension, essentially belonging to the object-category to which it is related" (ID III, 20 / H V, 22). The different ways in which objects are typically given is determined by their universal essence, which is theoretically articulated in the corresponding regional ontology (*ID* III, 21 / *H* V, 23). Thus the methodology of the empirical sciences is to be determined not only from the side of formal logic, through the development of rules for the production of knowledge in keeping with the principles of logic, but also from the side of regional ontology, which determines the mode of evidence appropriate to each object-domain.

3. TRANSCENDENTAL CONSCIOUSNESS AS THE GROUND OF THE SCIENCES

In the previous sections of this chapter on pure logic and regional ontology, we have been discussing the relation of phenomenology to what I have called the "conceptual foundations" of the sciences. In the development and construction of theories, the sciences constantly presuppose and make use of certain basic concepts. As a form of foundational research, phenomenology is to clarify those concepts by recourse to those mental processes in which the referents of those concepts are intuitively given.

A number of concrete examples of Husserl's method of phenomenological clarification can be found in the *Logical Investigations*. As a science, logic is based upon the primitive concepts of truth, proposition, relation, and the like. In especially the Sixth Logical Investigation we find Husserl's initial attempts at clarifying a number of these primitive concepts. Truth is clarified by recourse to the act of identifying synthesis where truth is actually given, where truth is experienced as the identity of the state of affairs as meant and the state of affairs as intuited. Such logical relations as conjunction, disjunction, and the like are clarified by recourse to those acts where such categorical objectivities are given, acts of "categorial intuition." These clarifications will also work together ultimately to show how logic as a science is possible. For logic claims to be a deductively organized body of knowledge; but knowledge, according to Husserl, can occur only in those contexts where the states of affairs judged are at the same time intuitively given. For any science, then, it is the task of phenomenology to disclose precisely the sense in which it can claim to count as knowledge by clarifying the manner in which its objects are given in the course of experience.

The phenomenological clarification of the conceptual foundations of the sciences remains one of the stated tasks of Husserl's phenomenology. But, as I indicated earlier, Husserl's concept of the ultimate foundations of the sciences underwent a process of radicalization as the question regarding the possibility of knowledge became global and as the implications of the ideal of philosophy as a rigorous foundational science became more apparent to him. In this section I will point out how a new dimension to the problem of the foundations of the sciences was disclosed in this process of radicalization. I will also attempt to indicate the shape the task of a phenomenological clarification of the foundations of the sciences was to take within this dimension. I will call this new dimension the "transcendental ground" of the sciences.

Husserl's turn to the transcendental dimension of the problem of the foundations of the sciences came about as a result of his reflections on the necessary prerequisites for any theoretical inquiry into the conditions of the possibility of scientific knowledge. All sciences are sciences of the world, or, at least, some part of it. Furthermore, the world, as given in prescientific experience, is constantly presupposed as a source of confirmation for theories in the empirical sciences. In both these ways the sciences presuppose, then, not only certain primitive concepts and indemonstrable propositions, but also the existence of the world. The presupposition of the existence of the world as the ultimate horizon for all possible objects of positive scientific research constitutes what Husserl identifies in *Ideas* I as the fundamental thesis of the "natural attitude." The natural attitude, however, is not the exclusive property of the sciences. It is shared with nontheoretical activity as well. The world is the arena not only of scientific research, but of practical life.

The aims of both theoretical and practical life are always specified in terms of the world, which is presupposed as simply "there." "Objective science, too," Husserl notes in the *Crisis*, "asks questions only on the ground of this world's existing in advance through pre-scientific life. Like all praxis, objective science presupposes the being of this world" (C, 110 / H VI, 112–13). But the world serves not only as the presupposition of the sciences, it serves as their object as well. "To cognize 'the' world more comprehensively, more reliably, more perfectly in every respect than naive experiential cognizance can, to solve all the problems of scientific cognition which offer themselves within the realm of the world, that is the aim of the sciences belonging to the natural attitude" (*ID* I, 57 / H III, 63; emphasis deleted).[9] Although prescientific experience may be considered naive when compared to the sophisticated explanations and methodological apparatus of the sciences, the sciences themselves are also naive insofar as they, like prescientific experience, are based upon the natural attitude. "In respect of its point of departure all natural science is naïve. The nature that it means to explore is for it simply there.

Without question physical things exist, exist as at rest, moving, changing, in infinite time. We perceive them, we describe them in pure and simple experiential judgments. To cognize these unquestioned data in an objectively valid, strictly scientific manner is the aim of natural science" (PSS, 19 / *PSW*, 18).[10]

In a discussion of science, it is difficult to circumvent the negative connotations of words like "naive" and "naïveté." But Husserl is not ascribing a naïveté to the positive sciences as if it were a fault, a theoretical defect. On the contrary, it is wholly appropriate, and perhaps even necessary, for the sciences to assume the existence of that which they seek to know. The assumption of the existence of the world becomes a defect—a fatal flaw, in fact—only when the epistemological question of the possibility of knowledge of the world is raised. For any answer to the question that itself presupposes the existence and knowledge of the world necessarily begs the question. The naïveté of the sciences is not so much a defect in the sciences of the world as it is an indication that such sciences are themselves in principle incapable of solving the basic epistemological problem. They need to be supplemented by another science that, in raising the question of the possibility of the scientific knowledge of the world, no longer presupposes the existence of the world or any scientific knowledge of it. Such a science Husserl calls "transcendental phenomenology."

The "transcendental turn" in Husserl's thinking, signaled by five introductory lectures delivered at Göttingen in 1907 and published under the title *The Idea of Phenomenology*, was executed for precisely the kind of epistemological reasons mentioned above. And it is to these lectures we will turn to see precisely how the global epistemological question of the possibility of knowledge of the world necessarily leads to the disclosure of pure consciousness as the transcendental ground of science.

In the opening lecture Husserl argues that epistemology, in the critical sense, is possible only as phenomenology. That is, it is only from the standpoint of the phenomenological attitude and through the use of phenomenological methods that the global question of critical epistemology pertaining to the relation of cognition to the world can be answered without presupposing precisely that which is to be made problematic by the question. The answer to the question of the possibility of knowing the world cannot presuppose knowledge of the world without begging the question. "If the very sense and value of positive knowledge *as such*, with *all* its methodological arrangements, with all its exact groundings, has become problematic, then this effects every principle drawn from the sphere of positive knowledge that might be taken as a point of departure as well as every ostensibly exact method of grounding" (*IP*, 21 / *H* II, 25). Any answer given to the global question of critical epistemology on the basis of the natural attitude already assumes the fact of knowing, the existence of the object of knowledge, the possibility of cognitive access to that object, and the correspondence of the cognition to that object (*IP*, 17 / *H* II, 20). In particular, any epistemology based upon explanatory psychology assumes that in this branch of scientific cognition we are in touch with the human mind as an object existing in the world, related to other objects in the world by way of causality. But the question of critical epistemology is directed to the possibility of cognition of the world on a global scale. To answer that question on the basis of a particular cognition of the world is, again, to assume the validity of precisely that which one is proposing to make problematic. Critical epistemology, then, cannot be conducted on the basis of the natural attitude. To think that this is possible, Husserl maintains, is to betray one's confusion as to the proper level of epistemological questioning (*IP*, 21 / *H* II, 26). This is the critical thesis that Husserl would direct to all forms of naturalized epistemology.

Up to this point, however, Husserl has assumed that the basic question of critical epistemology—the question of the possibility of knowledge per se—is both legitimate and coherent. But is it possible to answer this question without at the same time begging the question? Presumably any theoretically satisfying answer to the question of the possibility of knowledge must itself count as a piece of knowledge. But if this is the case, it looks as though the entire project of critical epistemology is misconceived from the outset.

In the second lecture Husserl takes up the problem of the point of departure for a critical epistemology that is truly consistent with its own level of questioning. Is it actually the case that "epistemology cannot get underway because it places knowledge as such in question and so must place any knowledge with which it begins in question as well" (*IP*, 26 / *H* II, 34)? Husserl's rejoinder to this objection—the Hegelian objection to critical epistemology—employs the Cartesian strategy of distinguishing within the domain of cognition those cognitive claims that are questionable from those that are not. The "global" epistemological question is then restricted to the former, while the answer is to be given on the basis of the latter. For although critical epistemology must begin with the resolve to question and to doubt all cognitions with respect to their claims to transcend themselves and make contact with an external object, it will nonetheless eventually discover a class of cognitions that is not questionable, that is indubitable. Cognitions that belong to this class possess the property of indubitability because their objects are not external to consciousness. Their objects are not transcendent, but immanent. By "immanent" Husserl means here that they are wholly given within the experience of them. Such objects are encountered in acts of reflection upon mental processes. Whereas the cognitive claims pertaining to transcendent objects exceed what is actually given in the experience of them, and so may turn out to be mistaken, the cognitive claims pertaining to immanent objects do not venture beyond available evidence. Mental processes are wholly given within the reflective apprehension of them. Here, "nothing that is meant fails to be given" (IP, 45 / H II, 61). In the face of such givenness, such evidence, it would be "absurd to persist in universal doubt" (IP, 23 / H II, 30). The reflective apprehensions of mental processes now count as "primary knowledge" (IP, 23 / H II, 29). Together they form the "absolute ground" for a theory of knowledge (IP, 24 / H II, 31). Being "first in themselves," they "can support the whole storied edifice of universal knowledge," as Husserl later puts it in *Cartesian Meditations* (CM, 14 / H I, 54). Here the "*epoché,*" the "epistemological reduction," abstaining from the use of any knowledge of transcendent objects for the sake of accounting for the possibility of the knowledge of transcendent objects, reveals another kind of knowledge, a knowledge whose objects are wholly "immanent" (IP, 30 / H II, 39). Such knowledge is therefore free of the problem of transcendence (IP, 45 / H II, 60).

Thus the resolve to refrain from utilizing any straightforward cognition of the world brings to the fore the reflective cognition of consciousness. This latter cognition would include cognition of the acts of cognition that make up in part a "highly ramified sphere of being that can be given to us absolutely" (IP, 24 / H II, 30). In this way the project of critical epistemology avoids universal skepticism by marking off a domain of cognition that is indubitable by virtue of the absolute givenness of its objects (IP, 27 / H II, 34). But now the account of the possibility of cognition of transcendent objects will have to be given solely on the basis of the reflective apprehension of the acts of cognition themselves if it is not, once again, to presuppose the cognition of transcendent objects. That is, the account of the possibility of a relation between cognition and its transcendent object will have to be developed on the basis of what is given within the act of cognition itself. If Husserl's strategy for critical epistemology is to be successful, there must be something essentially contained within the act of cognition by which it relates itself to its object. But what is it that belongs to the essence of the act of cognition such that the act makes contact with an object?

Husserl takes the central and basic question of critical epistemology to be the question of the possibility of knowledge as such, that is, the problem of the relation between cognition and its object (*IP*, 16–17 / *H* II, 19–20). This question is subsequently articulated into three subquestions: "How, then, can knowledge be sure of its agreement with the known objects? How can knowledge go beyond itself and reach its objects reliably? . . . How do I, the knowing subject, know—and how can I know for sure—that not only my experiences, these acts of knowing, exist, but also what they know exists?" (*IP*, 17 / *H* II, 20). These questions represent the three basic systematic problems of critical epistemology: (1) the problem of correspondence; (2) the problem of transcendence; and (3) the problem of objective existence.

Of these three problems, the problem of transcendence has a conceptual priority: "Transcendence remains both the initial and the guiding problem for the critique of knowledge. It is the riddle that stands in the way of positive knowledge and the impulse behind these new investigations. One could at the outset characterize the task of the critique of knowledge as one of providing a solution to the problem of transcendence" (*IP*, 28 / *H* II, 36). Husserl's solution to the problem of transcendence lies in the interposition of a third term—the sense (*Sinn*) of an act—which makes the reference of an act of cognition to an object possible. "Knowledge is, according to its essence, *knowledge of objectivity*, and it is such by virtue of the *sense* that is immanent to it, the sense by which it *relates* itself to objectivity" (*IP*, 16 / *H* II, 29). An act of consciousness refers to its object by way of its resident sense. And it is the task of the theory of knowledge "to solve the problems pertaining to the correlation of knowledge, its sense, and its object by inquiring into the essence of knowledge" (*IP*, 18 / *H* II, 22). Here we have the programmatic answer to the question posed above pertaining to the possibility of accounting for the possibility of cognition of a transcendent object through an exclusive examination of what's involved in the act of cognition itself. The act of cognition contains within itself a sense whereby it achieves a reference to an object. One need not go beyond what is phenomenologically available in the act itself in order to give an account of how it is related to an object. An act relates itself to its object by virtue of its own sense. The sense of an act can be reflectively captured, analyzed, and described. In this way an answer to the global question of critical epistemology with respect to the possibility of the cognition of transcendent objects can be given without presupposing the cognition of transcendent objects. The answer can be given solely on the basis of the cognition of immanent objects (i.e., the reflective apprehension of the acts of cognition together with their sense).

As Husserl was to emphasize repeatedly throughout his career subsequent to 1907, the reflective turn to consciousness through the adoption of the phenomenological attitude and the abstention from all judgments of worldly existence carry with them decisive implications for the status of consciousness. Within the phenomenological attitude, consciousness can no longer be considered to be a part of the world, in causal interaction with other parts of the world. For all judgments that posit the existence of the world and its causal relations have been suspended. Consciousness, then, can no longer be accepted as one entity among others in the world. It is nonworldly—yet the world appears "within" it. In this sense, consciousness is transcendental: it is the all-embracing horizon within which the world presents itself.

Transcendental consciousness is not in the world; but the world is in some sense "in" consciousness. Of course, the world cannot be in consciousness in any spatial or material sense. Rather, what Husserl means here is that the presumably existing world is now converted into a world-phenomenon. Within transcendental phenomenology, the world will be considered only insofar as it appears to consciousness by virtue of the sense-laden acts of consciousness that intend the world as such (*IP*, 55 / *H* II, 75). As phenomenon, the world is, in Husserl's language, "constituted" within transcendental consciousness (see, for instance, *FTL*, 268 / *H* XVII, 237). That is, the experience of the world, such that we are entitled to claim that the world is "there," is based upon the continuous and harmonious syntheses of mental processes within consciousness whereby the world appears to us.[11] "The world, as a 'phenomenon,' lies within me, and acquires its sense of being from me. Thus in transcendental subjectivity, lies the absolute pre-supposition [*Voraus-Setzung*] which gives sense to all presuppositions [*Voraussetzungen*]: the antecedent positing of my transcendental ego" (*FTL*, 276 / *H* XVII, 244). Any straightforward, objective claims we make about the existence of the world, or its disposition, presuppose the constitution of the world within transcendental consciousness.[12] This holds for the straightforward, objective claims of the positive sciences as well. In both cases, the final presupposition of transcendental consciousness must be explicated if cognition is to be completely clarified. For "every already existing thing," whether it be posited in natural life or in the context of scientific theory, "is a 'prejudice,' in the non-pejorative sense, and requires transcendental criticism, constitutive analysis, which only then can furnish knowledge and science in the strict sense" (*FTL*, 277 / *H* XVII, 244).

The transcendental basis of experience remains hidden, however, in the straightforward experience of the world. Only from the standpoint of the reflective phenomenological attitude does it become clear that "natural, objective world life is only a particular mode of the transcendental life which forever constitutes the world, [but] in such a way that transcendental subjectivity, while living on in this mode, has not become conscious of the constituting horizons and never can become aware of them. It lives in 'infatuation,' so to speak, with the poles of unity without being aware of the constituting multiplicities belonging to them" (*C*, 175–76 / *H* VI, 179). Thus we see that the sciences not only presuppose certain primitive concepts and first principles that reside in the foundations of their theoretical enterprise, but also the constitution of their research domains—the world together with all its regions and objectivities—within transcendental consciousness. "What science has before it as a province, given in advance for theoretical work, is, in respect of its sense and being, a province for the investigators (singly and in communion) by virtue of sources belonging to the (likewise separate and communalized) productivity of the investigators' own consciousness" (*FTL*, 15 / *H* XVII, 13). For "any straightforwardly constituted objectivity (for example: an Object belonging to Nature) points back, according to its essential sort (for example: physical thing *in specie*), to a correlative essential form of manifold, actual and possible, intentionality (in our example, infinite intentionality), which is constitutive for the objectivity" (*FTL*, 246 / *H* XVII, 217; emphasis deleted).

In all straightforward acts of experience and cognition, this universal a priori of intentional consciousness necessarily remains hidden. It is the ultimate presupposition of all experience, yet it remains unthematic in natural life and in the sciences based upon the natural attitude.

> While the corresponding intentionality is being executed, while it is flowing in this manner as an Objectivatingly productive living, it is "unconscious"—that is to say: it makes thematic, but it itself is, for that very reason and as a matter of essential necessity, non-thematic. It remains hidden, as long as it has not been uncovered by a reflection and has not thus itself become a theme, the theoretical theme of that logical research which is directed to the subjective. The subject which is straightforwardly judging or thinking in any manner ... has

"consciously" before him, thematically, only the formations undergoing production at that time. (FTL, 34–35 / H XVII, 30)

Because of the exclusive interest of the positive sciences in some particular objective field of research, their practitioners do not consider the subjective intentional correlate by which the field is constituted. "Thus the geometer," Husserl writes, "will not think of exploring, besides geometrical shapes, geometrical thinking" (FTL, 36 / H XVII, 32). "Intentional life," with all its goals and accomplishments, is taken for granted by all thinking (C, 113 / H VI, 115). This systematic disregard for the constitutive activity of transcendental consciousness amounts to the "transcendental naïveté" of the sciences.

Because of this ineluctable naïveté, the objective sciences "lack precisely the knowledge of what could procure the meaning and validity for the theoretical constructs of objective knowledge and thus gives them the dignity of knowledge which is ultimately grounded" (C, 119 / H VI, 121). With the disclosure of this previously hidden transcendental foundation of the sciences, then, comes the task of phenomenologically clarifying this foundation in the interests of making the sciences wholly perspicuous. "After all," Husserl states in the *Crisis*, "accomplishments can be understood only in terms of the activity that accomplishes them" (C, 117 / H VI, 119). Here lies the uniquely phenomenological mode of explanation: "Intentionality is the title which stands for the actual and genuine way of explaining [*Erklaren*], making intelligible. To go back to the intentional origins and unities of the formation of meaning is to proceed toward a comprehension which, once achieved (which of course is an ideal case), would leave no meaningful question unanswered" (C, 168 / H VI, 171). If the sciences are to be made fully intelligible, then, Husserl claims in *Formal and Transcendental Logic*, "we must rise above the self-forgetfulness of the theorizer who, in his theoretical producing [*Leisten*], devotes himself to the subject-matter, the theories, and the methods, and accordingly knows nothing of the inwardness of the producing—who lives in producing, but does not have the productive living itself as a theme within his field of vision. Only by virtue of a fundamental clarification, penetrating to the depth of inwardness that produces cognition and theory, the transcendental inwardness, does what is produced as genuine theory and genuine science become understandable" (FTL, 15–16 / H XVII, 14; typography corrected).[13] This is Husserl's phenomenological take on the Delphic injunction: "Know thyself!"

A similar programmatic statement can be found in the *Crisis*, where the locution "accomplishing life" is used to refer to the transcendental ground of the sciences. In this sense, accomplishing life is the "apodictically necessary and ultimate ground" of all scientific objectivity and makes the latter ultimately intelligible (C, 114–15 / H VI, 117). Thus, "one must fully clarify, i.e., bring to ultimate evidence, how all the evidence of objective-logical accomplishments, through which objective theory (thus mathematical and natural scientific theory) is grounded in respect of form and content, has its hidden sources of grounding in the ultimately accomplishing life, the life in which the evident givenness of the life-world forever has, had attained, and attains anew its pre-scientific ontic meaning" (C, 128 / H VI, 131; translation modified).

Up to this point we have followed Husserl in his acquisition of the concept of transcendental consciousness as a necessary prerequisite for a noncircular critical epistemology of objective knowledge drawn from pure evidence. As that within which the appearance of any objectivity is constituted, transcendental consciousness forms the ultimate presupposition of any objective cognitive claim, including the claims of the objective, or positive, sciences. As Joseph J. Kockelmans remarks, "It is only when we arrive at consciousness as the universal medium of access to whatever exists, including the life-world itself, that our search for foundations reaches its final destination."[14] If the foundations of the sciences are to be made fully transparent, the intentional processes upon which they are founded must be clarified. Such a clarification is the specific task of transcendental phenomenology.

But we have yet to indicate what form this clarification will take. According to Husserl, the judgments, or propositions, of science, as the "meanings" or "senses" of assertive acts, are themselves the complex products or results of intentional processes. Inscribed within them are the "sense-implications" of a genetic order by which they were produced on the basis of simpler, more original forms of experience. "Judgments as senses accordingly have a sense-genesis" (FTL, 207 / H XVII, 184; emphasis deleted). The phenomenological clarification of such judgments will then be a matter of uncovering "the hidden intentional implications included in judging and in the judgment itself as the product of judging" (FTL, 207 / H XVII, 184). Every judgment "points back" to the noetic activity by which it was produced and the noematic material (the sense material) from which it was compounded. A judgment, as a sense, refers back to prior senses upon which it was produced and the intentional act by which it was produced. The question of the intentional sense-implication can be traced back until one reactivates the original experience upon which the judgment in question is ultimately founded. In this way the judgment is to be made "materially evident" (*FTL,* 207 / *H* XVII, 184). This leads, quite naturally, to the notion that each intentionally founded judgment bears within itself a "sense-history," which is to be retraced in the process of clarifying it. "Judgments, as the finished products of a 'constitution' or a 'genesis,' can and must be interrogated with respect to their history. The essential peculiarity of such products is precisely that they are senses that bear within them, as a sense-implicate of their genesis, a sort of historicalness; that in them, level by level, sense points back to original sense and to the corresponding noetic intentionality; that therefore each sense-formation can be asked about its *essentially necessary sense-history*" (*FTL,* 208 / *H* XVII, 184). Here the search for foundations leads to an inquiry into origins—for Husserl, a genetic phenomenology of sense.

This form of clarification is to provide more than just an interesting account of the intentional career of a particular proposition. It is also a form of criticism. For the unraveling of the sense-moments of a proposition is guided by the question of the evidence for that judgment, that is, the question of the genetically first intentional experience where the state of affairs that corresponds to the proposition is itself given, and how it is given (*FTL,* 209 / *H* XVII, 185–86). Only when the intentional history of a judgment is analytically disclosed can the overall sense and justification of the judgment be assessed.

The phenomenological clarification of science as the intentional analysis of transcendental consciousness, then, has as its goal the step-by-step regressive inquiry into the genetically ordered layers of sense and corresponding intentional processes in transcendental consciousness by which science is built up and now appears as a "finished product." The phenomenology of science then becomes a kind of intentional archaeology, digging down through the sedimented layers of sense formations in order to recapitulate the intentional history of science so as to understand it and complete its reflective justification. This form of phenomenological excavation was carried out by Husserl himself in his justly famous "Galileo analysis" in section 9 of the *Crisis,* and in *Beilagen* III to that section, which was published in 1939 by Eugen Fink under the title "Die Frage nach dem Ursprung der Geometrie als intentional-historisches Problem" (The question of the origin of geometry as an intentional-historical problem).[15]

It would be inappropriate at this point, however, to launch into a detailed examination of Husserl's execution of the phenomenological clarification of the sciences in this genetic sense. The purpose of this section is only to review the philosophical considerations that led to Husserl's specific formulation of the task of phenomenological clarification of science. The *Crisis* text will be considered later, in chapter 5.

4. PHENOMENOLOGY AS THE ALL-EMBRACING FOUNDATIONAL SCIENCE

In the introduction to the *Cartesian Meditations*, Husserl represents the basic aim of Descartes's *Meditations* as the "complete reforming of philosophy into a science grounded on an absolute foundation" (*CM*, 1 / *H* I, 43). This project implied for Descartes a corresponding reforming of all the sciences because he conceived of the sciences as but "non-self-sufficient members of the one all-inclusive science, and this is philosophy" (*CM*, 1–2 / *H* I, 43–44). Husserl takes over the Cartesian project of establishing philosophy as an all-embracing foundational discipline, but rejects the Cartesian method for achieving it. Descartes's fundamental mistake, in Husserl's estimation, was to model the method of philosophy on one of the special sciences, namely mathematics (*C*, 73–78 / *H* VI, 74–80). The Cartesian reformation of philosophy was to take place by transforming it into a strictly deductively ordered discipline, taking its point of departure from self-evident axioms. But it was precisely here that Descartes failed to appreciate the methodological requirements for a truly foundational discipline. A foundational discipline cannot be deductive, for any deductive science is itself founded upon certain primitive concepts and axioms (*C*, 181 / *H* VI, 185). The attempt on the part of a deductive discipline to secure the validity of its own foundations through deduction will necessarily succumb to a circularity of first principles, as Antoine Arnauld was quick to point out.[16] Consciousness, as the domain of adequate evidence, cannot be taken as an axiomatic point of departure for the demonstration of its own validity. Rather, taking adequate evidence as the unquestionable principle of all rational discourse, a foundational discipline must proceed descriptively within the domain of consciousness and give an account of the possibility of genuine knowledge "from within" (*IP*, 43 / *H* II, 58). For this reason, "it is naturally a ludicrous, though unfortunately common misunderstanding, to seek to attack transcendental phenomenology as 'Cartesianism,' as if its *ego cogito* were a premise from which the rest of knowledge ... was to be deduced, absolutely 'secured.' The point is not to secure objectivity but to understand it" (*C*, 189 / *H* VI, 193).

It should be pointed out, however, that although phenomenology is not Cartesian in its method, it remains Cartesian in its ideal. It means to become a foundational discipline that embraces all the other sciences within itself. As Husserl represents it, phenomenology is the foundational discipline in the sense that one cannot meaningfully get behind the evidence offered in the reflective apprehension of transcendentally purified mental processes, mental processes considered strictly with respect to what is directly given in them. Because of its restriction to adequate evidence, it need not presuppose anything that would be in need of further clarification at a deeper level. It presupposes nothing that is not also given. "Accordingly, the realization of this philosophical self-examination that sees in everything given beforehand as existing an index for a system of uncoverable constitutive performances, is indeed the most extreme radicalness in striving to uproot all prejudice" (*FTL*, 276 / *H* XVII, 244; emphasis deleted). Moreover, it is a foundational discipline that bears its own foundation within itself. "Thus it must begin without any underlying ground. But immediately it achieves the possibility of creating a ground for itself through its own powers, namely, in mastery, through original self-reflection, of the naive world as transformed into a phenomenon or rather a universe of phenomena" (*FTL*, 276 / *H* XVII, 244).

Since all scientific cognition is carried out in acts of consciousness, phenomenology, as the science of the acts of consciousness, also includes all scientific cognition within its object domain. "It is the distinctive peculiarity of phenomenology to embrace within its sphere of its eidetic universality all cognitions and sciences" (*ID* I, 142 / *H* III 1, 133). Moreover, it is an all-embracing discipline in the sense that for every objectivity one could claim to know, there is necessarily correlated with it the intentional activity by which its givenness is constituted within consciousness (*C*, 114–15 / *H* VI, 117). Since the rationality of any claim to know is ultimately based upon the way in which the objectivity ostensibly known is given within consciousness, phenomenology is in the unique position of "carrying out every possible critique of reason" (*ID* I, 148 / *H* III 1, 136). For within each science, Husserl claims in the *Revue Internationale de Philosophie*, consciousness plays "le rôle de source de justification ultime."[17] In this way phenomenology sets philosophy on the road to the realization of the Cartesian ideal, for it is phenomenology as "the all-embracing science of transcendental subjectivity" that "gives a legitimate sense, and indeed the only conceivable sense, to the ideal of grounding cognition with an absolute freedom from presuppositions" (*FTL*, 272 / *H* XVII, 240–41; emphasis deleted). Understood in this way, "the whole of phenomenology is nothing more than the self-examination on the part of transcendental subjectivity" (*FTL*, 273 / *H* XVII, 241–42; emphasis deleted). Yet, in the exclusive turn to transcendental subjectivity, the existing world is not annulled so much as it is understood through the analysis and description of the acts by which it becomes available to us. "And in the same manner," Husserl writes, "positive science, as achieved by labors in common, becomes understood" (*FTL*, 275 / *H* XVII, 243). Transcendental phenomenology, in Husserl's book, counts as the ultimate self-elucidation of reason in all its applications.

PART TWO

Evidence and the Positing of Existence in Husserl's Phenomenology

CHAPTER THREE

TRUTH, EVIDENCE, AND EXISTENCE IN HUSSERL'S PHENOMENOLOGY

The first two chapters of this study provided a general orientation in Husserl's phenomenological philosophy of science. In this and the following three chapters, I will address the more specific question of the compatibility between Husserl's phenomenology and a robust appreciation of the theoretical dimension of the physical sciences. I will pose this question in terms of the distinction that has been drawn between the empirical and theoretical components of the physical sciences. On this distinction, empirical science remains within the domain of the observable. It seeks to identify and determine exact functional covariations of observable physical phenomena. The formulations of such functional covariations count as laws. In the ideal gas laws, for instance, pressure within a container is represented as directly proportional to temperature and inversely proportional to volume. Such laws, however, only state that a correlation exists and specify what that correlation is. They do not explain why such a correlation exists. The explanation of functional dependencies within the empirical domain calls for the development of a theory. And theories typically fulfill their explanatory task by postulating unobservable entities that tie the variables in question together by way of causality. As Stathis Psillos puts it in his study of scientific realism, scientific theories "explain and predict observable phenomena by reference to unobservable phenomena."[1] In the case of the ideal gas laws, for instance, we make use of the explanatory powers of kinetic theory. Positing the existence of molecules as the unobservable constituents of a gas, kinetic theory proceeds, under the standard Maxwell-Boltzmann interpretation, to understand temperature in terms of the average kinetic energy of the molecules and pressure in terms of the change of momentum as the molecules strike the inner surface of the container. As an increase in temperature represents a rise in the average kinetic energy, so the change in momentum increases, assuming the volume remains relatively constant. Hence the theoretical explanation of why pressure is directly proportional to temperature.

The move beyond what is observable in order to explain the behavior of what is observable distinguishes theoretical science from empirical science. Empirical science seeks to ascertain the lawlike regularities of observable phenomena; theoretical science seeks to explain why such lawlike regularities obtain. In doing so, it typically posits the existence of hidden, unobservable entities. Unobservable entities postulated by theoretical science are known as theoretical entities. To raise the question of whether such entities really exist is to raise the question of theoretical existence.

I will not claim that this bi-level account of the structure of scientific theories sketched out above is entirely unproblematic. The line between the observable and the unobservable, for instance, is notoriously difficult to draw. In addition, the lawlike behavior of theoretical entities often calls for additional levels of explanation. Thus the law/theory divide is not limited to the observable/unobservable divide. But I will employ the bi-level account because it has formed the conceptual frame for the debate between instrumentalist and realist interpretations of scientific theory.

Because phenomenology restricts itself to phenomena, to what is open to direct intuition, and because it ties knowledge to what is given in direct intuition, it might appear that phenomenology by its very nature is incompatible with a realistic interpretation of scientific theories. In the next three chapters I will argue that this is not the case. In this chapter I will take a line of approach to the question of theoretical existence afforded by Husserl's theory of truth. The connection between a theory of truth and the question of theoretical existence can be briefly formulated in terms of the necessary correlation Husserl recognized between truth and being. In section 62 of the "Prolegomena to Pure Logic" of the *Logical Investigations*, Husserl states that "nothing can be without being thus or thus determined, and that it is, and that it is thus and thus determined, is the self-subsistent truth which is the necessary correlate of the self-subsistent being" (*LI* I, 225–26 / *H* XVIII, B 228). "For the world," Husserl already claimed in section 36, "is merely the unified objective totality corresponding to, and inseparable from, the ideal system of all factual truth" (*LI* I, 143 / *H* XVIII, B 121). Thus there is, Husserl insists, an "a priori togetherness" of *Wahrheiten* and *Sachverhalten*, of truths and states of affairs (*LI* I, 225–26 / *H* XVIII, B 228). In section 6 of *Ideas* I, Husserl makes the same point in connection with eidetic truths and eidetic states of affairs. The latter are the necessary "correlates" of the former (*ID* I, 14 / *H* III 1, 16; see also *C*, 126 / *H* VI, 129 and *C*, 304 / *H* VI, 282).

We may formulate Husserl's thesis in the following way:

A proposition is true if and only if the corresponding state of affairs obtains.

Thus, if a scientific theory postulates the existence of theoretical entities and that theory is true, then those entities exist. Conversely, if the propositional component of a scientific theory that postulates the existence of theoretical entities is not true, then those entities, as postulated, do not exist.

The correlation between truth and being carries over into the context of justification as well. If we are justified in believing that the base assumption of a scientific theory that postulates the existence of certain theoretical entities is true, then we are justified in believing that those entities exist; if we are not justified in believing that base assumption is true, then, absent any other grounds, we are not justified in believing that those theoretical entities exist. The latter formulation can be quantified in different ways. It also admits of modal variation. The most interesting variant, anticipating the results of this chapter, is this one: if it is not possible for us to be justified in believing that any base assumption of a scientific theory that postulates theoretical entities is true, then it is not possible for us to be justified in believing that any theoretical entities exist. Obviously this statement holds true only if scientific theory is the only possible source of justification for belief in the existence of theoretical entities. For the purposes of this discussion, I will take this to be the case.

There is, then, a necessary correlation between truth and existence. If a proposition is true, then the corresponding state of affairs obtains; if a state of affairs obtains, then the corresponding proposition is true. "Truths do not, of course, produce the corresponding facts or things," Dallas Willard points out in commenting on the Husserl doctrine of truth, "but given the truths, those facts and things must exist; and conversely, given the facts (and things) the corresponding truth must obtain."[2] But there is also in Husserl's phenomenology a close connection between truth and evidence. Some commentators have maintained that this connection is also one of necessary correlation, and that Husserl rendered this correlation necessary by simply reducing truth to evidence. Günther Patzig, for example, claims that Husserl posits "a relation of identity between evident and true propositions and between evidence and truth in general," by "melting truth down into the medium of evidence, so to speak."[3] Similarly, Donn Welton takes Husserl's theory of truth to amount to the following: "What makes a statement (about the world at hand) true is not a magical union between two masses—a meaningful sentence and a thing—but a more or less adequate fit between the meaning intended in and through speech-acts and what is given in and through perceptual acts."[4] What is given through acts of perception counts as evidence for the meaning of a speech act, that is, a proposition. Contrary to what we had just established concerning Husserl's position on the necessary correlation between true propositions and existing states of affairs, Welton holds that what "makes" a statement true is the agreement, the "fit," between the proposition asserted in that statement and the perceptual givenness of the state of affairs to which that statement corresponds.

Now if the only thing that makes a proposition true is the fit between that proposition and the perceptual givenness of the corresponding state of affairs, then the necessary and sufficient condition of the truth of a proposition is an act of consciousness in which the corresponding state of affairs is perceptually given. If the state of affairs is not given, the proposition in question cannot be true, since what makes a proposition true is the fit between that proposition and the givenness of a corresponding state of affairs. The necessary correlation between truth and consciousness comes into play once we realize that Husserl defines evidence as an act of consciousness in which a state of affairs is itself given. On Welton's interpretation, then, a proposition is true if and only if there is a relevant case of evidence (i.e., an act of consciousness in which the corresponding state of affairs is perceptually given). On this view, evidence not only indicates that a proposition is true, it makes that proposition true. The domain of true propositions is thus restricted and determined by the scope of the states of affairs that are given in perceptual acts of consciousness, that is, in acts of evidence. Truth and evidence are made equivalent by reducing truth to evidence.

Theories that hold that some positive epistemic feature of a belief or proposition makes the belief or proposition true are known as epistemic theories of truth. The positive epistemic feature may range from warranted assertibility, to ideal consensus, to being evident. Those inclined to give an epistemic version of Husserl's theory of truth focus on being evident. We may summarize Patzig's and Welton's epistemic interpretation of Husserl's theory of truth in this way:

For any proposition p, p is true if and only if p is evident.

The phenomenological gloss on "p is evident" reads as follows:

p is evident if and only if the state of affairs to which p corresponds is given in an intuitive act of consciousness.

Thus the truth of p is not correlated here with the existence of the state of affairs to which p corresponds, but the occurrence of an act of consciousness in which the state of affairs to which p corresponds is intuitively given. In essential agreement with this line of interpretation, Louis Dupré maintains that, according to Husserl, "truth depends upon the fulfilling of a meaning-intention"; that is, "truth is constituted by the real presence of the object."[5]

This interpretation quite clearly commits Husserl to the position that truth is dependent upon states of consciousness. For if the truth is "constituted" by the presence of the object in perceptual consciousness, if propositions are "made" true by the perceptual givenness of the corresponding state of affairs in consciousness, then, apart from a consciousness in which an object is presented or a state of affairs given, there can be no truth.

Furthermore, this interpretation commits Husserl to a form of idealism, if we understand by idealism the claim that the existence of things is somehow dependent upon states of consciousness. The idealistic implication of the theory of truth here ascribed to Husserl becomes clear once we add the necessary correlation between evidence and truth to the necessary correlation between truth and existence earlier discussed. Let "A" stand for a state of affairs, and "p" for the corresponding proposition. According to Husserl's position on the necessary correlation between truth and existence:

> A obtains if and only if p is true.

But, on the above interpretation, Husserl is committed to the view that there is a necessary correlation between truth and evidence. Thus:

> p is true if and only if p is evident.

On Husserl's theory of evidence:

> p is evident if and only if A is intuitively given to consciousness.

Biconditional relations are transitive. Thus, bringing together the left hand of the first biconditional with the right hand of the last, on the assumption that p corresponds to A,

> A obtains if and only if A is intuitively given to consciousness.

There is, then, a necessary correlation between existence and evidence. If evidence is construed as an act of consciousness, then, on this interpretation, not only truth but also existence is dependent upon consciousness.

A number of Husserl commentators have drawn precisely this conclusion. A consideration of the relation between truth and evidence in Husserl, Henry Pietersma writes, will inevitably "involve the idealism of the Husserlian position: the scope of the mind defines reality."[6] Husserl's metaphysics "is determined by his epistemology ... the being of something is defined by the ideal epistemic situation for asserting it."[7] According to Patzig, the attempt to effect an identity between true and evident propositions by reducing truth to evidence is an essential part of Husserl's "turn to idealism."[8] On Husserl's view of truth, "it is obvious," Dupré claims, "that if one defines epistemological realism as the independence of the object from the act [of consciousness], Husserl can no longer be called a realist."[9]

I am inclined to reject these interpretations of Husserl's position on the relation between truth and evidence as both crude and unlovely—crude because they fail to make certain distinctions Husserl in fact makes; unlovely because they commit Husserl to a position with counterintuitive implications. Taking my cue from Pietersma's suggestion that "Husserl's views on the evident are to be understood in the context of a theory of justification,"[10] I will develop what I take to be a more sophisticated and philosophically attractive interpretation. On this interpretation, evidence will not be construed as a necessary and sufficient condition of the truth of a proposition, but rather as the necessary and sufficient condition for justified belief in the truth of a proposition. This interpretation of Husserl's theory of evidence makes his theory of truth compatible with the realist intuition that the truth about things, together with their existence, is generally independent of any consciousness of them. Evidence does not make a proposition true. But it does make us justified in believing that it is true. At least for any internalist theory of justification it does. Likewise, existence does not depend upon consciousness; rather, the justification with which we posit existence depends upon consciousness.

How are the preceding considerations related to the question of theoretical existence in the sciences? Given his position on the necessary correlation between truth and existence, Husserl would hold that theoretical entities exist only if it is true that they exist. On the crude interpretation of Husserl's theory of truth, it can be true that theoretical entities exist only if it is evident that they exist. But it can be evident that they exist only if they can be given in an intuitive act of perception. However, as long as theoretical entities are by definition unobservable, it could never become evident, in the required phenomenological sense, that they exist. It follows that it could never be true that they exist. Hence they do not exist. On the crude interpretation of Husserl's theory of truth, phenomenology is incompatible with a realist construal of scientific theories.

On the interpretation I propose, the question of theoretical existence in the context of Husserl's theory of truth and evidence must be recast in terms of justification. Thus, if it is the case that theoretical entities could never be given to perceptual consciousness, if it could never become evident in the phenomenologically preferred way that they exist, then we could never be justified in believing that they exist. On this account, it is still possible that such entities exist. But it would not be possible for us to be justified in believing that they exist.

This conclusion assumes, however, that for Husserl direct intuition is not only the ultimate but also the only source of justified belief in science. That is, ultimately, we are justified in believing only that which we can in some sense directly see to be the case. I will challenge this assumption in the next chapter. Granting this assumption for the moment, however, the strongest antirealist claim that could be made on the sophisticated interpretation is that we are not justified in believing that theoretical entities exist. In this way the sophisticated interpretation takes us from the question of whether it is true that theoretical entities exist to the question of whether we are justified in believing that it is true that they exist. In the next chapter I will lay out Husserl's theory of justification. In this chapter I will stay focused on his theory of truth.

I. KNOWLEDGE, EVIDENCE, AND TRUTH

Intentionality, Husserl claims, is the general heading for all problems taken up within the discipline of phenomenology (*ID* I, 199–201 / *H* III 1, 168–70.). Phenomenology is the descriptive eidetic science of transcendentally purified consciousness (*ID* I, 167 / *H* III 1, 156); and intentionality names the most general structure of all acts of consciousness (*ID* I, 199 / *H* III 1, 187).[11] To claim that all acts of consciousness are intentional is to claim that every act of consciousness is directed toward some object (*ID* I, 200 / *H* III 1, 188). Being directed toward an object is an essential property of all acts of consciousness

(*ID* I, 73 / *H* III 1, 73–74). Every act of perception has an object perceived; every act of love has an object loved; every act of hate has an object hated; every act of thought has an object thought; every act of imagination has an object imagined. Name any act of consciousness—it will refer to some object or state of affairs.

Although all acts of consciousness are directed toward an object, they are not all directed toward an object in the same manner. In merely thinking of an object, or speaking of it, I intend that object "emptily." In such a circumstance, the object is not intuitively present. I have referred to the object in thought or speech, but there is no intuitive content to the act that refers to it. If, on the other hand, I were to imagine that object—say, the Taj Mahal—then that act would contain a degree of intuitive content or "fullness." The Taj Mahal is not merely referred to, but to some degree intuitively given, although in an act of imaginative representation the Taj Mahal is not given as "bodily present." An intuitive presentation of the latter kind for a physical object like the Taj Mahal is achieved only in an act of perception.

There are, then, different ways in which acts intend objects. In acts of thought or speech, the object is emptily intended. In acts of imagination or perception, there is a measure of intuitive content whereby the object is presented. Acts can also enter into various relations with one another. The most important, for our present purposes, is the relation of "fulfillment" (see *LI* II, 675–706 / *H* XIX 2, B2 8–47). When an act of empty reference to an object is accompanied or followed by an act of imaginative or perceptual presentation of that same object, then the latter act is said to fulfill the former. Having read about the Taj Mahal, I may form the belief that the tomb chamber, where the body of Mumtaz Mahal resides, is octagonal in shape. In itself, however, such a thought would be devoid of intuitive content. If I were then to imagine an octagonal tomb chamber, the thought would be more or less intuitively fulfilled. If I were to travel to Agra and enter the tomb chamber of the Taj Mahal, then the thought would be more or less intuitively fulfilled through the perceptual presentation of the tomb chamber itself as bodily present.

The fulfillment relation is of utmost importance for Husserl's theory of knowledge. In essential agreement with the tradition, Husserl holds that knowledge is a matter of justified true belief (*LI* I, 135 / *H* XVIII, B 110; *LI* I, 61 / *H* XVIII, B 13–14). The mere belief that the tomb chamber of the Taj Mahal is octagonal does not count as knowledge, even if that belief is in fact true. The truth of the proposition believed, although a necessary condition, is not a sufficient condition for knowledge. The person to whom the belief in the proposition belongs must also be justified in holding that belief. In keeping with the internalist tradition of epistemology,[12] Husserl maintains that a person is justified in holding a belief just in case the belief in question is accompanied by evidence. An act of believing p on the part of a person S, then, will count as knowledge if and only if the truth of p is evident to S (*LI* I, 61 / *H* XVIII, B 13–14). Evidence marks off baseless opinion from genuine knowledge (*LI* I, 61 / *H* XVIII, B 14). It is the "crown of knowledge" (*LI* II, 777/ *H* XIX 2, B2 133). Since evidence, for Husserl, is a mental act that provides intuitive fulfillment for an empty intention, "all talk of knowledge refers to a relationship between acts of thought and fulfilling intuitions" (*LI* II, 837 / *H* XIX 2, B2 204). "Knowledge always has the character of a fulfillment" (*LI* II, 777–78 / *H* XIX 2, B2 134).

But precisely what is "evidence" on Husserl's account? What would it mean for the truth of a proposition to become "evident"?[13] It can be argued that Husserl has two distinct concepts of evidence: monothetic and synthetic.[14] In the former, evidence is represented as an act whereby an object or state of affairs is intuitively given as bodily present. It is a "mode of consciousness that consists in the self-appearance, the self-exhibiting, the self-giving, of an affair, an affair-complex (or state of affairs), a universality, a value, or other objectivity, in the final mode: 'itself there,' 'immediately intuited,' 'given *originaliter*'" (*CM*, 57 / *H* I, 92). Evidence, for Husserl, is not in the first place a belief that supports another belief; rather, "evidence is, in an extremely broad sense, an 'experiencing' of something that is, and is thus" (*CM*, 12 / *H* I, 52). It is a "seeing" in which the object itself is given (*IP*, 44 / *H* II, 59). In other words, evidence is an act of perception. For "the primitive mode of the giving of something-itself is perception" (*FTL*, 158 / *H* XVII, 141; emphasis deleted). By "perception" here, Husserl not only means sensuous perception of physical objects. For mental processes and ideal objects can also be perceived, that is, immediately intuited.

With respect to physical objects, the evidence afforded by perception will, of course, admit of degrees. For the perception of any transcendent object is always and necessarily partial, one-sided, adumbrated, less than fully adequate, and therefore open to revision in the light of subsequent experience. A perception where the entire object is given at once, where the evidence is wholly adequate, remains an ideal. This ideal serves as the "epistemologically precise" sense of evidence (*LI* II, 765 / *H* XIX / 2, B2 121). It is the "adequate self-givenness of the object" (*IP*, 44 / *H* II, 59). The Husserl of the *Ideas* will claim that this ideal can be realized in the reflective apprehension of the acts of consciousness (*ID* I, 95–96 / *H* III 1, 92–93). Being nonspatial, the acts of consciousness bear within themselves no hidden sides or dimensions. As "immanent objects," they are completely given in the act that apprehends them—hence the epistemologically privileged position of the phenomenological science of consciousness. Its claims, and only its claims, can be grounded in adequate evidence (cf. *LI* II, 866 / *H* XIX 2, B2 240; *IP*, 48 / *H* II, 60; and *CM*, 36 / *H* I, 74). The Husserl of the *Ideas* will make similar claims for essences. Being nonspatial, they, too, can be adequately given in an act of intuition. For that reason phenomenology can be a science of the essence of the acts of consciousness—an eidetic science—and remain entirely within the realm of complete evidence and certainty.

The synthetic concept of evidence, on the other hand, represents evidence as a complex act that combines an act of empty reference with an act of perception in such a way that the object as referred to is seen to be in agreement with the object as perceived. Here evidence is construed not as a simple act of perception, but as a "synthesis of fulfillment" (*LI* II, 765 / *H* XIX 2, B2 121–22). In the Sixth Logical Investigation, Husserl characterizes evidence in the epistemologically precise sense as "that act of most perfect fulfillment," where "the object is not merely meant, but is the strictest sense given and given as it is meant" (*LI* II, 765 / *H* XIX 2, B2 122). Evidence is an act of consciousness that takes place when an act that emptily intends an object is combined with an act in which the object itself is intuitively given in such a way that the latter "fulfills" the former. In such an act the object as emptily intended is seen to be the same as the object as intuitively given (*LI* II, 765 / *H* XIX 2, B2 121–22). For that reason, Husserl calls evidence a synthetic act of identification:

> In general, when judging goes right ahead naturally, the process will be such that the judger goes on accepting the accepted objectivity, even while he is being guided by his need to verify; so that, when he ends with the evidently seen object "itself," he says: "The object is actual, is actually qualified thus, stands actually in these relationships," and the like. With the transition, there takes place here as an identifying coincidence between, on the one hand, the objective affair (and ultimately the total judgment-complex, the syntactically formed affair complex, or state-of-affairs) that was already believed in previously and, on the other hand, the objective affair now given—as it itself, the fulfilling actuality—in the believing with evidence, the

> believing that fulfils the intention aimed at cognition. Thus it is, in
> the case of successful verification. (*FTL*, 122 / *H* XVII, 109)

The synthetic version of the act of evidence, then, involves at least three acts: the act of empty intention, the act of intuitive fulfillment, and the act of identifying the state of affairs intended in both of those acts as the same.

It should be pointed out here, however, that the state of affairs that serves as the object of the act of evidence, understood as the synthetic act of identification, is not the original state of affairs emptily intended. It is rather the complex state of affairs of the state of affairs emptily intended being identical with the state of affairs intuitively given. The conceptual significance of this fact will become apparent once we relate the synthetic concept of evidence to the necessary correlation between truth and being.

On the basis of the synthetic concept of evidence, the Husserlian analysis of our example of the Taj Mahal would take the following form: Upon reading about the Taj Mahal, I form the belief that the tomb chamber of the Taj Mahal is octagonal. That is, I emptily intend the state of affairs: the being octagonal of the tomb chamber of the Taj Mahal. If I now travel to Agra and enter the tomb chamber of the Taj Mahal, I will have a more or less adequate perceptual presentation of the state of affairs: the being octagonal of the tomb chamber of the Taj Mahal. When these two acts are brought together in a synthesis of fulfillment by a synthetic act of identification, a new state of affairs is experienced, to wit: the being octagonal of the tomb chamber as emptily intended being identical with the being octagonal of the tomb chamber as intuitively given. This act of identification is what Husserl calls "evidence" in the synthetic sense. When the tomb chamber is intuitively presented in agreement with the way in which it was emptily intended, I can then judge with evidence that the tomb chamber is octagonal. The truth of the proposition that the tomb chamber is octagonal is evident. I am now justified in the belief that the tomb chamber is octagonal. I can now claim to know that the tomb chamber is octagonal. Or so it would seem.

What precisely is the relation between evidence, thus understood, and truth? In section 38 of the Sixth Logical Investigation, Husserl introduces truth as the objective correlate of the synthetic act of evidence. "Truth," Husserl writes, "as the correlate of an identifying act is a state of affairs, as the correlate of a coincident identity it is an identity: the full agreement of what is meant with what is given as such. This agreement we experience in evidence, in so far as evidence means the actual carrying out of an adequate identification" (*LI* II, 765 / *H* XIX / 2, B2 122). On this conception, truth is just that complex state of affairs to which we alluded above. It is the being identical of the state of affairs as emptily intended with the state of affairs as intuitively given. This complex state of affairs is an ideal entity, an "Idea" in the language of the *Logical Investigations*. It is the "Idea" of the identity between said states of affairs. We can experience this Idea in and through the act of identification. Hence there is a sense in which we can experience the truth (*LI* I, 195 / *H* XVIII, B 190). Truth is not a hidden relation of agreement between thought and being, between a proposition and a state of affairs; it is rather the phenomenon of agreement between the state of affairs as emptily intended and that same state of affairs as directly intuited.

We should be careful to note that here truth is not construed as a property of a proposition. It is rather a state of affairs in which an identity relation holds between a state of affairs under two different modes of givenness (*LI* II, 765 / *H* XIX 2, B2 122). It is the being identical of a state of affairs as emptily intended with a state of affairs as intuitively given. This new, complex state of affairs, however, is not identical with the state of affairs identified, but with the identity of that state of affairs. The proposition asserted in the judgment "The tomb chamber of the Taj Mahal is octagonal" corresponds to the state of affairs: the being octagonal of the tomb chamber of the Taj Mahal. The complex state of affairs—the being identical of the tomb chamber as emptily intended with the tomb chamber as intuitively given—corresponds to the proposition that would be asserted in the judgment "The tomb chamber as emptily intended is the same as the tomb chamber as intuitively given." If the complex state of affairs obtains, then the latter proposition is true. But the latter proposition is not identical or equivalent to the former proposition. The former proposition predicates a property of the tomb chamber of the Taj Mahal, namely, being octagonal. But the latter proposition asserts an identity relation between two states of affairs.

Husserl himself recognizes this distinction when he claims that the "being" expressed in an affirmative categorial judgment is not the same as the "being" experienced as the truth. "For we must observe that in the case of an evident judgment, i.e. of an evident predicative assertion, *being in the sense of truth is experienced but not expressed*, and so never coincides with the being meant and experienced in the 'is' of the assertion" (*LI* II, 767 / *H* XIX 2, B2 124; translation modified). In terms of our example, the being octagonal of the tomb chamber of the Taj Mahal is not the same as the being identical of the tomb chamber of the Taj Mahal as emptily intended and as intuitively given. Precisely for this reason the latter "being" experienced in the act of evidence does not serve to verify the proposition originally expressed, namely, "The tomb chamber of the Taj Mahal is octagonal." Rather, it is the verifying state of affairs for the unexpressed proposition that corresponds to it. This proposition, of course, could in turn be expressed. But if a second-level act of evidence were to be carried out with respect to this new intention, the objective correlate of this act would not verify the expressed proposition, but an even more complex unexpressed proposition—"und so weiter," Husserl adds (*LI* II, 767 / *H* XIX 2, B2 124).[15]

This is a significant conceptual problem. It turns out that the concept of truth as the objective correlate of a synthetic act of identification will not help us if we set out to capture the relation between evidence and the truth of any particular proposition under explicit consideration. For the synthetic act of evidence carried out with respect to that proposition will never present the verifying state of affairs for that proposition. It will never present the truth of that proposition, but rather the truth of a more complex, unexpressed proposition. In each experience of the truth, the proposition originally up for verification gets left behind. Although the synthetic concept of the act of evidence has often been hailed as Husserl's unique phenomenological contribution to the theory of truth, this conceptual problem is alone enough to render it a nonstarter.

What is it, then, that makes a proposition under consideration true? To answer that question we must turn to the third and fourth concepts of truth discussed in section 39 of the Sixth Logical Investigation. In that section Husserl lists four concepts of truth (and he rejects none of them): (1) the state of affairs consisting of the identity of what is meant with what is given; (2) the ideal unity of the corresponding acts of meaning and givenness; (3) the object that is given in the fulfillment of a meaning intention; (4) the correctness of the propositional content of a judgment. The fourth concept of truth is the traditional concept of truth as a property of a proposition. It is the "correctness" (*Richtigkeit*) of a proposition. "The proposition 'directs' itself to the thing itself, it says that it is so, and it really is so" (*LI* II, 766 / *H* XIX 2, B2 123). The third concept of truth pertains to the object as intuitively given in the act of evidence. This object, Husserl claims, can also be called "true," or the "truth." Furthermore, as the "ideal fullness" for an intention, it is experienced as that which makes the corresponding proposition, as the epistemic essence of an intention, true (*LI* II, 766/ *H* XIX 2, B2 123). The object given is that by virtue of which the truth conditions of the corresponding proposition are satisfied. If we follow Husserl's monothetic formulations of the concept of evidence, then here we can say that it is the object given in the act of evidence that makes the corresponding proposition true. For this object is not the complex states of affairs of the synthetic act of evidence, but the state of affairs as intended by way of the proposition under consideration. It is the tomb chamber given in the act of perception that makes the proposition asserted in the judgment "The tomb chamber is octagonal" true.

But the "object given," which makes the relevant proposition true, can itself be given two significantly different interpretations. On the one hand, we might take it that Husserl means to claim that it is the *object* that is given that makes the proposition true. This interpretation refers us back to the necessary correlation Husserl posited between truth and being, and to the fourth definition of truth as simply a matter of getting the world right. If a proposition is true if and only if the state of affairs to which it corresponds obtains, then there is some sense in which the object for which the state of affairs obtains makes the proposition true. The tomb chamber's being octagonal makes true the judgment: "The tomb chamber is octagonal." On the other hand, we might take Husserl to be asserting that it is the *givenness* of the object that makes the relevant proposition true. This refers us back to the crude interpretation, which posits a necessary correlation between truth and evidence. For here it is not the existence of the object, but its givenness in an act of consciousness that bestows truth upon the corresponding proposition.[16] The former interpretation is consistent with realism; the latter commits Husserl to some form of idealism, as indicated above.

In what follows I will argue that the correlation in fact posited by Husserl between the truth of propositions and monothetic acts of evidence is not a correlation between truth and occurrent cases of evidence, but rather between truth and the ideal possibility of evidence. This is the distinction overlooked by the crude interpretation of Husserl's theory of truth. Furthermore, I will show that, with respect to occurrent cases of evidence, there can be no necessary implication from evidence to truth. This follows from the later Husserl's insistence on the essential inadequacy of all occurrent cases of evidence. I will then suggest that the relation between truth and occurrent cases of evidence must be understood in a justification-theoretic ("j-theoretic") context. Finally, I will indicate why Husserl takes it that the lack of a necessary connection between truth and occurrent cases of evidence does not lead us down the path of skepticism.

2. EVIDENCE AS AN IDEAL POSSIBILITY

Proponents of the crude interpretation of Husserl's theory of truth are given to such locutions as the following: the real presence of the object constitutes the truth; or, the fit between the object as emptily intended and the object as given in an act of perception makes the relevant proposition true. It seems most natural to take such proponents as making claims about the relation between truth and occurrent cases of evidence. But such claims commit Husserl to a philosophically unlovely position. For if it is the case that the occurrent perceptual givenness of the object makes the relevant proposition true, then the relevant proposition is not true (i.e., it is false), when the object is not perceptually given. When evening comes, and the Taj Mahal is closed up for the day, and the last attendant walks out of the tomb chamber, it is suddenly no longer true that the tomb chamber is octagonal. The tomb chamber is not being perceptually given to some consciousness. Hence, on the crude interpretation, it cannot be true at that time that the tomb chamber is octagonal. If I am reading about the Taj Mahal, and the author claims that the tomb chamber is octagonal, and if, at the same time, the tomb chamber is not being perceptually given to some consciousness, then the author has misled me. If, several hours later, someone chances to glance at the tomb chamber, the author's veracity is suddenly restored. Things would get even more counterintuitive if we indexed evidence to my experience alone. Nothing I read about could be true if that thing was not at the same time being given to me in an act of perception. Surely no self-respecting philosopher would want to hold such a position.

In the "Prolegomena to Pure Logic," Husserl explicitly rejects the premises that would lead to such counterintuitive conclusions. In section 51 he states that "as in the realm of perception, the unseen does not at all coincide with the non-existent, so lack of evidence does not amount to untruth. The experience of the agreement between meaning and what is itself present, meant, between the actual sense of an assertion and the self-given state of affairs, is evidence: the Idea of this agreement is truth, whose ideality is also its objectivity" (*LI* I, 195 / *H* XVIII, B 191–92; translation modified). Here Husserl denies that the truth of a proposition is necessarily tied to the act of evidence in which the state of affairs to which that proposition corresponds is perceptually given. In fact, in this passage, it is not tied to evidence at all. Truth is here defined as the Idea of the agreement between a proposition and a state of affairs, what is itself present.[17] This agreement can be experienced in the act of evidence, but the Idea of truth is not the Idea of this experience. Later, I will suggest that the experience of the agreement between a proposition and the corresponding state of affairs is what makes us justified in believing that the proposition is true. But clearly Husserl here holds that it is not the experience of evidence that makes the proposition true. The lack of evidence does not make for a lack of truth on the part of the proposition.

Nonetheless, Husserl does make the claim elsewhere that truth and evidence are "correlates" (*CM*, 12 / *H* I, 52). What can this mean? In the light of Husserl's statements above, it cannot mean that truth is correlated with actual cases of evidence. For then, in the absence of an occurrent case of evidence, a proposition would not be true. What he has in mind, rather, is a correlation between truth and the possibility of evidence. For every case where there is an agreement between a proposition and a state of affairs, it is possible that such an agreement be perceptually given (*LI* I, 190–91 / *H* XVIII, B 185). Ernst Tugendhat brings this point out clearly in commenting on this facet of the relation between truth and evidence in Husserl: "Of course every proposition to the effect that 'A is true' can be transformed into the proposition 'It is possible that anyone can judge with evidence that A is the case.' But this gives expression only to an *ideal* condition, namely, that the *possibility* of evidence essentially pertains to all judgments. From this it does not follow that every true proposition must be evident to some *real* person (my translation)."[18] Dallas Willard concurs when he states that "so far as cognition is concerned, to each truth there corresponds the possibility of an evident judgment. It is true that P if and only if it is ('in principle') possible for there to be an evident judgment that P."[19]

Furthermore, the possibility of evidence correlated to truth must not be construed as a real possibility for specifically human consciousness. There is no reason to think the domain of true propositions should be limited by the factual constraints on the perceptual powers of a particular species inhabiting this planet. Rather, truth is necessarily correlated to the ideal possibility of evidence. Husserl makes this point in his argument against psychologism in the "Prolegomena to Pure Logic." There he admits that any true proposition can be converted into an equivalent statement about the possibility of evidence. Thus p is true if and only if it is possible that p is evident. But the possibility of evidence must be construed in the ideal sense, as the possibility for some consciousness, not as a possibility tied to human beings—for "such possibilities of inner evidence are, however, real ones, and what is psychologically impossible may very well be ideally possible" (*LI* I, 191 / *H* XVIII, B 185). Husserl makes a similar point with respect to the possible truth of a proposition. A proposition is possibly true if and only if it is possible that the corresponding state of affairs be given in an act of imagination. But again, he is careful to say that this is the case, "whether we ourselves, as particular empirical individuals, succeed in thus realizing it or not" (*LI* II, 760 / *H* XIX 2, B2 116).

The necessary correlation between truth and evidence, then, obtains only between truth and evidence as an ideal possibility. The truth of a proposition is not dependent upon the actual occurrence of evidence in some existing consciousness. Nor is it dependent upon the real possibility of an occurrence of evidence in some existing kind of consciousness, be it human consciousness or otherwise. It is dependent upon only the ideal possibility of the actual occurrence of evidence in some possible consciousness. In this sense the equivalence relation between truth and evidence is almost entirely nonrestrictive.

3. THE FALLIBILITY OF OCCURRENT CASES OF EVIDENCE

Contrary to the crude interpretation of Husserl's theory of truth, I maintain that Husserl ties truth to the possibility of evidence, not the actuality of evidence, or even the possibility of evidence for some actual consciousness. It could be false that p is in fact evident and nonetheless true that p is true. Nonetheless, if p is true, then it must be the case that it is ideally possible that p is evident. We now turn to the question of the relation between actual cases of evidence and truth. Does Husserl hold that if p is in fact evident, then p is true? In the light of Husserl's mature theory of evidence, the answer is negative. For Husserl holds, in the final analysis, that all occurrent cases of evidence are fallible.

The fallibility of evidence makes its debut in Husserl's phenomenology in connection with the experience of transcendent objects. By a necessity rooted in the essence of the experience of transcendent objects, such objects are only partially given. There is always more to the object than is given in any particular experience of it. For that reason, the evidence available in the experience of transcendent objects is always and necessarily inadequate. The future course of experience may reveal that the position taken on the existence or the character of the object was mistaken. It may reveal that the preceding evidence was illusory or deceptive. Thus, Husserl states, "any experience [of a transcendent object], however extensive, leaves open the possibility that what is given does not exist in spite of the continued consciousness of its own presence 'in person.' According to eidetic law it is the case that physical existence is never required by the givenness of something physical" (*ID* I, 102 / *H* III 1, 97). I may take myself to be perceiving a transcendent object. But because the evidence involved in the perception of that object is inadequate, it is always possible that the object itself does not exist. Given the necessary correlation between truth and existence, it follows that if the object in question does not exist, then the proposition p that claims or presupposes it exists is not true. Thus it is possible for p to be evident—inadequately evident—and at the same time fail to be true.

With respect to adequate evidence, however, the situation is entirely otherwise. In an act of adequate evidence, the object is wholly given. Thus the positing of the existence of an object on the basis of adequate evidence cannot be mistaken. Here the existence of the object given is guaranteed by its givenness (*IP*, 65 / *H* II, 8). If a state of affairs is adequately given, then the corresponding proposition cannot fail to be true. It would appear, then, that the question of the relation of occurrent cases of evidence to truth must be divided into the question pertaining to inadequate evidence and the question of adequate evidence. With respect to inadequate evidence, it does not follow that if p is evident, then p is true; with respect to adequate evidence, it does.

The Husserl of the *Ideas* claims that there are in fact cases of adequate perceptual evidence. Such are to be found in the reflective apprehension of the acts of consciousness. An act of consciousness is wholly given in the reflective apprehension of it. It is given "absolutely." In this sense the act of consciousness is "immanent." There is nothing more to the act that is not given in the reflective apprehension of it. For this reason, the positing of the existence of an act of consciousness on the basis of the reflective apprehension of it cannot be mistaken. Upon the occurrence of a tree perception, it is possible that the tree fails to exist. The "givenness" of the tree does not guarantee the existence of the tree. But with the reflective apprehension of the tree perception, it is not possible for the tree perception to fail to exist, even in the existential absence of the tree perceived. Hence the epistemic privilege of a science based upon the reflective apprehension of the acts of consciousness. For here can adequate evidence be found. Here states of affairs can be given in such a way that the corresponding propositions must be true.

As we pointed out in chapter 1, however, Husserl came to deny the real possibility of adequate evidence. Even in the *Ideas* Husserl admitted that, strictly speaking, the evidence involved in the reflective apprehension of the acts of consciousness could not be adequate. This is not because acts of consciousness are spatial, but because they are temporal. "It is the case also of a mental process that it is never perceived completely, that it cannot be adequately seized upon in its full unity. A mental process is, with respect to its essence, in flux which we, directing the reflective regard to it, can swim along after it starting from the Now-point, while the stretches already covered are lost to our perception" (*ID* I, 97 / *H* III 1, 93). Acts of consciousness may not be spread out in space, but they are spread out in time.

Although in the passage immediately following the above Husserl claims that lack of adequacy in the reflective apprehension of the acts of consciousness is essentially different from the lack of adequacy in the perception of transcendent objects, he does not explain why the former lack of adequacy does not introduce that same measure of fallibility into the reflective apprehension of the acts of consciousness as it does into the perception of transcendent objects (*ID* I, 97 / *H* III 1, 93). As Elisabeth Ströker has shown, however, subsequent attention to the temporal horizon of all experience led Husserl to conclude that even the ostensibly adequate evidence contained in the reflective apprehension of the acts of consciousness contains "unfulfilled intentions."[20] "Husserl thereby established," Ströker maintains, "that all evidence—far from offering absolute certainty and security against deception and error—has an irrevocably presumptive character."[21] As a direct consequence, Tugendhat points out, "adequate evidence remains, in the widest sense, barred to all. In all concrete cases it is only a regulative idea" (my translation).[22]

The lack of adequacy on the part of evidence is to be found in the context not only of assertoric claims, but of apodictic claims as well. Once the method of ideation was developed into a process of imaginative variation over possibilities, the evidential grounds for apodictic claims became open-ended and subject to revision. Thus evidence, in all it forms, is never to be achieved in a single flash of intellectual insight (*FTL*, 157 / *H* XVII, 140). Rather, it is built up through the course of harmonious experience—in perception or imagination—of a certain object or state of affairs. It is always open to revision; it is always possible that some new evidence will contradict the old. "This holds for every evidence," Husserl claims in *Formal and Transcendental Logic*, "even an ostensibly apodictic evidence can be disclosed as deception and, in that event, presupposes a similar evidence by which it is 'shattered'" (*FTL*, 156 / *H* XVII, 140).

In Husserl's later theory of evidence, then, adequate evidence is converted into "an Idea lying at infinity."[23] It can be approximated, but never achieved. This holds for evidence in the context of claims pertaining to essence as well as existence. Thus, even if it were true that in cases of adequate evidence, p is evident entails p is true, it turns out, on Husserl's analysis, that for us there can be no real occurrent cases of adequate evidence. Given that every occurrent case of evidence is necessarily inadequate, it is not true that if p is evident, p is true.[24] Once the idea of adequate evidence is idealized, the identity of truth and evidence is, as Edward G. Ballard aptly put it, "infinitely postponed."[25]

4. EVIDENCE AND JUSTIFICATION

Given that all occurrent cases of evidence are fallible, what is to be made of the connection between occurrent cases of evidence and truth? I contend that the connection is indirect. We have established the fact that, for Husserl, actual cases of evidence do not guarantee the truth of the corresponding proposition. They do not make the corresponding proposition true. Nonetheless, evidence is the only indication we have that a proposition is true. Thus, although an occurrent case of evidence does not make the relevant proposition true, it does make us justified in believing that it is true. The connection between evidence and truth can be made only by way of a theory of justification.

In her article on Husserl's principle of evidence, Elisabeth Ströker chides those who take Husserl to claim that "truth can be derived from the experiences of evidence" for having failed to take into account the specific sense in which Husserl raises the issue of truth. Husserl is not proposing a theory of truth *simpliciter*; rather, he is conducting a phenomenological clarification of the *sense* of truth.[26] The question of the sense of truth is the question of how, in the course of experience, a proposition comes to acquire the status of being true *for us*. It is the question of how the truth of a proposition is commended to us within experience. On Husserl's phenomenological account, a proposition acquires the status of truth for us when the corresponding state of affairs is perceptually given. In *Ideas* I he writes, "Truth can only be given in an actual evidential consciousness" (*ID* I, 335 / H III 1, 323). For evidence is "the experience in which the correctness [truth] of his judgment is brought home to a judging subject" (*LI* I, 191 / H XVIII, B 186). Husserl's phenomenological account of truth, then, is not a theory of truth conditions for a proposition, but of conditions under which a proposition comes to acquire the sense of truth "for us" (*CM*, 59 / *H* I, 94). That is, it does not state the conditions under which a proposition is true, but the conditions under which we are justified in taking a proposition to be true. Thus, in a j-theoretic context, "it is clear that truth or the true actuality of objects is to be obtained only from evidence, and that it is evidence alone by virtue of which an 'actually' existing, true, rightly accepted object of whatever form or kind has sense for us. . . . Every rightness [in the sense of being justified: every *Recht*] comes from evidence" (*CM*, 60 / *H* I, 95). Likewise, Husserl claims that without evidence, and the possibility of returning to evidence, no world—real or ideal—would exist for us: "Both of these exist for us thanks to evidence" (*CM*, 60 / *H* I, 96). Here again, Husserl is not stating existence conditions for objects, but pointing to the conditions under which objects acquire the sense of existing for us. He is formulating the conditions under which we are justified in believing that an object exists, not the conditions for the existence of that object (cf. *CM* 65 / *H* I, 99). For this reason, Husserl refers to evidence as the original source of justification, as a *Rechtsquelle* (*ID* I, 338 / *H* III1, 326, and *ID* I, 44 / *H* III 1, 51; cf. *FTL*, 159 / *H* XVII, 142). Evidence is connected to truth by way of justification.

5. THE RATIONAL INDUBITABILITY OF THE PRINCIPLE OF EVIDENCE

At this point we have established that, for Husserl, what I believe with justification to be true on the basis of inadequate evidence may be false. We have also seen that, for the mature Husserl, all actual cases of evidence are inadequate. It follows that anything I believe on the basis of evidence may be false. But as soon as we foreswear the idealist identification of truth with occurrent cases of evidence, do we not open ourselves up to the threat of skepticism? After all, the only way we can tell if a proposition is true is by way of evidence. If it is not necessarily the case that evident propositions are true, then some evident propositions may be false. It follows that we might be justified in believing that which is false. Moreover, if there is no necessary connection between truth and evidence, it may be the case that all evident propositions are false. Remember Descartes's evil genius. The principle of evidence as a source of justification for belief may be, for all we know, systematically misleading. How, then, could we claim to know that something is true if it is possible that the sole basis for that claim—evidence—is in all respects deceptive? In allowing this chasm to open up between truth and evidence, has Husserl not opened the door wide to skepticism? If evidence does not make a proposition true, then what guarantee do we have that what we are justified in believing to be true on the basis of evidence is in fact true? What guarantee do we have that evidence is a reliable indicator of truth?

Husserl has no answer to these questions. But that does not mean he has no response. He simply rejects them as philosophically malformed. In this section I will show why Husserl, rather than attempting to assuage such skeptical worries with a philosophical demonstration of the reliability of evidence, rejects them as "rationally unmotivated" and, moreover, why he takes any skeptical denial of the epistemic reliability of evidence to be self-referentially incoherent. Thus the lack of a necessary connection between truth and evidence does not, in itself, constitute a reason for doubting the general epistemic reliability of evidence. Here Husserl steers a steady realist course between idealism and skepticism.

Husserl's argument runs as follows: When one asks for a guarantee for the reliability of evidence, one is in effect asking for what evidence we have for the reliability of evidence. Any answer to this request would necessarily presuppose what it seeks to demonstrate. For if we were to oblige the questioner by providing evidence for the epistemic reliability of evidence, we would already be depending upon the epistemic reliability of evidence.

But if we cannot, as a matter of principle, demonstrate the epistemic reliability of evidence without reasoning in a circle, are we obliged to doubt the epistemic reliability of evidence? If evidence is the source of all justified belief, and we have no evidence for the reliability of evidence that does not already presuppose the reliability of evidence, is our belief in the reliability of evidence then unjustified? Are we rationally compelled to doubt the reliability of evidence in general? By no means, Husserl would reply. For it is not possible to doubt rationally the principle of evidence. Of course, it is possible that what I believe in any specific case to be true on the basis of evidence is in fact false. But it would be irrational for me to doubt the truth of what I believe on the basis of evidence for that reason alone. For although I have reason to believe that it is *possible* that what I believe on the basis of evidence is false, apart from any concrete evidence to the contrary I have no reason for believing that it probably *is* false. (Here I take it that to doubt p means to believe that p is probably false.) It would be irrational, if not psychologically impossible, for me to believe that what I take to be true on all available evidence is in fact probably false. Rational doubt, Husserl maintains, must be motivated by some form of specific counterevidence (*ID* I, 332 / *H* III 1, 320). If I have no evidence that would lead me to believe that a certain proposition is false, then it would be wholly irrational for me to believe that that proposition is probably false.

If rational doubt must be motivated by some form of evidence, then clearly it would be impossible to doubt rationally the principle of evidence in general. The rational doubt of the epistemic reliability of evidence in general would require some evidence for thinking that evidence is unreliable. But such a requirement is clearly incoherent, for it presupposes the reliability of that which it seeks to discredit. It would be self-defeating, then, to argue or claim that evidence is unreliable, for the only thing that could speak for the truth of such a claim is evidence (cf. *IP*, 49 / *H* II, 61). Evidence is all we have to rely on for the rationality of our beliefs. Hence it would be irrational to doubt the principle of evidence. "To deny self-givenness [i.e., evidence] in general," Husserl writes in *The Idea of Phenomenology*, "is to deny every ultimate norm, every basic criterion that lends sense to knowledge . . . and thus get involved in the absurdity of skepticism" (*IP*, 45 / *H* II, 61). When I have evidence, Husserl states in the *Logical Investigations*, "all doubt would be mistaken. I therefore find myself at a point which I have either to recognize as the Archimedian point from which the world of doubt and unreason may be levered on its hinges, or which I give up at the peril of sacrificing all reason and knowledge" (*LI* I, 159 / *H* XVIII, B 143; translation modified).

As the source of all justified belief and rational assertion, evidence can be argued neither for nor against. To argue for it is to presuppose the reliability of that which one is seeking to establish—and that is to beg the question; to argue against it is to discredit the basis of one's own argument—and so to refute one's self. As the Scottish philosopher Thomas Reid put it in his *Inquiry*: To reason against evidence is absurd, and to reason for evidence is absurd. For evidence is a first principle.[27] It is, according to Husserl, the ultimate condition of rational discourse (*ID* I, 338 / *H* III 1, 326). For precisely that reason it must be simply accepted as trustworthy, "for if we no longer trust in evidence, how can we continue to make and maintain assertions rationally?" (*LI* I, 166 / *H* XVIII, B 152; my translation). Once we doubt the epistemic reliability of evidence, we "should have to pack in all rational striving for truth, all assertion and all demonstration" (*LI* I, 159 / *H* XVIII, B 143).[28]

6. SUMMARY AND TRANSITION

Theoretical science postulates the existence of unobservable entities in order to explain the lawlike behavior of observable objects. Such theoretical entities cannot be directly given in a perceptual act of human consciousness. Do we nonetheless have good reasons for thinking that the theoretical entities postulated by a well-confirmed theory really exist? To answer this question in the affirmative is to advance a realist interpretation of scientific theories.

Is Husserl's phenomenology compatible with a realist interpretation of scientific theories? On the crude version of Husserl's concept of truth, the answer would have to be negative. Husserl, this version holds, reduces truth to evidence. Given Husserl's concept of evidence, this means that a proposition is true if and only if the corresponding state of affairs is given in a perceptual act of consciousness. If theoretical entities cannot, by definition, be given in a perceptual act of consciousness, then any propositions corresponding to such states of affairs cannot be true, including existential propositions. Hence it cannot be true that theoretical entities exist, since the existence of theoretical entities cannot be given in the required sense. But if it cannot be true that theoretical entities exist, they cannot exist. It follows, then, on the crude version of Husserl's concept of truth, that the realist construal of scientific theory is incompatible with Husserlian phenomenology.

I rejected the crude version of Husserl's concept of truth for having failed to appreciate the specific modal qualification of Husserl's claims about the relation between truth and evidence. The necessary correlation between truth and evidence holds not between truth and occurrent cases of evidence in human consciousness, nor does it hold between truth and possible cases of evidence in human consciousness. Rather, it holds between truth and possible cases of evidence in some possible consciousness. The correlation between truth and evidence, then, must be formulated in the following way:

> p is true if and only if it is possible that the state of affairs corresponding to p be given to some possible consciousness.

More briefly:

> p is true if and only if it is ideally possible that p is evident.

When it comes to occurrent cases of evidence, the principle "If p is evident then p is true," holds—if at all—only for cases of adequate evidence. But the later Husserl held that all occurrent cases of evidence are necessarily inadequate. Thus, whenever p is in fact evident it does not follow that p is true, since inadequate evidence is fallible. I then suggested that the relation between truth and occurrent cases of evidence must be set in a justification-theoretic context. Hence, although it does not follow that if p is evident to S, p is true, it does follow that if p is evident to S, then S is justified in believing that p is true.

In this way the question of theoretical existence in connection with Husserl's concept of truth and evidence led us to Husserl's theory of justification. It does not follow from the fact that theoretical entities cannot be given to human consciousness that theoretical entities do not exist. But if theoretical entities cannot be given to human consciousness, can human beings be justified in believing that they exist? From the principle cited above—if p is evident to S, then S is justified in believing that p is true—it does not follow that if p is not evident to S, then S is not justified in believing that p is true. To be entitled to that conclusion, we would have to draw upon a stronger formulation of the principle, namely: S is justified in believing that p is true if *and only if* p is evident to S. Nor does it follow from the principle that if p can be evident to S, then S can be justified in believing that p is true, that if p cannot be evident to S, then S cannot be justified in believing that p is true. Again, we would need a stronger formulation of the principle, namely: S can be justified in believing that p is true if *and only if* p can be evident to S. If Husserl's theory of justification commits him to the stronger formulations of these principles, then his phenomenology would be incompatible with the realist construal of scientific theories. Not that it is in a position to deny the existence, or the possibility of the existence, of theoretical entities. But it would be constrained to deny that we are justified, or ever could be justified, in believing that theoretical entities exist.

CHAPTER FOUR

• •

EVIDENCE, RATIONALITY, AND EXISTENCE
IN HUSSERL'S PHENOMENOLOGY

In the preceding chapter on evidence and truth, I suggested that while an occurrent case of evidence does not make the corresponding proposition true, it does make us justified in believing that the corresponding proposition is true. Evidence is that experience whereby a proposition can acquire the sense of being true such that we are justified in making it the object of our assent. Thus a consideration of Husserl's conception of the relation between evidence and truth leads us directly to a consideration of the relation between evidence and justified belief.

The major statement of Husserl's theory of justification is to be found in part 4 of *Ideas* I, titled "Reason and Actuality" (Vernunft und Wirklichkeit), especially in the second chapter of that part, "Phenomenology of Reason" (Phänomenologie der Vernunft). There Husserl lays out a phenomenological theory of rationality. The general task of a theory of rationality is to specify those conditions under which a belief is justified. More precisely, for any proposition p, a theory of rationality is to specify the conditions under which a person, S, is justified in believing p. It is persons who are justified in having beliefs. In our examination of part 4 of *Ideas* I, I will distinguish between a weak and a strong statement of the rationality condition. I will then indicate why the weak statement is so weak as to make it practically useless as a condition for person rationality. I will then argue that the strong statement—which is very strong indeed—is not intended as a statement of a rationality condition that is to hold for all cognitive subjects in general. Rather, it is a statement of the condition for philosophical rationality. It holds only for some cognitive subjects at some times, namely, philosophers when they philosophize. Although it appears as if Husserl is developing here a general theory of rationality, there are indications in his other works that what he has in mind here is something quite specific.

Expanding on such indications, I will argue that Husserl's concept of rationality is differentiated with respect to epistemic project. I will then show why the strong statement of the rationality condition is not binding in the domain of positive scientific research. Thus, while it may be the case that if p is evident to a practicing empirical scientist, that scientist is justified in believing p, it does not follow that a scientist is justified in believing p if and *only if* p is evident. Such a restriction on justified belief holds, if at all, only for the philosopher in pursuit of philosophy as a rigorous science. If justified belief in the context of positive scientific research is not restricted to what is evident in the Husserlian sense, then it is least possible that the practicing scientist is justified in believing in the existence of entities that cannot be directly given in an intuitive act of evidence. I will argue, then, that on Husserl's own account, such a scientist—together with the scientifically educated—may be justified in believing in the existence of theoretical entities even if such entities cannot be given in the phenomenologically required sense.

1. HUSSERL'S THEORY OF RATIONALITY: *IDEAS* I

In part 4 of *Ideas* I, the problem of rationality is initially posed in terms of the question of the relation between the noetic-noematic components of experience and the putative object of experience. In part 3 Husserl sketched out the major contours of the correlation between the noetic and noematic dimensions of consciousness. The ontological identity of the noema is a matter of huge disagreement in Husserl scholarship. I will have more to say about it in chapter 6. Here suffice it to say that every intentional act of consciousness (noesis) intends its object in a particular way, under a particular description (noema). Every element in the act by which an object is presented will find its correlate in the noema of that act. In part 4 Husserl takes up the issue of the relation between the noetic-noematic complex of consciousness and the object intended by consciousness. He begins by reasserting the point that consciousness and reality represent two distinct "realms of being, which are radically opposed and yet essentially related to one another" (*ID* I, 307 / *H* III 1, 295). He also claims that noemata are not to be found on the side of reality: all noemata fall under a unique genus, different from the genera of real objects (*ID* I, 307 / *H* III 1, 295). Now the question arises: How does consciousness achieve a relation to an object that is ontologically distinct from the act of consciousness and its noema? (*ID* I, 308 / *H* III 1, 295–96; *ID* I, 310 / *H* III 1, 299). Husserl contends that the answer to this question is to be given in terms of the core component of the noema, known as its "sense" or "content," by which an act achieves a reference to an object. "Every noema has a 'content,' namely its 'sense,' and through it directs itself upon 'its' object" (*ID* I, 309 / *H* III 1, 297; my translation). Again: "The noema bears within itself an objective reference by virtue of the 'sense' which belongs to it" (*ID* I, 308 / *H* III 1, 296; my translation). On the noetic side of an act of consciousness we find the claim (*die "Prätention"*) to be actually related to an object, to be in touch with reality. The task of the phenomenological theory of rationality is to investigate the noetic-noematic conditions under which such a claim is justified (*ID* I, 308 / *H* III 1, 297).

It is important to appreciate from the outset the specific sense of a phenomenological inquiry into the conditions for justified belief. Consciousness of an object is achieved in and through the synthetic unity of the acts of consciousness. For "no object is conceivable without there also being conceivable multiple intentional experiences, connected in continuous or in proper synthetical (polythetical) unity—processes in which 'it,' the object, is intended to as an identical object" (*ID* I, 314 / *H* III 1, 302; translation modified). The core of the noema makes such a synthetic unity possible. In such a synthetically unified course of experience, an object is "constituted." That is, the flux of mental processes is synthetically unified such that there is a coherent experience of a selfsame object. Does it follow, however, that an object so constituted actually exists? Upon the unified and harmonious experience of an object, does it follow that there is an object such that the experience is actually related to it? Husserl asks precisely this question at the end of the first chapter of book 4: "There is necessarily consciousness of the X [the object] as the same in the different acts or act-noemas furnished with differing 'determination-contents.' But is it actually the same? And is the object itself 'actual'? Can it not be non-actual while the manifoldly harmonious and even intuitively fulfilled posita—posita of any essence-content—still flow off in the way peculiar to consciousness?" (*ID* I, 324 / *H* III 1, 312). More succinctly, does the unified and harmonious consciousness of an object guarantee the posited actuality of that object? (*ID* I, 325 / *H* III 1, 313).

In response to these questions, Husserl makes the striking concession that, in one sense, an object can be constituted in the synthetically unified concatenations of consciousness "whether or not it is actual" (*ID* I, 325 / *H* III 1, 313). Under what conditions, then, Husserl asks, does the object referred to as actually existing actually exist? He does not undertake to answer the question immediately. Rather, he postpones the question until after a discussion of the various forms of evidence and the conditions of justified belief (see below). At that point the question is posed in terms of the relation between the rational positing of an object as actual and the actuality of the object. Husserl's answer: the "object to be rationally posited" and the "truly existing object" are equivalent. We may put the claim this way: for any object x, x truly exists if and only if x is to be rationally posited. In the following paragraph, Husserl explicates the "to be" (*zu*) locution. "Of essential necessity . . . to every 'truly existing' object there corresponds the idea of a possible consciousness in which the object itself is seized upon originarily and therefore in a perfectly adequate way. Conversely, if this possibility is guaranteed, then *eo ipso* the object truly exists" (*ID* I, 341 / *H* III 1, 329).

It does not follow from this principle, however, that if an object is in fact rationally posited, it truly exists. The principle holds only for cases where the positing is motivated by adequate evidence. But, as we have seen, the later Husserl converted adequate evidence into a Kantian Idea, admitting that all occurrent cases of evidence only approximate this Idea. Of course, positing existence on the basis of inadequate evidence can be rational to some degree. But positing on the basis of inadequate evidence does not count as rational positing in the sense specified in the principle, where Husserl speaks of seizing upon an object in a "perfectly adequate way." The idea of a possible consciousness where the object is adequately given is an ideal that any actual finite consciousness can only approximate. In any actual finite consciousness the evidence of existence will always be inadequate; hence the actual positing of existence will always be fallible. The necessary correlation between existence and evidence, then, holds only for adequate evidence as an ideal possibility.

Furthermore, we must be careful to mark the specific sense of "actual" and "truly existing" within the discipline of phenomenology. At the end of chapter 1 of part 4, Husserl says that in one sense the synthetically unified concatenations of consciousness have the power to make the actuality of the object necessary. In another, broader sense, there can be such concatenations of consciousness, bringing about a consciousness of an object, whether or not that object is actual (*ID* I, 325 / *H* III 1, 313). I will take it that in the broad, ordinary sense, the actuality of the object refers to a mode of being of the object. If an object is actual, it exists. In the narrower, phenomenological sense, however, "actuality" refers to a noematic component by which an object is intended as actual. Thus we must make a distinction between actuality as a mode of being of the object that is intended and "actuality" as a noematic characteristic of the object as intended. It is then entirely possible that the object as intended acquire the noematic characteristic of being "actual" (in the narrow sense), and yet fail to be actual (in the broad sense) (*ID* I, 325 / *H* III 1, 313). There is no necessary relation between being rationally posited as "actual" and being actual. The only necessary relation here is in fact a species of the necessary correlation between noesis and noema, between positing an object as actual and that object having the posited noematic characteristic of being actual. Within the discipline of phenomenology, within "the limits of the phenomenological reduction" (*ID* I, 345 / *H* III 1, 334), one never goes beyond the noetic-noematic correlation. To do so would be to go beyond what is, strictly speaking, given within the reflective apprehension of the acts of consciousness. The question of the actuality of the object must become the question of how an object "shows itself" (*erweist sich*) as actual within consciousness (PSS, 25 / PSW, 21). Thus the speculative question of the relation between the noema and the object is converted into the phenomenological question of the internal structure of the noema. "Everywhere 'object' is the name for eidetic concatenations of consciousness; it appears first of all as noematic X, as the subject of sense pertaining to different essential types of sense and posita [existential status, for example,actual, possible, probable]. Moreover, it appears as the name, 'actual object,' and is then the name for certain eidetically considered rational concatenations in which the sense-conforming, unitary X inherent in them receives its rational position" (*ID* I, 347 / *H* III 1, 336). Here it is no longer the existence of the object in the straightforward sense that is the necessary correlate of rational positing, but the sense of existence; no longer the actuality, but the sense of actuality. "Phenomenology actually encompasses the whole natural world and all of the ideal worlds which it excludes: phenomenology encompasses them as the 'world sense' by virtue of the eidetic laws connecting any object-sense and noema whatever with the closed system of noeses, and specifically by virtue of the eidetic connections of rational positing the correlate of which is the 'actual object' which, thus, on its side, always exhibits the index for the wholly determined system of teleologically unified formations of consciousness" (*ID* I, 347–48 / *H* III,1 336–37; translation modified). I will have more to say about Husserl's use of quote marks around such words as "actual" and "object" in chapter 6. Here suffice it to say that they convert references to objects to references to noemata by which objects are intended.

A phenomenological theory of rationality, then, sets out to identify the noetic and noematic conditions under which one is justified in positing an object as actual. But those conditions are not, at the same time, the conditions for the actuality of the object. Rather, they are the conditions under which the object acquires the sense of actuality in the course of experience. There is not, nor can there be, a necessary correlation between an object being rationally posited as actual and the actuality of that object in the broad sense outlined above. The lack of such a necessary correlation in itself, however, is no warrant for doubt in the existence of an object when we are justified in positing it as existing. For if, on balance, one were justified in positing an object as existing, it would be irrational to doubt that it exists. This is a variation of the point we made at the end of the previous chapter.

Taking all this into consideration, precisely what are the noetic-noematic conditions of justified belief? In the opening paragraphs of chapter 2 of part 4, Husserl lays down a rationality condition: "If one speaks simply of objects, one normally means actual, truly existing objects. . . . No matter what one says about such objects, that which is meant and stated must—if one speaks rationally—be something which can be 'grounded,' 'shown,' directly 'seen,' or mediately seen 'intellectually'[*muss sich* . . . *"begrunden," "ausweisen," direckt "sehen" oder mittelbar "einsehen" lassen*]" (*ID* I, 326 / *H* III,1 314).

The first thing to note in the formulation of this condition is that it pertains to person rationality, not proposition rationality. It is important to take this into consideration because there may be many true propositions that are perfectly rational, in the sense of being supported or entailed by other true propositions, which nonetheless could not be rationally believed or asserted by a given person. That person may have no cognitive access to the propositions from which the proposition in question follows. For most people, most of the theorems of S5 modal logic probably fall into this category. Given the axioms of S5, the theorems of S5 are perfectly rational in the sense that they follow from those axioms, yet it would be safe to say that most people have no access to the relevant evidence for these theorems. For these people, simply asserting the theorems of S5 modal logic without further ado would be wholly gratuitous and irrational, although the theorems themselves may be perfectly rational. In part 1 of *Ideas* I, Husserl speaks of the rationality of sciences as systems of propositions apart from the persons who might believe them (*ID* I, 17 / *H* III 1, 21–22). But in part 4 he is addressing himself to the question of the rationality of persons.

Let us formulate the first statement of the rationality condition (RC) in the following way:

> RC1: A person, S, is justified in believing a proposition p if and only if p can either be evident or be demonstrated on the basis of what is evident.

Here we take "grounded," "shown," and "directly seen" to be appositives captured by the term "evident," followed by the disjunct "mediately seen intellectually," which we will take to mean demonstrated by way of logical inference. For the purposes of this discussion, we also take it that the conditions of rational belief are identical with the conditions of rational assertion.

The second thing to note about this formulation is its modal qualification. It does not assert that a person, S, is justified in believing p if and only if p is evident or has been demonstrated by S on the basis of what is evident. Rather, the justification of the person's belief is tied to the question of whether p *can be* evident or demonstrated on the basis of what is evident (*"sich . . . direckt 'sehend' oder mittelbar 'einsehen' lassen"* [*ID* I, 326 / *H* III 1, 314]). Thus the rationality of believing p does not depend upon an act or any accomplishment on the part of the person who believes. It depends, rather, on a property of the proposition believed. It must be possible that this proposition be evident or demonstrated on the basis of what is evident.

Third, it is important to note what kind of possibility for evidence or demonstration a proposition must possess. Husserl does not claim that if a proposition is to be a candidate for justified belief it must be possible that the proposition be evident to or demonstrated by the person who believes it. Neither does he claim that it must be possible that the proposition be evident to or demonstated by some other existing person. He states only that it must be capable of being evident or demonstrated. In fact, he explicitly states that "the possibility of the rational showing referred to here should be understood, not as empirical, but as 'ideal,' as an essential possibility" (*ID* I, 326 / *H* III 1, 314). Thus the possibility of evidence or demonstration with respect to the proposition in question must not be limited by any empirical considerations pertaining to the historical situation, education, mental capabilities, or perceptual faculties of any particular person.

Construed in this way, the first statement of the rationality condition would seem to be exceedingly weak. For a person, S, to be justified in believing a proposition, that proposition need not be evident to S, nor need it be possible that it be evident to S, nor need it be possible that it be evident to any existing person belonging to the same historical community or even the same species as S. It need only be possible that it be evident to or demonstrated in some possible consciousness. Thus the first formulation of the rationality condition can be explicated in this way:

> RC1*: S is justified in believing p if and only if it is ideally possible that p is evident or demonstrated on the basis of what is evident.

If we invoke the principle we established in the last chapter, which posits a necessary correlation between truth and the ideal possibility of evidence, it follows that, on this statement of the rationality condition, S is justified in believing p if and only if p is true. That is, a person is justified in believing any proposition, just as long as that proposition is true. But this allows for the rational belief in a proposition apart from any evidence the person who believes the proposition actually has or could ever hope to have. The only condition on the rationality of the belief is that the proposition believed can be evident; and the possibility of its evidence is not to be limited by any empirical considerations, for Husserl insists that he is here speaking only of ideal possibility.

A clue as to why Husserl states the rationality condition in such a weak form can be found in the opening paragraph of chapter 2. There he states that "in the logical sphere, in the sphere of statement, 'being truly' or 'actually' and 'being something which can be shown rationally' are necessarily correlated" (*ID* I, 326 / *H* III 1, 314). That which actually or truly exists and that which is "rationally showable" stand in necessary correlation. Otherwise stated: a state of affairs A obtains if and only if A can be given in an act of evidence or demonstrated on the basis of what can be given in an act of evidence. Invoking the equivalence relation between existence and truth established in the last chapter, we can reformulate the principle in this way: p is true if and only if it is possible that p be evident or demonstrated on the basis of what is evident.

The possibility of evidence and demonstration here, however, must be understood as an ideal possibility. If the possibility of evidence in this principle were tied to a particular empirical person, S, then it would turn out that a proposition p could be true if and only if p could be evident to S or demonstrated by S on the basis of what is evident to S. But this would yield entirely unacceptable results. For instance, if the proposition that Edmund Husserl was born in 1859 could not be evident to S, it would not be true that Edmund Husserl was born in 1859. Likewise, if S received a poor education or was mentally deficient in some important respect and, as a result, could not prove that the sum of the interior angles of a triangle is equal to 180 degrees, then it would not be true that the sum of the interior angles of a triangle is equal to 180 degrees.

But we should want to reject any principle that leads to such conclusions, as does the early Husserl, who asserts in the *Logical Investigations*, "What is true is absolutely true, true 'in itself': truth is one and the same, whether men or non-men, angels or gods apprehend it in judgment [or not] . . . [truth is an] ideal unity, set over against the real multiplicity of races, individuals and experiences" (*LI* I, 140 / *H* XVIII, B 117–18; my translation). When the possibility of evidence is correlated with truth as a property of propositions, that possibility must be construed in the ideal sense. "The solution of the generalized '3-body problem,' or 'n-body problem' may transcend all human cognitive capacity, but the problem has a solution, and the evidence which relates to it is therefore possible" (*LI* I, 191 / *H* XVIII, B 185). Thus the principle in question must be read as follows: p is true if and only if it is ideally possible that p is evident or demonstrated on the basis of what is evident.

So far, so good. The problem arises when the ideal possibility of evidence and demonstration is laid down not only as a necessary and sufficient condition for the truth of a proposition but also as a necessary and sufficient condition for the justified belief in a proposition. The resultant rationality condition is far too weak, I maintain, for it holds, in the last analysis, that any belief is justified just in case the proposition believed is true. On this condition, a person may be justified in believing a proposition in the absence of any actual evidence; more paradoxically, a person may be justified in believing a proposition contrary to all available evidence. For the only condition on the rationality of the belief is that the proposition believed is true. Given the fallibility of all occurrent cases of evidence, it is entirely possible, on RC1, that a person holds a justified belief contrary to all available evidence. Once evidence is construed as an ideal possibility, it can no longer serve as a sufficient condition for person rationality. For, presumably, the conditions under which a person is justified in holding a belief will incorporate a number of contingent and experiential factors that pertain to that person.

While the rationality condition stated in the opening paragraph of chapter 2 appears to be overly permissive, the rationality condition implied in the section immediately following—section 136—is exceedingly strong. There

Husserl undertakes to indicate precisely what "rational showing" (*vernunftige Ausweisung*), or "rational consciousness" (*Vernunftbewusstsein*), amounts to. He does so by introducing a number of eidetic distinctions. For both essential and individual states of affairs, there is a difference between the consciousness in which those states of affairs are originally presented and the consciousness in which they are not. With respect to an individual state of affairs, say, a particular landscape, there is a difference between perceptual and memorial consciousness. With respect to an essential state of affairs, for example, "a + b = b + a," there is a difference between judging that state of affairs with "insight" and judging it "blindly." Within these different forms of consciousness, the core "sense" (*Sinn*) remains the same. The difference pertains to the question of whether the sense is fulfilled by a corresponding act of intuition. In addition, there are differences to be noted in the way the sense is intuitively fulfilled, perceptually or nonperceptually (*ID* I 327 / *H* III 1, 315).

With such distinctions firmly in hand, Husserl then claims that the noematic moment of intuitive fulfillment serves as the basis (*Unterlage*) for the noematic posited being-characteristic. Thus the perception of the landscape, in which the landscape appears "in person," serves as a basis for the posited characteristic of the landscape's "being actual" (*ID* I 327 / *H* III 1, 315). Moreover, the posited characteristic acquires its rational character (*Vernunftcharacter*) "if and only if it is a position on the basis of a fulfilled, originarily presentive sense and not merely on the basis of just any sense" (*ID* I 327 / *H* III 1, 315–16). Here the rationality condition is given a strict formulation: it holds that the posited being-characteristic is rational not only if the sense to which this characteristic is attached can be intuitively fulfilled, but also only if it is actually so fulfilled.

It must be pointed out here, however, that this formulation of the rationality condition does not immediately concern the rationality of a person. Rather, it bears upon the rationality of the positional characteristic of the noema. As such it deals with the question of rationality prior to the level of belief and assertion. It might seem, then, that the strong and the weak forms of the rationality condition do not conflict or stand in tension with each other, since they are posed at different levels, the prepredicative and the predicative.

But this way of reconciling the formulations would be ill-advised. For in *Experience and Judgment*, Husserl holds that predication, the act of judging, is drawn from the prepredicative sphere of experience where the state of affairs judged is already given in a polythetic act (*EJ*, 197–215 / *EU*, 231–55).

It follows, then, that if the posited being-characteristic lacks the property of being rational, then the act of belief or judgment in which that characteristic is asserted also lacks that property. Moreover, given the correlation between the noetic and noematic dimension of consciousness, if the posited characteristic lacks the property of being rational, the noetic act by which that characteristic is posited would also lack that property. But if the prepredicative act of positing that characteristic is not rational, then neither is the predicative act that asserts that characteristic rational.

The way Husserl characterizes the situation in the passage under consideration supports this interpretation. For here he places the act of predication in apposition to the act of positing. Both are "motivated" by evidence (*ID* I, 328 / *H* III 1, 316). Hence, if a state of affairs A is given in an act of perception, the positing of A as actual is rational. But if the positing of A as actual is rational, the belief in the proposition corresponding to A is also rational. If this is indeed the case, then the strong form of the rationality condition, initially set forth on the level of prepredicative experience, entails the strong form on the predicative level.

The second formulation of the rationality condition can then be represented in the following manner:

RC2: A person, S, is justified in believing a proposition p if and only if p is evident to S.

It should be immediately apparent that RC2 is stronger than RC1 in a number of respects. For it holds that a person is justified in believing a proposition not only if the corresponding state of affairs could be evident to some person, not only if the corresponding state of affairs could be evident to that person, and not only if the corresponding state of affairs has been evident to that person, but only if the corresponding state of affairs *is* evident to that person. While the weak formulation allows for the rationality of asserting any true proposition, the strong allows for the rationality of asserting only one proposition, namely the one for which the corresponding state of affairs is being intuitively given to the one asserting it. On the strong formulation, I am not justified in believing in the vast majority of propositions, which I normally take myself to be justified in believing—that Edmund Husserl was the founder of the phenomenological movement, that President Gerald R. Ford came from the city of Grand Rapids, Michigan, that there is such a country as China, that I had oatmeal for breakfast this morning, that my membership in the Funky Buddha Yoga Hothouse is about to expire, or the like. It would seem, then, that the weak formulation is too weak, while the strong formulation is too strong—at least if the strong formulation is intended as a statement of a general rationality condition, holding for all persons at all times.

Sensing, perhaps, the stringency of the strong formulation, Husserl proceeds to dilute it. Although it remains the case that originary presentation is the privileged form of evidence, states of affairs not presented in this fashion can take on "secondary" rational characteristics (*ID* I, 328 / *H* III 1, 316). Husserl does not attempt, at this point, to give an exhaustive list of such secondary rational characteristics, but he does mention the re-presentation (*Wiedervergegenwartigung*) of an essential cognition as an example. Thus, believing that the square of the hypotenuse of a right triangle is equal to the sum of the square of the other two sides not on the basis of current intellectual insight into the corresponding eidetic state of affairs, but rather on the basis of a memorial modification of that insight, counts as a rational noetic act in the derivative sense. In this way Husserl brings those propositions that have been evident, or demonstrated on the basis of what was evident, into the circle of possible objects of justified belief.

I have been formulating the second statement of the rationality condition in terms of person rationality. In this passage, however, Husserl stresses that the kind of rationality under discussion is the rationality of the noetic act of positing and, correlatively, the noematic *positum*. A noetic act of positing is rational, in the primary sense, if and only if it is motivated by the intuitively fulfilled sense of its noematic correlate. Likewise, that which is posited is rational in the primary sense if and only if it is "based" upon the fulfillment of the sense to which it is attached. Thus the entire discussion of rationality takes place within the scope of the two eidetically correlated dimensions of consciousness, with no reference to a "factually existing ego" (*ID* I 333 / *H* III 1, 322). By tying the question of rationality to the eidetic relations that hold for consciousness, and not to actual persons, Husserl severs any dependency relation between the rationality of an act and the contingent circumstances pertaining to a particular person. The form of the rationality condition is not, "A person, S, is justified in believing p if and only if . . . ," but, "A noetic act of positing x as actual is justified if and only if . . ."

But are there not person rationality implications embedded in the act rationality formulation? It would seem that there are. The act rationality formulation is more general than the person rationality formulation. For the act rationality formulation does not state that the act in question must occur in a human, or any other specific form of consciousness. But the person rationality formulation can be seen as a specification of the act rationality formulation. The latter states a necessary and sufficient condition for the rationality of an act. But if that condition is to be met, it must be met by an occurrent act in some consciousness. And that act may be the act of a person. Where this is the case, it follows that if the act is rational, the person to whom the act can be ascribed is, *eo ipso*, rational. What else could person rationality be other than a specific case of act rationality?

Furthermore, the person rationality formulation also makes no reference to existing persons and their contingent circumstances. It states only the necessary and sufficient condition that must be met if a person is to be rational in his or her belief. The contingent circumstances of a particular person come into play only with respect to the question of whether that person is justified in his or her beliefs (i.e., whether a state of affairs is or can be given to that person such that the person is or can be justified in believing the corresponding proposition). Although the term "person" appears, suitably enough, in the person rationality formulation, it still makes no reference to existing persons and their contingent circumstances. The latter become relevant only in the application of the rationality condition to particular cases.

The second statement of the rationality condition, in either its act or its person rationality formulation, remains exceedingly strong and restrictive. It allows for rational positing, believing, or asserting only with respect to those states of affairs that are being, or have been, originarily presented. Where such givenness is absent, the rational characteristics are also lacking. It would seem, then, that only the proto-*doxa*, only belief with certainty motivated by evidence, counts as rational belief. Yet Husserl maintains that other modalities of belief, although not themselves rational, can partake of rationality (*an der Vernunft Anteil hat*). This is the case when the proto-*doxa* "speaks on their behalf" (*ID* I, 334 / *H* III 1, 322; cf. *CM*, 58 / *H* I, 93). Although a certain state of affairs may not present itself in consciousness such that we would be justified in taking it to be actual, it is possible that the probability, or the likelihood, of the actuality of the state of affairs could be so presented. The assertion "It is likely that p" could partake of rationality if it were evident that p is likely. Here the straightforward assertion of "p" would not be rational. But, if the likelihood of p is originarily presented to consciousness, the assertion "It is likely that p" would, at least, have a share of rationality.

At this point Husserl does not discuss, describe, or explain how likelihood, or probability, is to be given in an act of evidence. His intent here is programmatic rather than analytic. But clearly the idea is that the rationality of all other modalities of belief is to be ultimately referred back to the proto-*doxa*—"the unmodalized primal form of the mode of believing" (*ID* I, 251 / *H* III 1, 240)—where what is posited is based upon evidence in the sense of originary presentation (*ID* I, 334 / *H* III 1, 324). The phenomenological concept of evidence, then, admits of differentiation according to the modalities of belief and, correlatively, the modalities of being (*ID* I, 250 / *H* III 1, 239).

2. THE STRONG FORMULATION AND PHILOSOPHICAL RATIONALITY

Statements of the strong formulation of the rationality condition can be found in other passages of *Ideas* I as well. In part 1 Husserl states that "immediate 'seeing,' not merely sensuous, experiential seeing, but seeing in the universal sense as an originarily presentive consciousness of any kind whatever, is the ultimate legitimizing source of all rational assertions" (*ID* I, 36 / *H* III 1, 43). One can also find similar statements in other works. For instance, in *Formal and Transcendental Logic*, Husserl maintains that "anything that we intend to state rationally should be drawn from evidence" (*FTL*, 201 / *H* XVII, 179). Such statements, in themselves, carry no qualifications. It appears as if Husserl is laying down a general condition of rationality that is to hold for all cognitive subjects at all times. But if we examine the context in which these statements are made together with other, similar statements, it becomes clear that what Husserl has in mind is a specific form of rationality, namely, "philosophical" rationality.

In the introduction to the *Cartesian Meditations*, Husserl sets the strong formulation of the rationality condition in the context of the decision, on the part of a cognitive subject, to become a philosopher. According to Husserl, the decision to become a philosopher is the decision to become personally and wholly responsible for one's beliefs. I am not to accept beliefs on the say-so of others; neither am I to hold beliefs that go beyond the evidence I have for them. Rather, all my beliefs must be grounded in and restricted to the evidence that I myself have achieved. In my life qua philosopher, reason is to become wholly autonomous, accepting only that which it has seen for itself. "Must not the demand," Husserl asks, "for a philosophy aiming at the ultimate conceivable freedom from prejudice, shaping itself with actual autonomy according to ultimate evidences it has itself produced, and therefore absolutely self-responsible—must not this demand, instead of being excessive, be part of the fundamental sense of genuine philosophy?" (*CM*, 6 / *H* I, 47). This is indeed a tall order for mere mortals, but if it is the case, then "anyone who seriously intends to become a philosopher must 'once in his life' withdraw into *himself*, to overthrow and build anew all the sciences that, up to then, he has been accepting. Philosophy—wisdom (*sagesse*)—is the philosopher's quite personal affair. It must arise as his wisdom, as his self-acquired knowledge tending toward universality, a knowledge for which he can answer from the beginning, and at each step, by virtue of his own absolute insights" (*CM*, 2 / *H* I, 44).

A similar passage can be found in the *Crisis*. There Husserl refers to Descartes's strong foundationalist concept of philosophical knowledge: "Philosophical knowledge is, according to Descartes, absolutely grounded knowledge; it must stand upon a foundation of immediate and apodictic knowledge whose evidence excludes all conceivable doubt. Every step of mediate knowledge must be able to attain the same sort of evidence" (*C*, 75 / *H* VI, 77; translation modified). Given that Descartes's received beliefs do not measure up to this rigorous standard of philosophical knowledge, he is compelled to begin with a radically skeptical attitude—and so must anyone else, Husserl adds, "who seriously seeks to be a philosopher.... Once in his life every philosopher must proceed in this way" (*C*, 75–76 / *H* VI, 77).

It is important to note that in each of these passages, the strong formulation is given out on the antecedent condition that one has decided to be a philosopher. If one commits oneself to the ideal of philosophy, then the strong formulation of the rationality condition holds: I ought not to accept any belief apart from direct evidence. Husserl does not say that the strong formulation holds for everyone who would attain knowledge, but only for those dominated by the will to philosophical knowledge. This qualification is judiciously included in Dorion Cairns's statement of the phenomenological rationality condition, the "fundamental methodological principle of phenomenology": "No opinion is to be accepted as *philosophical* knowledge unless it is seen to be adequately established by observation of what is seen as itself given 'in person.'"[1] Here the rationality condition is specified with respect to a particular kind of knowledge. It represents the condition that must be met if one is to claim to be in possession of philosophical knowledge. It is not set forth as a necessary condition for knowledge in general.

The same point can be made in connection with Husserl's discussion of science and scientific rationality. Here science is to be understood in the traditional, philosophical sense, as *scientia*, as "the idea of genuine science grounded on an absolute foundation" (*FTL*, 7 / *H* XVII, 6). If one takes up the idea of science as an ideal for epistemic striving, then one will resolve "not to accept any cognition unless it is justified absolutely" (*FTL*, 7 / *H* XVII, 6). For the "first methodological principle" to be analytically derived from the idea of science is "that I, as someone beginning philosophically, since I am striving toward the presumptive end, genuine science, must neither make nor go on accepting any judgment as scientific that I have not derived from evidence, from 'experiences' in which the affairs and affair-complexes in question are present to me as 'they themselves'" (*CM*, 13 / *H* I, 54). The scientist qua scientist in this particular sense "intends to let no judgment be accepted by himself or others as 'scientific knowledge,' unless he has grounded it perfectly and can therefore justify it completely at any time by a freely actualizable return to his repeatable act of grounding" (*CM*, 11 / *H* I, 51). For "genuine science and its own genuine freedom from prejudice require, as the foundation of all proofs, immediately valid judgments which derive their validity from originally presentative intuitions" (*ID* I, 36 / *H* III 1, 42).

Phenomenology, in its direction and method of research, represents Husserl's attempt to set philosophy on the path toward the realization of the idea of genuine science (cf. *C*, 113 / *H* VI, 115). In its turn to consciousness and adoption of the phenomenological attitude, phenomenology seeks to establish itself as a foundational discipline based on the only domain where adequate evidence can be found (*IP*, 48 / *H* II, 60; *CM*, 36 / *H* I, 74). Thus the norm for phenomenological rationality is but a specification of the genuine sense of the norm for scientific rationality. In section 59 of *Ideas* I, Husserl expresses this norm as follows: "To avail ourselves of nothing but what we can make essentially evident to ourselves through consciousness itself in its pure immanence" (*ID* I, 136 / *H* III 1, 127; emphasis deleted; my translation). But again, this norm applies to us "as phenomenologists" (*ID* I, 136 / *H* III 1, 127).

Thus does the phenomenological theory of rationality turn out to be a theory of phenomenological rationality. It does not claim to be a statement of a rationality condition for cognitive subjects in general. Rather, it lays down a condition that is to serve as a norm for belief on the part of the cognitive subject that has taken up the ideal of a particular kind of knowledge—"genuine science" or "philosophical knowledge." The conditions of justification for that particular kind of knowledge will not, however, hold for all kinds of knowledge. In other contexts persons may be justified in their beliefs apart from direct evidence. Yet the phenomenologist remains in a position to describe the noetic-noematic conditions under which others, in these contexts, are justified in holding beliefs from which the phenomenologist qua phenomenologist must abstain. Thus the phenomenologist can identify and delimit those conditions under which a person would be justified in believing in the existence of transcendent objects, even though the phenomenologist does not participate in such beliefs due to the inadequacy of their evidence (*ID* I, 331 / *H* III,1 319).[2] This is precisely what Husserl does in section 138 of *Ideas* I. Moreover, he holds that the phenomenologist is in the unique position to develop a critique of all forms of rationality—theoretical, axiological, and practical (*ID* I 333–36 / *H* III 1, 289–92).

Knowledge in general is justified true belief (Gettier problems aside). But if it is the case that there are different kinds of knowledge—philosophical knowledge as opposed to other kinds of knowledge—then the conditions of justified belief may vary according to the kind of knowledge being sought. That Husserl's statement of the strong formulation of the rationality condition is always given in connection with a particular kind of knowledge—"philosophical knowledge," "scientific judgment," "genuine science"—serves as an indication that he has a specific, not a general, condition of rationality in mind.[3] His concept of rationality is differentiated with respect to epistemic project.

3. RATIONALITY IN NONTHEORETICAL CONTEXTS

In the first of his *Meditations on First Philosophy*, Descartes claims that Reason persuades him that he should withhold his assent "from opinions which are not completely certain and indubitable."[4] In his letter to Hyperaspistes of August 1641, however, Descartes states that there are times when one ought to believe that which is not completely certain and indubitable. To make his point, he asks Hyperaspistes to consider the following hypothetical situation:

> Suppose that a man decided to abstain from all food to the point of starvation, because he was not certain that it was not poisoned, and thought that he was not bound to eat because it was not clearly established that he had the means of keeping alive, and it was better to wait for death by abstaining than to kill himself by eating. Such a man would be rightly regarded as insane and responsible for his own death. Suppose further that he could not obtain any food that

was not poisoned, and that fasting was beneficial to him; none the less, if the food appeared harmless and healthy, and fasting appeared likely to have its usual harmful effects, he would be bound to eat the food and thus follow the apparently beneficial course of action rather than the actually beneficial one. This is so self-evident to all that I am surprised that anyone could think otherwise.[5]

Is Descartes being inconsistent here? Is he privately retracting what he publicly put forward elsewhere? By no means. For in the First Meditation, Descartes states that "reason now leads me to think that I should hold back my assent from opinions which are not completely certain and indubitable."[6] When is the "now" that Reason leads him to think such things? The context makes it clear: when he undertakes to demolish his opinions in order to establish a firm foundation for the sciences.[7] That is, the strict rationality condition laid down in the *Meditations* is not intended as a general condition governing belief in all contexts, but as a condition that holds for one who endeavors to establish philosophy as a genuine science. It obtains only in a highly specific context of theoretical activity. In practical life, as indicated by the letter, it would be absurd to put such strictures on justified belief. As Descartes cautions in the opening articles of the *Principles of Philosophy*, the will to doubt everything that might possibly be false should be "employed solely in connection with the contemplation of truth. As far as ordinary life is concerned, the chance for action would frequently pass us by if we waited until we could free ourselves from our doubts."[8] One who holds that we are justified in believing only that which is certain would have to acknowledge, as Hume points out in his *Enquiry*, "that all human life must perish, were his principles universally and steadily to prevail" (*Enquiry*, section 12, part 2). For human beings "must act and reason and believe; though they are not able, by most diligent enquiry, to satisfy themselves concerning the foundation of these operations, or to remove the objections, which may be raised against them" (*Enquiry*, section 12, part 2). Beliefs function not only in theoretical contexts in which the cognitive value of certainty may predominate, but in practical contexts as the basis of actions that are directed toward values other than truth and certainty. In such contexts decision and action are often called for before the truth of the relevant beliefs can be made entirely evident. On the basis of prior experience and present appearances, I could claim to know that the bread before me is healthy and nutritious, even if I were not certain, in some scientific sense, that it is. A belief justified in this context would also count as knowledge—not scientific or philosophical knowledge, but "practical" knowledge. Such knowledge would not be absolutely certain, Descartes admits, but it would be "morally" certain—that is, its certainty would be "sufficient to regulate our behavior."[9]

Husserl makes similar concessions when it comes to belief, and the justification of belief, in nontheoretical contexts. In "Philosophy as a Rigorous Science," he writes that "in the urgency of life that in practice necessitates adopting a position, man could not wait until—say, after a thousand years—science would be there, even supposing that he already knew the idea of rigorous science" (PRS, 138 / PSW, 63–64). For, as he explains elsewhere, "life, after all, consists in decisions of the 'moment,' which never has time to establish anything with scientific rationality" (FTL, 6 / H XVII, 5). What has been scientifically established can have an impact on practical life. But the practical exigencies of life require that decisions be made and actions carried out on the basis of beliefs that often fall outside the pale of what has been established with the certainty of science. At any point in its development, science cannot speak to the full range of present human concerns. The idea of science is an "infinite idea." That is, it functions as an Idea in the Kantian sense, regulating theoretical activity of successive generations, eternally approximating the idea but never arriving at it (PRS, 136 / PSW, 61).

In the meantime, practical life requires answers to vital questions. It cannot wait for science (PRS, 139 / PSW, 65). It requires a form of wisdom, as opposed to science, which is suitable for the regulation of practice in the present. The idea of wisdom, then, is a finite idea. It can be and is achieved by various human communities. And within those communities there are wise individuals who represent the considered wisdom of the community. They know how to assess, weigh, deliberate, and decide within the manifold practical orientations of life. But their wisdom, for the most part, is not based upon, or derived from, science. The theoretical articulation of such wisdom is what Husserl calls a *Weltanschauung* philosophy, as opposed to a rigorously scientific philosophy (PRS, 132–33 / PSW, 58–59). Such a philosophy gives expression to the wisdom of the age, and, in the absence of a fully developed scientific philosophy, provides immediate practical guidance in the affairs of life.[10]

Husserl does not reject this practical form of philosophy on the basis of its unscientific character: "The value of *Weltanschauung* stands with utmost firmness on its own foundations" (PRS, 143 / PSW, 68). Even philosophers stand in need of thinking, deciding, and acting where scientific philosophy has, as yet, nothing to say. "It is certain that we cannot wait. We have to take a position, we must bestir ourselves to harmonize the disharmonies in our attitude to reality—to the reality of life, which has significance for us and in which we should have significance—into a rational, even though unscientific, 'world-and-life-view.' And if the *Weltanschauung* philosopher helps us greatly in this, should we not thank him?" (PRS, 141 / PSW, 66). *Weltanschauung* philosophy has its independent source of value and its distinct function. In its own sphere, it is both necessary and legitimate (PRS, 143 / PSW, 68). As Gary G. Gutting points out, "in addition to the rigorous descriptions of phenomenology, there is room and need for more speculative world-views that are developed on the level of the natural attitude and hence do make existential commitments. . . . The important point for us to realize is that such speculation has its own, less rigorous, methodology and must not be confused with truly scientific philosophy—i.e. phenomenology."[11]

Non-scientifically justified belief in the practical context has its own integrity. It is not merely a deficient form of science. For it does not set out to do what science does. "For prescientific life . . . this type of acquaintance [practical knowledge] suffices, as does its manner of converting the unknown into the known, gaining 'occasional' knowledge on the basis of experience . . . and induction. This suffices for everyday praxis" (C, 124 / H VI 126). Such knowledge, when compared to science, is often disparaged, acquiring the status of "mere opinion," "the disdainful coloring of the *doxa*" (C, 124 / H VI 126). But, Husserl maintains, "in prescientific life itself, of course, it has nothing of this; there it is a realm of good verification and, based on this, of well-verified predicative cognitions and of truths which are just as secure as is necessary for the practical projects of life that determine their sense" (C, 125 / H VI, 127–28). It is a form of knowledge that "the scientist himself must be satisfied with . . . whenever he has recourse, as he unavoidably must have recourse, to it" (C, 125 / H VI, 127–28).[12] Again, Husserl's concept of rationality is differentiated with respect to epistemic project.

4. POSITIVE SCIENTIFIC RATIONALITY

In practical life, then, we are not only required but often justified in going beyond what is, strictly speaking, evident to us. But, Husserl maintains, this is not only the case in practical life. It is also true in the pursuit of positive science. For positive science is also a form of human activity (C, 118 / H VI, 120;

C, 133 / H VI, 135). Similar concessions must be made to human finitude. Practicing scientists do not have time to conduct a regressive inquiry into the foundations of their discipline prior to getting on with positive research. If practicing scientists were required, qua scientists, to recapitulate and justify the entire development of their discipline for themselves step-by-step, science itself would surely come to a grinding halt. Neither does a practicing scientist need to conduct such an inquiry. For "even the mathematician, the physicist, and the astronomer need not understand the ultimate grounds of their activities in order to carry through even the most important scientific performances" (*LI* I, 58 / *H* XVIII, 25). "Simple positivity," Husserl writes in *Formal and Transcendental Logic*, "as a naive devotedness, not only of the practical but also of cognitive living, to the world that is indeed given beforehand, has in it a legitimacy—unclarified, to be sure, and therefore still undelimited, but nevertheless a legitimacy" (*FTL*, 226 / *H* XVII, 200).

As we noted in chapter 2, Husserl recognized a division of intellectual labor between science and philosophy. While the positive scientist begins with the discipline as given and seeks to carry it forward into new developments that presuppose the old, the philosopher is to make a regressive inquiry into the ultimate foundations of the discipline in particular and into the possibility of knowledge in general. There are both positive and critical directions of theoretical inquiry. But the scientist need not engage in critical reflection prior to positive research. Nor need the scientist wait until those engaging in critical reflection deliver wholly secure results. There is something entirely appropriate about the "dogmatic," epistemologically unreflective attitude of the practicing scientist, about "that position which sets aside with full awareness all skepticism together with all 'natural philosophy' and 'theory of knowledge,' and takes cognitive objectivities where one actually finds them—no matter what difficulties an epistemological reflection on the possibility of such objectivities may always point out afterwards" (*ID* I, 47 / *H* III 1, 54; emphasis deleted). Thus, "in the present situation, and as long as there is indeed lacking a highly developed cognitive critique which succeeds in perfect rigor and clarity, it is at the least right to close the boundaries of dogmatic research to 'critical' modes of inquiry" (*ID* I, 48 / *H* III 1, 54–55; emphasis deleted).[13]

As in practical life, so in positive science: justified belief cannot be restricted to what is directly evident. The practicing scientist qua scientist need not inquire into the ultimate conditions of the possibility of science in general, nor into the specific conceptual and theoretical foundations of his or her own discipline. As a matter of fact, scientists typically do not acquire the bulk of their scientific belief on the basis of evidence personally achieved, but rather on the basis of authority in the context of formal education and apprenticeship. Physicists are not individually required, qua physicists, to reinvent the discipline of physics from the ground up. They are not required to overthrow all their scientific beliefs and readmit them only on the condition that they are wholly evident, certain, and indubitable. This is not only a matter of fact, but also a matter of propriety. For if scientists are to make a contribution to their own field, they simply do not have the time to establish the foundations of their discipline together with the conditions of the possibility of science in general. Taking things on the say-so of others is a positive condition for progress and development within a given research tradition. If each scientist were required to become autonomous in the philosophical sense, science itself would be placed in permanent abeyance. Science is a social enterprise.[14]

The scientist is justified, then, in going beyond what is actually evident. This is not only the case for what a scientist is entitled to assume from the tradition, but also in the context of current work. For "the *de facto* course of our human experience is such that it constrains our reason to go beyond intuitionally given physical things . . . and base them upon the 'truth of physics'" (*ID* I, 105 / *H* III, 1, 99). Here what is given serves as a basis for forming beliefs about what is not given. What cannot be observed by human beings can nonetheless be detected on the basis of what is observed by human beings. "When engaged in natural science we effect experientially and logically ordered acts of thinking in which these actualities [experienced physical things], being accepted as they are given, become conceptually determined and in which likewise, on the basis of such directly experienced and determined transcendencies [external objects], new transcendencies are inferred" (*ID* I, 114 / *H* III 1, 107). The empirical scientist is therefore justified in making methodological use of hypotheses (PRS, 139 / *PSW*, 64), and in drawing inferences from what is directly experienced to what is not experienced (*IP*, 13 / *H* II, 17). Through the use of symbolic means, science goes far beyond the narrow confines of the intuitable (*LI* I, 201 / *H* XVIII, 201–2), given the fact the "objects are certainly possible, that in fact lie beyond the phenomena accessible to any human consciousness" (*LI* I, 428 / *H* XIX 1, B 219). "We in fact know only too well," Husserl writes in the *Logical Investigations*, "that the overwhelming majority of general statements, and in particular those of science, behave meaningfully without any elucidation from intuition, and that only a vanishing section, even of the true and the proven, are and remain open to complete intuitive illumination" (*LI* II, 777 / *H* XIX 2, B2 133).

Yet, Husserl maintains, "should intuition fall wholly away, our judgment would cease to know anything" (*LI* II, 777 / *H* XIX 2, B2 133). Knowledge in the strict sense, for Husserl, is always a matter of the intuitive fulfillment of an empty intention. "Ohne Einsicht kein Wissen" (Without insight, no knowledge) (*LI* I, 166 / *H* XVIII, B 152). It would seem, then, that if empirical science were a purely theoretical enterprise aiming at knowledge and knowledge only, it should strictly adhere to what can be presented directly in intuition. If science, in its laws and hypotheses, goes beyond what is intuited and intuitable, can it be said that it still strives for knowledge? Is it that science has some goal other than knowledge in the strict sense? Does it seek to realize some other value?

To answer these questions, we turn to Husserl's Galileo analysis in section 9 of the *Crisis*. In his phenomenological inquiry into the foundations of modern mathematical physics, Husserl also characterizes the aims that are being sought in and through its development. The idealization of natural shapes into geometrical figures, the development of methods for the exact quantitative measurement and determination of physical events and processes, the postulation of a correlation between the idealized world of pure physical events and real qualitative appearances—in short, the conversion of the natural world into a "mathematical manifold"[15]—carried with it something of decisive significance for practical life. The covariation between idealized quantities could be determined with mathematical precision; these quantities can also be correlated with sensuous qualities and events in the intuitively given lifeworld. Following the mathematically determined functional covariations, one could bring the corresponding intuitions vividly "to mind" (*C*, 43 / *H* VI, 42). One can also, given the appropriate values for the variables of a particular formula, determine the remaining unknown quantity. "Thus one can outline the empirical regularities of the practical life-world which are to be expected. In other words, if one has the formula, one already possesses, in advance, the practically desired prediction of what is to be expected with empirical certainty in the intuitively given world of concretely actual life, in which mathematics is merely a special praxis. Mathematization, then, with its realized formulae, is the achievement which is decisive for life" (*C*, 43 / *H* VI, 43).

The mathematization of nature, its conversion into a quantitatively determinable manifold, makes it possible to develop "formulae," mathematically exact statements of functional covariation within the physical world. Such formulae, in turn, make prediction of events in the perceptual world possible to a greater degree than without them. In this context, however, predictive success functions as a nonepistemic value; it is a value located in practical life; it is "practically desired." The practically motivated desire for the means of more accurate and farther-reaching prediction is what gave rise to the "passionate interest of the natural scientist" in developing such formulae and the proper method of acquiring and grounding them in a rationally compelling manner (C, 43 / H VI, 43). What is developed by the mathematical techniques of modern physics is "nothing but prediction [*Voraussicht*] extended to infinity," Husserl writes (C, 51 / H VI, 51). Here Husserl shows his solidarity with the then-dominant positivist understanding of science and its tendency to limit the physical sciences in particular to the formulation of laws that govern observable phenomena and enhance the powers of prediction. "What every scientist seeks, and seeks alone," writes Moritz Schlick in his 1932 essay "Positivism and Realism," "are ... the rules which govern the connection of experiences, and by which alone they can be predicted."[16]

Thus it would seem that, on Husserl's view, the primary value sought in the development of modern mathematical physics and allied disciplines is not the theoretical values of truth and certainty, but the practical values of predictive success and the control of nature. The law that states that the rate of acceleration for a free-falling body at or near the surface of the earth is 9.8 meters per second squared is valuable not primarily because is true that free-falling bodies undergo this rate of acceleration. After all, as we saw in chapter 1, exact laws in the empirical sciences are but "idealizing fictions" (*LI* I, 106 / H XVIII, B 72). In reality, there are no free-falling bodies. But this formula is nonetheless valuable because it, in conjunction with other formulae, enables us to predict and control with a high degree of accuracy such things as the point of projectile impact. Such laws are valuable as devices, or instruments, of prediction and control.

What Husserl offers here is clearly an instrumentalist interpretation of the laws of empirical science. The cardinal virtue of scientific laws is not truth, but predictivity. Technically false because they are "idealizing fictions," they are nonetheless to be valued as instruments of prediction. In *Ideas* I he writes, "Any cognition in physics serves an index to the course of possible experiences with the things pertaining to the senses and their occurrences found in those experiences. It serves, therefore, to orient us in the world of actional [practical] experience in which we all live and act" (*ID* I, 85 / H III 1, 83). Laws and formulae in science are not about real, actually existing objects, processes, or events. Rather, they are means, methods, or instruments by which more or less accurate predictions about real, actually existing objects, processes, and events can be made. What is of epistemic import is the prediction produced, not the means of producing it. Nonetheless, Husserl claims that the predictions about perceived states of affairs generated by science count as knowledge (*ID* I, 85 / *H* III 1, 83). His instrumentalism does not "negate" the truth-claims of the sciences en bloc, as Hans Wagner suggests.[17] It only limits them. The apparatus by which such knowledge is produced is itself denied epistemic status. Laws are not about the real world, but they can produce more or less accurate knowledge about the real world.

The question we want to pursue is whether the grounds that led Husserl to adopt an instrumentalist interpretation of empirical science also committed him to an instrumentalist interpretation of theoretical science. Is it also the case that theoretical science is just a more powerful way of making predictions about occurrences in the perceivable world? Granted, the idealized objects of empirical laws do not exist. Is it also the case that the entities postulated in scientific theories do not exist? Are they also convenient fictions that serve only to facilitate prediction and control? To answer these questions, we must turn to Husserl's ontological analysis of physical objects. This we do in the next chapter.

PART THREE

The Problem of Theoretical Existence in Husserl's Philosophy of the Physical Sciences

CHAPTER FIVE

PHYSICAL THINGS, IDEALIZED OBJECTS, AND THEORETICAL ENTITIES

Henry Pietersma once remarked that much of the secondary literature on Husserl is both confused and confusing.[1] This is especially the case with respect to Husserl's alleged "instrumentalism." As I pointed out in the introduction, there is little agreement on the question of whether Husserl was an instrumentalist. Moreover, scant attention is paid to the particular sense of his instrumentalism on the part of those who hold that he was an instrumentalist. As an unfortunate but inevitable result, Husserl's stated position on the epistemic nature and status of the physical sciences has been subject to one misunderstanding after another.

In this chapter I will attempt to sort out some of the basic ontological issues underlying this confusion. I will claim that Husserl was indeed an instrumentalist. But I will also claim that he was an instrumentalist only in a restricted and relatively nonstandard—if not uncommon—sense. Furthermore, I will claim that his version of instrumentalism is entirely compatible with a realist interpretation of scientific theories.

In the contemporary Anglo-American philosophy of science, instrumentalism is typically set forth and debated as an interpretation of scientific theories.[2] Roughly speaking, the instrumentalist position holds that scientific theories are nothing but highly sophisticated syntactical machinery for generating new and scientifically interesting predictions concerning observable events.[3] Theories should not be taken as straightforward statements about unobservable entities. Rather, they are tools for generating conditional statements about relations between observable states of affairs. Consequently, theoretical entities ostensibly postulated in scientific theories are to be understood as convenient fictions that merely serve to enhance the predictive scope and power of empirical science. Theoretical terms by which such concepts are expressed are to be countenanced in science only if they can be given at least a partial interpretation in a language that refers only to observable states of affairs by way of correspondence rules.[4] Thus, to assign a straightforward semantics to scientific theories would represent a serious misreading of their nature and intent. They themselves are not true or false. They are only more or less empirically adequate, more or less reliable.[5]

Instrumentalism, then, is a form of antirealism with respect to theoretical entities. It holds that they do not exist—or, at least, that the theoretical component of science provides us with no reasons for thinking that they do. In this chapter I intend to show that while instrumentalism in Anglo-American circles is an interpretation of scientific theories, Husserl's instrumentalism is an interpretation of scientific laws. For when he turns to the physical sciences, he is primarily concerned with the epistemic status and existential import of their laws. The primary impetus behind the development of the empirical sciences in general is, according to Husserl, the practical interest in the ability to predict and control the future course of natural events (*C*, 43 / *H* VI, 43). Empirical science is "more concerned with practical results and mastery than with essential insight" (*LI* I, 245 / *H* XVIII, 255). The laws of empirical science, then, are to function as finely honed instruments of prediction. Physics, with its statements of lawlike regularities, "serves as an index to the course of possible experiences with the things pertaining to the senses and their occurrences found in those experiences. It serves, therefore, to orient us in the world of current experience in which we all live and act" (*ID* I, 85 / *H* III 1, 73; translation modifed).

Moreover, like Stephen Toulmin, Husserl maintains that when laws are given a mathematically exact formulation, they hold only for idealized objects—free-falling bodies, frictionless planes, incompressible fluids, perfectly elastic bodies, ideal gases, ideally efficient engines, and the like.[6] But these objects, Husserl contends, do not exist in the physical sense. That is, they do not exist in the real causal nexus of space and time. Idealized objects are abstract constructs that serve to make an exact, but always approximate, knowledge of real objects possible. The original aim of empirical science was to develop precise, objective, and predictive knowledge about the real physical world. The construction of a world of idealized objects and relations is a necessary step in the attainment of that epistemic goal. But the idealized world will never be more than a convenient fiction, a device, for making scientific knowledge of the real world possible. As Gary G. Gutting put it, "idealizations are employed only as *instruments* for achieving, by a series of increasingly accurate approximations, a precise description of the world."[7]

Husserl's brand of instrumentalism, thus construed, is not intended as a form of antirealism with respect to theoretical entities. It does not intend to deny the existence of a certain class of real objects whose existence is in question. More specifically, it does not amount to the denial of the existence of such theoretical entities as atoms, protons, quarks, strong and weak nuclear forces, and the like. Husserl's instrumentalism is, if anything, an "anti-reificationism." Opposed to treating idealized objects as if they were real, its point is not so much existential as categorical. It seeks to remind us that ideal objects are not real physical objects, and therefore do not and cannot constitute the real world of nature. It therefore also opposes the Platonizing tendency to reduce perceptually given real objects to the status of mere appearances of ideal objects represented in the discipline of mathematics.

If the exact sciences of nature are, strictly speaking, about the world of ideal objects, it follows that they are not about the real world.[8] But this analysis does not mean that Husserl's instrumentalism "negates" the truth-claims of the natural sciences, as Hans Wagner suggests.[9] Rather, it means that the claims of the exact sciences of nature will always be indirect and only approximately true of the real world. In order to achieve a mathematically exact and objective representation of the real physical world, the physical sciences first resort to ideal cases, and then proceed to approach real cases through a process of "successive approximation."[10] One begins with a free-falling body as an ideal case, and then adds in the resistance of the medium. One begins with frictionless planes, and then adds the coefficient of friction. Through abstraction and idealization there is an initial movement away from real objects and processes, and then a return to real objects and processes by way of application (cf. C, 32 / H VI, 30).[11] Exact knowledge is possible only by a passage through the ideal; but precisely for that reason, it will never be more than an approximate knowledge of the real.[12]

Husserl's chief concern in the *Crisis* is that the idealized representation of nature in the modern physical sciences has been effectively substituted for the real world—the world given to us in perceptual experience (C, 48–49 / H VI, 48–49). True to Platonic form, the real world, the world that we perceive, is then degraded to the status of mere subjective appearance. The world as conceived in the exact science of physics now counts as the objective world that "really" exists; the world as perceived in everyday life—the lifeworld—is the subjective world that doesn't really exist at all.[13] The temptation to commit such a category mistake presents itself once the idealized version of the physical world has been established in the tradition and thereby takes on a semblance of self-subsistence. The initial processes of abstraction and idealization, constantly presupposed in the present practice of the exact physical sciences, have already been accomplished and thus, to a large degree, forgotten. Their results have been passed down through the modern scientific research tradition. The idealized natural world now serves as a presupposition, a point of departure, for the scientific representation and explanation of the real world. As long as the intentional origins of the idealized natural world remain hidden, however, the tendency will be to take this world as the real, objectively existing world, independent of any human activity, while the real world is reduced to the status of mere subjective appearance.

In line with this ontological reversal, the epistemic roles of real and ideal worlds are also exchanged. The real (now only "apparent") world then functions as the means for developing scientific knowledge about the ideal (now "objective") world governed by mathematically exact laws (C, 48 / H VI, 48). The constant tendency, Husserl warns, in the development and use of such laws is to take them and their "formula meaning" for the "true being of nature itself" (C, 43 / H VI, 44). Here "we take for true being what is actually a method—a method which is designed for the purpose of progressively improving, *in infinitum*, through 'scientific' predictions, those rough predictions which are the only ones originally possible within the sphere of what is actually experienced and experienceable in the life-world" (C, 51–52 / H VI, 52). Thus what is in fact only a means or a method for predicting real events and occurrences in the world is taken to express something of the true nature of the world. In this way there comes about the "surreptitious substitution of the mathematically substructed world of idealities for the only real world, the one that is actually given through perception, that is ever experienced and experienceable—our everyday life-world" (C, 48–49 / H VI, 48–49). What began as a method for providing predictive knowledge of this world—by which Husserl means the perceivable world—has now turned into a science of some other, imperceptible world, which, Husserl claims, does not exist in the physical sense. In opposition to this development, he insists, "all knowledge of laws could be knowledge only of predictions, grasped as lawful, about occurrences of actual or possible experiential phenomena" (C, 50 / H VI, 50).

The contribution Husserl thought phenomenology could make in rectifying this situation consists in showing how what is usually taken as the objectively existing physical world was constituted in and through the mental processes of abstraction and idealization, mental processes that take their point of departure in the perceptual givenness of the lifeworld. After this phenomenological elucidation, it would then be clear that the original aim of science, in its passage to the ideal, was knowledge of the real, perceivable world. The idealized or "mathematicized" nature of physical science would then be exposed as the construct it always was—not the final object of knowledge, but the means for knowledge (C, 48 / H VI, 48).

This, however, represents a phenomenological strategy based upon Husserl's late position on the nature of modern mathematical physics, the position of the *Crisis*. In the period surrounding the composition of the *Ideas*, he did not take mathematics to be a science of a separate world of idealized objects; nor did he see the employment of exact methods in general within the physical sciences as opening up the possibility of the ontological reversal he sought to expose in the *Crisis*. Rather, in the *Logos* article of 1910, "Philosophy as a Rigorous Science," Husserl saw the scientific concept of the objective "physical thing," as opposed to the physical thing as it appears to the subject, as entirely in keeping with the perceptual "sense" and experience of physical objects (PSS, 41 / PSW, 34–35). In *Ideas* I he argues that the physical thing of science, moreover, is not other than, or hidden behind, the apparent object of everyday perception. That is, physical science posits no imperceptible thing beyond the object of everyday perceptual experience. Later I will argue that the shift in Husserl's conception of the primary referent of the physical sciences is a result of a shift in his analysis of the categorial status of geometrical objectivities. In *Ideas* I, they represent the eidetic spatial forms of real material things; in the *Crisis* they are exact ideal objects. But first we turn to his earlier conception of the physical thing and its relation to the perceived object.

I. THE PHYSICAL THING

In the section of "Philosophy as a Rigorous Science" devoted to naturalism, Husserl addresses himself to the distinction between physical and mental being with respect to the way in which they are given in experience, their "modes of givenness." Unlike mental processes, the physical thing is always given in and through a series of appearances. Thus we can distinguish between the thing that appears and its appearances. The appearances of a thing can change as the spatial orientations of the thing and the percipient vary with respect to each other, as the sensory apparatus of the percipient varies, or as the real conditions of the perceptual situation vary. Yet, through the multiplicity of its changing appearances, the physical thing is experienced as one and the same. It is given as a unity "throughout changes in its appearances" (PSS, 47 / PSW, 35). What a physical thing is "in itself," then, must be distinguished from its appearances. It is not to be identified with any one of its phenomenal properties, or even with the unity of the totality of its phenomenal properties. It retains its identity through its shifting phenomenal properties, and is intersubjectively accessible as the same because, Husserl says, it is a unity of real, causal properties in one all-embracing space and time (PSS, 47 / PSW, 35). Its appearances, its phenomenal properties, are not objective, if we mean by "objective" belonging to the object itself, but subjective insofar as they are relative to the orientation and sensory constitution of the perceiving subject.

Following up on this distinction, already available in reflection upon the everyday perceptual experience of physical things, the physical sciences seek to penetrate the "vague medium of appearances" in order to make an exact determination of what the physical thing is "in itself" (PSS, 47 / PSW, 35). Such a determination will always be carried out on the basis of the way the physical object appears, but in such a way as to leave the appearances behind (PSS, 48 / PSW, 36). "Physics eliminates the phenomenal in order to seek for the Nature that presents itself therein" (PSS, 42 / PSW, 31). Every consistent inquiry into the nature of the physical thing "necessarily leads over into causal complexes and terminates in the determination of corresponding Objective properties subject to law. Natural science, therefore, only follows up consistently the sense of what the physical thing itself as experienced, so to speak, 'claims' to be; and it calls this, obscurely enough, 'elimination of secondary qualities,' 'elimination of the merely subjective moment in the appearances' while 'retaining the qualities that are left, the primary ones'" (PSS, 47 / PSW, 34–35).[14]

This understanding of the physical sciences as moving through the appearances of a thing to determine its real properties, as opposed to its phenomenal properties, is echoed in a later text. In the "Preparatory Considerations" of *Formal and Transcendental Logic*, Husserl states that the physical sciences restrict themselves to a determination of those properties that belong to the physical object as such. In their pursuit of a wholly objective representation of the thing, they will eliminate many subject-relative factors that initially appeared, in prescientific experience, as objective. This will include the sensuous qualities of a thing, which are variously determined by the sensory constitution of the perceiving subject and its relation to the object:

> This plane of theory delimits the themes of science, and does so to such a degree that the positive sciences make a conscious effort to frame the concept of theoretical objectivity even more rigorously: in such a manner that the positive sciences will exclude, as merely subjective, many a thing that the pre-scientifically experiencing and thinking subject finds as an Objective theme. In this manner the scientific investigator of Nature excludes "sensuous qualities." The single experiencing subject finds natural Objects as sensuously qualified, but nevertheless as Objects, as existing in and by themselves, not affected in their existence by the reflectively apprehensible acts of experiencing and of experiential thinking, neither determined nor determinable by the contents of those acts. Yet, with the effecting of an intersubjective communion of experiencing and thinking, the contents of sensuously experienced Objectivity and the descriptive concepts fitted to its contents show a dependence on the experiencing subjects; though the identity of the Objects in question nevertheless remains intersubjectively cognizable and determinable. A purely Objective science aims at a theoretical cognizing of Objects, not in respect of such subjectively relative determinations as can be drawn from direct sensuous experience, but rather in respect of strictly and purely Objective determinations: determinations that obtain for everyone and at all times, or in respect of which according to a method that everyone can use, there arise theoretical truths having the character of "truths in themselves—in contrast to mere subjectively relative truths." (*FTL*, 37-38 / H XVII, 33)[15]

The physical sciences, then, seek to determine the object with respect to those properties it has "in itself," not with respect to properties it has only in relation to perceiving subjects. If an object appears green to us, it is not because it is green, but because it is of such a nature (that is, possesses a reflectance property) as to appear green to the likes of us. To say that such an object is green is to express what Husserl calls a "subjectively relative truth," that is, the truth that the object typically appears green to a standard perceiving subject of a certain kind under conditions that have been intersubjectively established as normal. Physical science seeks to determine the "objective truth" about the thing, the truth that holds irrespective of the way the thing appears to a particular subject or subjects of a particular kind.[16] In the physical sciences, then, the so-called secondary qualities are taken to be mere appearances. They are not determined by the object itself, but in its relation to a perceiving subject whose sensory apparatus just happens to be constituted in a certain way (*ID* III, 53 / *H* V, 62). In seeking to determine the object "objectively," the physical sciences countenance only those determinations of the object that would hold for all subjects at all times. Such objective determinations, then, will be "intersubjectively valid."

But if the intersubjective community for which these determinations are to hold is construed as the community of human beings, the physical sciences have yet to achieve the form of objectivity to which they aspire. For while this form of intersubjective validity will overcome the subjectivity of the human individuals, it does not transcend the subjectivity of the human species as a whole. As Husserl indicates in *Ideas* III, the scope of the intersubjective community that constitutes the sense of objectivity in the physical sciences must be expanded to include not only all actual human percipients, but all possible percipients of whatever sensory constitution. Although the objective properties of the thing will always be determined on the basis of some specific form of sense experience, the properties themselves must be independent of all sense experience (*ID* III, 54 / *H* V, 63).[17]

Thus the objectivity of nature, as conceived in natural science, is essentially correlated to an ideal plurality of all possible perceiving subjects (*ID* III, 55 / *H* V, 64). What objectively belongs to the physical object is what "any possible subject of the pre-delineated ideal community can bring out and determine in rational experiential thought on the ground of his 'appearances' and the communications of others concerning their 'appearances'" (*ID* III, 55 / *H* V, 64). The world as perceived by human beings then receives the status of an appearance of "objective nature exclusively determined by 'exact' mathematical-physical predicates, absolutely not intuitable, not experienceable" (*ID* III, 56 / *H* V, 65). In this way there arises a "unique physical nature, with the one objective space and the one objective time, consisting of nothing but physical things that are characterized purely by concepts having the exactness ascribed in physics" (*ID* III, 56 / *H* V, 65).

The physical thing as conceived in the physical sciences is thus distinguished from the perceived object. The perceived object is a "mere appearance" of the thing of physics. The thing of physics is, in some important sense, never perceived (*ID* III, 58 / *H* V, 68). This distinction between the "physical thing" and the "perceived object" quite naturally leads to the question of the relation between the two. Is it the case that the thing as conceived in the science of physics represents a "hidden entity" behind the perceived thing? Must the physical thing then be construed as the hidden cause of the perceived object? Husserl addresses himself to these questions in section 52 of *Ideas* I, titled "The Physical Thing as Determined by Physics and the 'Unknown Cause of Appearances.'" We now turn our attention to Husserl's conception of the physical thing in this section.

The exposition of the essential differences between consciousness and reality in the sections immediately preceding section 52, by which Husserl sought to establish the ontological priority and absolute character of consciousness, took into consideration only the reality of the objects of direct perceptual experience. At the beginning of the exposition Husserl explicitly excludes any reference to things as they are determined by the physical sciences—things conceived of quite differently than they are perceived. In section 41 he writes, "Let us therefore exclude the whole of physics and the whole domain of theoretical thinking. Let us remain within the limits of simple intuition and the syntheses belonging to it, among which perception is included" (*ID* I, 86 / *H* III 1, 84). The initial burden of the exposition is to establish the fact that even the thing as it appears in perception, the appearance of which is considered to be "subjective," is nonetheless transcendent to consciousness; it is not a real part or component of the mental processes by which it appears; therefore, it is not to be identified with the subjectively immanent sensations by which it appears.

At the end of the exposition, however, Husserl returns to the question of the thing as it is determined by the physical sciences. Is it transcendent not only with respect to subjective mental processes, but also with respect to the appearing thing of sensuous intuition? If so, if it is removed from the reach of consciousness by a kind of double transcendence, does it then exist independently of consciousness? Could it then be construed as the hidden cause of the appearances, as the hidden cause of the consciousness of the perceived object? In section 41 Husserl demonstrated that the appearing physical thing is not identical with the subjective mental process by which it appears; in section 43 he argued that it would contradict the sense of the perceived thing to conceive of it as an internal picture, image, or even a sign of the objective physical thing as determined by the science of physics. Granting all this, could we nevertheless take it that the appearing thing is an appearance of something else that is ontically distinct from it? If y were the appearing thing, could it count as the appearance of another thing, x, where y is not identical with x? Furthermore, would the existence of y justify, in a scientific context, the belief in the existence of x, which does not directly appear, but is hypothetically postulated in order to explain the appearance of y—that is, postulated as the hidden cause of the y-appearance?

But we must be precise in the formulation of this question. For what Husserl has in mind here is not the question of whether x causes y, but whether x causes the appearing of y (i.e., the mental processes by which y appears). The question, then, is not whether the physical thing x exerts a causal agency on the perceived object y in any straightforward manner, but rather whether x exerts its causal agency upon a percipient S such that S perceives y, and y is not identical with x. If this were the case, then y would count as an appearance of x only in the indirect sense. For what is directly perceived is not x, but y. But since the perception of y is caused by x, y would function as an image or, at least, an indicative sign of x. It would seem, then, that as long as we hold to the nonidentity of x and y, we are committed to some version of the representational theory of external perception. X is hypothetically postulated in order to explain the course of mental processes whereby y appears; y then counts as a representation of x, not by virtue of its identity with x, but by virtue of some causal linkage to x.

In section 52 Husserl rejects this way of setting up the relation between the perceived object and the physical thing. It not only conflicts with the manifest sense of the perceived object together with the essence of the experience of physical things, it also leads to an infinite regress. His argument takes the following form: if the hidden physical thing, x, exists, then it must, by essential, *de re* necessity, be perceivable—if not by us, then by some other possible subjects with more suitably adapted sensory apparatus (*ID* I, 119 / *H* III 1, 111). But, if x is perceivable, it must, in turn, be perceivable by means of its appearances. If x were to appear, then, it would require the postulation of some other hidden entity, say, z, which, as a hidden cause, would account for the appearance of x. But if z exists, it, too, must be perceivable. And if z is perceivable, it must be so by means of its appearances, which would require the postulation of another hidden cause (even though, in this case, we're at the end of the alphabet), and so on. Thus, Husserl concludes, if we posit x as a hidden cause of its own appearances, "we should fall into an inevitable infinite regress" (*ID* I, 119 / *H* III 1, 111).

But is Husserl's argument as cogent and effective as we might hope it could be? I will argue that it is not, and that it trades on an ambiguity in the term "perceivable."

If we claim that an object, x, is perceivable, then, presumably, it is precisely that object that we can perceive. If we say that x is perceivable by means of its appearances, then, presumably, it is still x that we perceive—albeit by means of its appearances. Let us call this the "direct" form of perception. On the other hand, if we maintain that there is a distinction to be made between the apparent object and the object that brings about its appearance, then we have something quite different in mind. For now we are dealing with two objects: the one that appears, y, and the one "behind" the appearance, x. Here it is not x that is directly perceived. Only y is. But if x is the cause of the appearance of y, we may say, nonetheless, that x is perceived in an indirect sense. That is, on the basis of the direct perception of y, there is an indirect perception of x.

Here the indirect perception of x ought to be understood as a propositional attitude (i.e., as a belief directed toward a proposition). Accordingly, we would say that on the direct perception of y, we have some propositional attitude concerning x. Such an expanded sense of perception is reflected in everyday speech when, for instance, we say that we "see that" something is the case. We see that a person is in pain. What we see directly is not the pain, but a certain facial expression, say, a wince. But, against the background of repeated experiences of a correlation between physical winces and the sensations of pain, the direct perception of the wince serves as the occasion for the indirect perception of the pain—we see that a person is in pain when we see him wince. Thus the distinction between direct and indirect perception is roughly parallel to the distinction between seeing and seeing that. Indirect perception involves a direct perception plus a propositional attitude.

Now the position that Husserl seeks to refute takes the perception of physical things to be a case of indirect perception: perceiving a physical thing x is actually a matter of directly perceiving the apparent object y, where the perceiving of y is the result of the causal agency of x upon a percipient S such that S forms some propositional attitude concerning x. I look out my window. I see that there is a tree outside. But what I see directly is the tree-appearance (the perceived object) brought about by the causal agency of the tree (the physical thing) upon my sensory apparatus. I do not see the tree itself, the physical thing; rather, I see the tree-appearance. The tree itself is the hidden cause of the tree-appearance. And the former is what gets determined by the physical sciences, since the physical sciences deal with the "hidden cause" of appearances.

But if this is what the analysis of indirect physical thing perception comes to, it does not inevitably lead to an infinite regress. For, on this analysis, it will never be the case that x, the physical thing itself, is directly perceived. Only an x-surrogate, that is, some other object that counts as an appearance of x, will be directly perceived. So, for any percipient S, x will only be indirectly perceivable. As percipients are differently constituted with respect to sensory apparatus, they will indirectly perceive x on the basis of different appearances of x—if not of the y sort, then, say, of the z sort. Here the same entity, x, appears differently to differently constituted percipients by way of different appearances. What is directly perceived are appearances y and z. In both cases the selfsame x remains the hidden cause of the course of mental processes whereby y and z appear. But here there is no regress. For in both cases, and in all relevantly similar cases, it is the same entity, x, which is being perceived in the indirect sense—that is, on the basis of an apparent object that is ontically distinct from it. There may be multiple appearances of x, perhaps infinitely many appearances of x. But these appearances do not form a regressive chain because there is, and can be, on the indirect analysis, no instance where x itself is converted into the apparent object that would in turn require the postulation of another hidden cause in order to explain or account for its appearance.

To make the regress work, one must deny the premise that one was initially willing to grant in order to derive the regress, namely, that things are indirectly perceived on the basis of the direct perception of appearances that are ontically distinct from them. Husserl makes this move when he asserts that if the hidden cause of our perceptual mental processes exists, it must be possible for other subjects differently constituted with respect to sensory apparatus to perceive x. Here, however, he means "perceive" in the direct sense where x itself is that which appears. But this is to give the direct, rather than the indirect, analysis of perception. Immediately reinstating the indirect analysis in order to initiate the regress, he then says that if x were perceived, then it, too, would be perceived by means of appearances ontically distinct from it. But this instance of indirect perception would then require the postulation of a *new* hidden cause. This hidden cause, in turn, would have to be (directly) perceivable by some other perceptual subjects, which would be a matter of (indirect) perception by way of appearances and thus require the postulation of a new hidden cause, and so on ad infinitum. But when he insists that the perception of the hidden cause must also be by way of appearances, he reinvokes the indirect analysis that he temporarily suspended in order to allow for a direct perception of x on the part of other perceptual subjects. Thus the infinite regress depends upon the alternating affirmation and denial of the major premise of the indirect analysis. But each time the premise is denied, the question of whether the physical thing is being directly perceived is begged. Stated otherwise, the regress argument depends on the ambiguity between the direct and the indirect senses of the term "perceive."

Even if Husserl had shown the absurdity of taking the physical thing to be the hidden cause of its own appearance, he has not developed a case against the postulation of hidden entities in general. Nor has he shown why the postulation of hidden entities is inappropriate in the explanation of perception. For even if it is the case that the physical thing is what is perceived by means of its appearances such that what one sees is the physical thing itself and not some intermediate object, the postulation of hidden entities in order to explain the appearance of the physical thing is not ruled out of hand. In such explanations it is not the physical thing itself that is taken to be the direct cause of its own appearance for the perceptual subject, but some third entities, like Locke's imperceptible corpuscles or the photons of modern physics. These third entities themselves do not appear, neither are the appearances that they bring about appearances of them. Rather, the appearances that they bring about are the appearances of the physical thing to which they are causally related. This leaves open the possibility that it is the physical thing itself that is perceived by means of its appearances, and nevertheless its appearances are brought about by hidden causes. Here x is not the hidden cause, for it is precisely x that is perceived. But those entities that bring about the appearance of x such that it is perceived are hidden. They are postulated in order to explain the appearance of x, while x is neither hidden nor postulated. I look out my window. I see the tree. But I do not see the entities or processes that bring about the appearance of the tree whereby I see it.

The postulation of hidden entities in order to explain the perception of a physical thing does not entail that the physical thing itself is hidden. Furthermore, while the hidden entities are hidden to us, it does not follow that they are necessarily hidden. In fact, Husserl holds that if they exist, then they must be perceivable in the ideally possible sense (*ID* I, 119 / *H* III 1, 111). Now if they were in fact perceived by subjects differently constituted than us, it may be necessary to postulate other hidden entities in order to explain their appearance. If these hidden entities are in turn to be perceived, then other hidden entities may be postulated, and so on. But this state of affairs does not lead to an infinite regress. Such a regress would require an identity on the part of the perceptual subject. But here we are speaking of different perceptual subjects. For any one of them there is no question of perceiving hidden entities, which would require the postulation of a second round of hidden entities, for the hidden entities with respect to any one kind of perceptual subject are, and will remain, hidden. Thus there is no need to explain the perception of them through the postulation of other entities.

Whatever our assessment of his argument may be, it is clear that in rejecting the notion of the physical thing as the hidden cause of its own appearance, the Husserl of *Ideas I* wants to maintain the identity of the physical thing and the perceived object. The physical thing itself is given in "sensuous modes of appearance" (*ID* I, 120 / *H* III 1, 112). Moreover: "The physical thing which he [the physicist] observes, with which he experiments, which he continually sees, takes in his hand, puts on the scales or in the melting furnace; that physical thing, and no other, becomes the subject of the predicates ascribed in physics, such as weight, temperature, electrical resistance, and so forth" (*ID* I, 120–21 / *H* III 1, 113). According to Husserl in the *Ideas*, then, the physical thing as determined by the physical sciences is identical with the physical thing as perceived in everyday life. "The perceived physical thing itself is always and necessarily precisely the thing which the physicist explores and scientifically determines following the method of physics" (*ID* I, 119 / *H* III 1, 111–12; emphasis deleted). Although the physical thing as exclusively determined by the physical sciences is not perceivable, it is in fact identical with a perceivable object. The sensuous intuition of a thing delivers a "mere This," an "empty X," which then "becomes the bearer of the exact determinations ascribed in physics which do not themselves fall within experience proper" (*ID* I, 119 / *H* III 1, 112). The exact determinations ascribed to a physical thing cannot themselves be perceived, but they are nonetheless determinations of a perceivable thing; although the thing is determined quite differently in the physical science than in straightforward sensuous intuition, the determinations are of the same thing and, moreover, "quite compatible" (*ID* I, 120 / *H* III 1, 112).[18]

As such, these statements represent a reaffirmation of Husserl's position as indicated already in section 40 of *Ideas* I, where he claims that "the experienced physical thing proper provides the mere 'This,' an empty X, which becomes the bearer of mathematical determinations" (*ID* I, 85 / *H* III 1, 83). The perceived object and the physical thing are not two ontologically distinct objects, the latter causing the appearance of the former. Rather, they are one and the same thing with categorically distinct, but nonetheless compatible, sets of determinations. It would simply be a mistake to assign ontically distinct objects to the differing sets of determinations and then relate the two objects by way of causality such that the sensuously intuited object becomes the mere sign of the physical thing (*ID* I, 120 / *H* III 1, 112). Rather, the causal relation is not between two different objects, but between two different sets of determinations of one and the same object. In a sense, then, the object becomes a "sign for itself" (*ID* I 121 / *H* III 1, 113). That is, "the physical thing appearing with such and such sensuous determinations under the given phenomenal circumstances is, for the physicist . . . an indicative sign of a wealth of causal properties belonging to one and the same physical thing which, as causal properties, makes themselves known in phenomenal dependencies of various sorts" (*ID* I, 121 / *H* III 1, 113).

The determinant physical properties of a thing make themselves known through an ordered array of appearances under changing physical conditions (*PP*, 77 / *H* IX, 101). The thing reveals itself as a unity of properties that manifest themselves in their causal environment according to a rule. Thus, Husserl claims, we can speak of the objective color of a thing, which manifests itself in a variety of hues, shades, and tones according to its causal environment. The series of color-appearances is regulated by the identical color property (*ID* II, 45 / *H* IV, 42). Real properties are "unities with respect to manifolds of schematic [appearance] regulations in relation to corresponding circumstances" (*ID* II, 46 / *H* IV, 43). Appearances do not hide the property, they manifest it. Without appearances we would not be aware of the property. There are "real properties" of the physical object, and there are "manifest properties" (appearances) functionally dependent upon the real properties (*ID* II, 59 / *H* IV, 54).[19]

Husserl's position on the identity of the perceivable and the physical thing is itself both manifest and clear. But it can be given two different interpretations. One way to construe Husserl's claim is as follows: When the physical sciences seek to determine the physical properties of a perceived thing, they are not positing another thing, hidden behind the perceived thing, as the bearer of those exclusively physical properties. Rather, they are determining the physical properties of that perceived thing. It does not follow from this claim, however, that the physical sciences deal only with perceivable things. Rather, what is being asserted here is that when the physical sciences deal with perceivable things, it is precisely those things they determine. The example Husserl uses in section 52 of *Ideas* I is a case in point. There he speaks of the physical thing as that which the physicist handles, weighs, places in the furnace, and the like. The claim concerning the identity of the perceivable and physical thing is made with respect to a molar physical object that is also perceivable. On this construal, the claim is ontologically nonrestrictive—it does not limit the domain of the physical sciences to the humanly perceived or perceivable.

On the other hand, in his insistence upon the identity of physical and perceivable things, Husserl might be taken to be making the claim that the physical sciences deal only with those objects that are at the same time perceived or, at least, perceivable. Although the physical determinations of the perceived thing are not themselves perceivable, the physical thing that is determined is always perceivable. Under no circumstances do the physical sciences posit imperceptible entities that serves as hidden causes of perceivable objects, events, and processes. Let us call this the "restrictive construal" of Husserl's claim.

Although the restrictive construal is not forced by the considerations Husserl brings to bear on the question of the relation between the perceived object and the physical thing, there is some textual evidence that it is indeed close to his intent. In section 52, for instance, we find Husserl referring in passing to what are usually taken to be imperceptible physical entities—atoms and ions—not as imperceptible physical entities, but as imperceptible determinations of perceivable things (*ID* I, 121 / *H* III 1, 113 and *ID* I, 123 / *H* III 1, 115). Now atoms and ions are classical examples of theoretical entities postulated by the physical sciences in order to explain the lawlike behavior of observable objects. But they are posited not as imperceptible determinations, or properties, of perceivable things, but as imperceptible parts or constituents of perceivable things. Yet here Husserl refers to atoms and ions as "determinations" of perceived physical things, or, more precisely, as theoretically constructed categories (*kategorialen Denkbestimmungen*)—like mass, temperature, moment, and so on—by which physical objects and processes are determined (*ID* I, 121 / *H* III 1, 113). By categorically reinterpreting imperceptible entities as imperceptible properties of perceivable things, Husserl then makes it possible to claim that the physical sciences deal only with perceivable things. Theoretical entities are not themselves things, but only determinations of physical things that can, in turn, be given in perception. But on this point he is just plain wrong.[20]

Further evidence for the restrictive construal of Husserl's claim is provided by the fact that he seems to think that the preceding considerations of the physical concept of the thing show conclusively that the physical sciences do not deal with imperceptible things. In section 52 he asserts that "even the higher transcendency characterizing the physical thing as determined by physics does not signify reaching out beyond the world which is there for consciousness" (*ID* I, 121 / *H* III 1, 113; emphasis deleted). Again: "The transcendency belonging to the physical thing as determined by physics is the transcendency belonging to a being which becomes constituted in, and tied to, consciousness" (*ID* I, 123 / *H* III 1, 115). In maintaining the identity of the thing as determined by the physical sciences with the thing as given in straightforward perceptual experience, Husserl takes himself to be demonstrating that not even the science of physics deals with things that are beyond the ken of perceptual consciousness. We have shown, he states, that "the thinking pertaining to physics establishes itself on the foundation laid by natural experiencing (or by natural positings which it effects). Following the rational motives presented to it by the concatenations of experience, it is compelled to effect certain modes of conception, and to effect them for the theoretical determination of sensuously experienced things" (*ID* I, 212 / *H* III 1, 113). The physical sciences seek to determine the imperceptible causal properties of things given in perceptual experience. But in doing so they do not posit a hidden world of imperceptible things. Rather, the imperceptible determinations remain determinations of perceptible things.[21]

Given the underlying identity between the object of perceptual experience and the object as determined by the physical sciences, it would be a colossal mistake, Husserl holds, to convert the totality of objects as determined by the physical sciences into a hidden world of a separate physical reality, hypothetically postulated for the sake of explaining the perceived world (*ID* I, 121 / *H* III 1, 114). This mistake would be seriously compounded if, in addition, the perceived object was identified with the subjective mental processes by which it is perceived (*ID* I, 121 / *H* III 1, 114), thereby converting the supposed causal relation between the physical thing and the perceived thing into a "mythical bond" between reality and consciousness, between the objective physical world and the subjective world of mental contents.

But this is precisely what has taken place in the modern tradition, Husserl maintains. By making such a move, the moderns transformed the relation of causality from a relation that holds between the objective correlates of consciousness to a relation between things transcendent to consciousness and mental processes immanent to consciousness. Thus they have "absolutized" the world as conceived in the physical sciences, and "relativized" consciousness to that world (*ID* I, 122 / *H* III 1, 114). But such a move is absurd, Husserl claims. For in the preceding sections of *Ideas* I (41–49), he had demonstrated that consciousness is absolute and that the physical world, in its existence, is relative to it. Consciousness is that region of being "to which, according to their essence, they [all other regions of being] are relative and on which they are therefore all essentially dependent" (*ID* I, 171 / *H* III 1, 159). To "absolutize" the physical world is to take that which is relative and dependent in its existence upon something else as if it were independent; to "relativize" consciousness is to take that which is absolute and independent in its existence as if it were dependent upon something else.

The thesis of identity between the perceived thing and the physical thing may then be seen as a tactical move in the overall strategy Husserl employs in his argument for the absolute character of consciousness. It serves to defuse any objections that might be brought against this argument by a reference to those things that the physical sciences ostensibly posit beyond the constitutive reach of perceptual consciousness. Our purpose in this section, however, is to examine Husserl's pre-*Crisis* ontology of the physical object irrespective of its text-specific tactical significance. In the next chapter I will take up the question of the absolute character of consciousness and the relative character of all physical things. There I will argue that the phenomenological sense of the absolute character consciousness is entirely consistent with the belief in the independent existence of physical things, both perceptible and imperceptible.

My main concern here, however, is to underscore the fact that, in the *Ideas*, Husserl takes the exact determinations delivered by the physical sciences to be determinations of real, perceivable, physical things existing in space and time. In the *Crisis*, on the other hand, Husserl takes the exact determinations of the physical sciences to be determinations not of perceivable real objects, but of imperceptible ideal objects—objects that do not exist in physical space and time, and which, therefore, have no real physical existence. What accounts for this shift in conception? As I indicated at the outset of this chapter, this shift is tied to a change in Husserl's conception of the ontological status of geometrical objects.

2. GEOMETRY AND THE PHYSICAL THING

In part 1 of *Ideas* I, Husserl treats the relation between geometry and physical science as a special case of the relation between eidetic and empirical science in general. It is a matter of principle, Husserl claims, that every empirical science is founded upon those eidetic disciplines that pertain to the essence of the abstract genera to which the objects of its research domain belong. In fact, the realization of the ideal of a completely rational empirical science, where "every particular included in it has been traced back to that particular's most universal and essential grounds" (*ID* I, 19 / *H* III 1, 24), depends upon the development of the relevant eidetic disciplines. Thus the completion of the empirical sciences of nature depends upon the development of the regional ontology of nature. The more "rational" a science becomes, the more it approximates the ideal of an exact nomological science, the greater its scope and power will be (*ID* I, 19 / *H* III 1, 25). Moreover, the rationalization of a science is directly proportional to the degree to which the foundational eidetic disciplines have been developed and utilized. "This is confirmed by the development of the rational natural sciences, the physical sciences of Nature. Their great era began in the modern age precisely when the geometry which had already been highly developed as a pure eidetics in antiquity (and chiefly in the Platonic school) was all at once made fruitful in the grand style for the method of physics. People made clear to themselves that the material thing is essentially *res extensa* and that geometry is therefore the ontological discipline relating to an essential moment of material thinghood, namely the spatial form" (*ID* I, 19 / *H* III 1, 25). In *Ideas* I Husserl refers to geometry as an eidetic science pertaining to the abstract genus "space." Since space, together with time and causality, is a constituent of the unified concrete genus "material thing," the science of space—geometry—is the science of the spatial essence of material things. Geometrical objects, then, are to be construed as universals that admit instantiation on the part of real, material individuals. The exact determination of physical things gained through the employment of geometry and allied mathematical disciplines provides access to the determinations of real physical things.

Husserl gives the same analysis in *Ideas* III: the science of geometry deals with the essence of the spatial forms of empirically intuitable material things. "[The geometer] turns usual empirical intuition of spatial things into the eidetic, whether it be figures on the board or even models that he gets out of the model closet. His interest is directed to the spatial shape, but not the experienced shape or the shape quasi-experienced in his phantasy, but rather the 'pure' spatial shape, i.e. the shape-essence to be grasped in the eidetic attitude on the ground of empirical apprehension. To the extent that shape is a basically essential moment of the material thing as the *res extensa*, the geometrician, the essence-investigator of possible thing-shapes, is *ep ipso* simultaneously a rational physicist" (*ID* III, 36–37 / *H* V, 42). Although the science of geometry attends to "pure" shapes, and not to shapes as perceived, they are nonetheless the shapes of possible material things. They pertain to the essence of material things. For that very reason, "physics was raised to a new level when it took geometry as a regional ontology of the material thing, expressing a priori truths which hold unconditionally of all physical things" (*ID* III, 37–38 / *H* V, 43). Modern mathematical physics, on the analysis given in the *Ideas*, yields exact determinations of the essential structure of the physical world.

In Husserl's later works, *Formal and Transcendental Logic* and *The Crisis of European Sciences*, we find a markedly differently analysis. The exact determinations of the physical sciences are not determinations of real, physical things, but of idealized objects. Here the physical sciences posit imperceptible objects, not just imperceptible forms of perceptible objects. In *Formal and Transcendental Logic*, Husserl discusses the difference between the world as straightforwardly perceived in everyday life and the world as conceived in the exact physical sciences. There he makes it quite clear that the physical sciences do not deal with perceivable objects at all, but rather with idealized objects:

> As a level founded on the *logos* of the aesthetic world, there rises the *logos* of the Objective worldly being, and of science, in the "higher" sense: the *logos* of the science that investigates under the guidance of the ideas of "strict" being and strict truth, and develops correspondingly "exact" theories. As a matter of fact, there grows up—first in the form of exact geometry and then in the form of exact natural science (Galilean physics)—a science with a consciously new style, not a science that reduces "observable and describable" (that is: aesthetic) formations, data of pure intuitions, to types and comprehends such formations in concepts, but an idealizing-logicizing science. Historically, we all know this science first took shape as, and was afterwards guided by, the Platonizing geometry, which talks, not about straight lines, circles, and the like in the "aesthetic" sense, not about "their" Apriori, the Apriori of what appears in actual and possible appearances, but rather about the (regulative) idea applying to a space that so appears, about "ideal space" with its "ideal straight lines" and the like. The whole of "exact" physics operates with such "idealities"; thus, beneath actually experienced Nature, beneath the Nature dealt with in actual living, it places a Nature as an idea, as

a regulative ideal norm, as the logos, in a higher sense, belonging to actually experienced Nature. (*FTL*, 292–93 / *H* XVII, 257)[22]

In the *Crisis*, Husserl asserts that the "objective" world as conceived by the physical sciences is exclusively populated by idealized objects (*C*, 129 / *H* VI, 132), and, for that very reason, is in principle imperceptible. "The contrast between the subjectivity of the life-world and the 'objective,' the 'true' world, lies in the fact that the latter is a theoretical-logical substruction, the substruction of something that is in principle not perceivable, in principle not experienceable in its own proper being, whereas the subjective, in the life-world, is distinguished in all respects precisely by its being actually experienceable" (*C*, 127 / *H* VI, 130). While in the *Ideas* Husserl wanted to underscore the identity of the thing as determined in the physical sciences and the perceived thing, in the *Crisis* he emphasizes their difference and assigns them to ontologically distinct camps. "The bodies familiar to us in the life-world are actual bodies, but not the bodies in the sense of physics" (*C*, 139 / *H* VI, 142). For the bodies in the sense of physics are "theoretical idealizations," "hypothetical substructions" (*C*, 140 / *H* VI, 143).

The basis of the shift in Husserl's concept of the ontological status of the referents of the modern mathematical physical sciences lies in his analysis of the mental processes and correlative objectivities that lie at the basis of their founding mathematical disciplines—especially geometry. In the *Ideas* geometry was represented as an eidetic science of space. On the basis of an ideating abstraction performed on the empirical intuition of material bodies, geometry seizes upon the essential spatial structures and relations of the physical world (*ID* III, 36–37 / *H* V, 42). But in the *Crisis*, Husserl maintains that the science of geometry is not based upon an ideating abstraction, an eidetic reduction from spatial fact to spatial essence, but on the process of idealization. This shift is of crucial significance. For the two processes in question here yield categorically different objectivities: one, a universal; the other, an ideal object. Moreover, to the degree that modern physics is mathematical, this shift has direct consequences for Husserl's position on what, precisely, modern mathematical physics is about.

Already in the *Logical Investigations*, Husserl makes a distinction between the process of ideation and that of idealization, together with their distinct objects. Here he anticipates his later position on the status of geometrical objectivities: "Plainly the essential forms of all intuitive data are not in principle to be brought under 'exact' or 'ideal' notions, such as we have in mathematics. The spatial shape of the perceived tree as such, taken precisely as a 'moment' found in the relevant percept's intentional object, is no geometric shape, no ideal or exact shape in the sense of exact geometry. . . . The essence which direct ideation elicits from intuitive data are 'inexact essences,' they may not be confused with the 'exact' essences which are Ideas in the Kantian sense, and which . . . arise through a peculiar 'idealization'" (*LI* II, 450–51 / *H* XIX 1, B1 245).

While ideating abstraction produces a consciousness of an essence that admits of instantiation on the part of real individuals, idealization yields an ideal object, or "Idea" in the Kantian sense. As a matter of principle, the latter cannot be instantiated by real individuals. It can only be approximated. Thus ideas, or ideal objects, will never be given to sensuous intuition. "For a figure understood geometrically is known to be an ideal limit incapable in principle of intuitive exhibition in the concrete" (*LI* II, 777 / *H* XIX 2, B2 133). On the basis of sensuous intuition of round objects, ideating abstraction delivers the concept of the inexact essence "roundness," which is, in turn, instantiated by round objects. But round objects are always more or less circular. The extension of the concept of roundness is thus inexact and therefore open to difference in subjective interpretation. What counts as round to one person may not count as round to another. And there seems to be no exact method that in principle could be performed by all persons that would decide the issue. Inexact concepts—"fuzzy predicates"—then, are not "objective" in the strict sense. They cannot produce or compel intersubjective agreement with respect to their precise extension.

Idealization, by contrast, delivers an exact concept. Its extension is not a cluster of real objects bound together by mutual resemblance, but the unique ideal object constituted in the act of idealization. In idealization, empirically given and imaginable real objects are aligned in a series converging on an ideal limit where real variation in one respect or another is reduced to zero. The idealized object, then, emerges at infinity as the limit of the series. This idealized object, it must be emphasized, is not real, but ideal. As a limit, it differs qualitatively from the series that converges upon it. To refer back to our example of round objects, the process of idealization aligns more or less round objects in a series converging on an ideal limit where the variation in distance between center and all points on the circumference is reduced to zero. Thus there arises a consciousness of the circle in the geometrical sense. But the circle as an idealized object is not the spatial essence of real round objects. It is not instantiated by them. Nor could it be. Real objects are always round, that is, more or less circular. But they are never circles in the mathematically exact sense. In the world of actual perceptual experience, "we find nothing of geometrical idealities, no geometrical space or mathematical time with all their shapes" (C, 50 / H VI, 50). The exact concept of the circle has a perfectly definite extension: the circle, an ideal object, an Idea in the Kantian sense (cf. ID I, 166 / H III 1, 155). Real objects may approach the circle by way of approximation, but never instantiate it (cf. ID I, 167 / H III, 1 156). Being exact, the concept of the circle is also objective in the scientifically preferred sense: one can always tell whether an object is a circle or not; its extension is clear-cut.

Thus we have two very different conceptions of the nature of geometry, the mental processes by which its objects are constituted, and the ontological status of those objects. If geometry is based upon the mental process of ideation, then its objects count as the essences of real, material things given in perception. If geometry is based upon the mental process of idealization, then its objects are Ideas in the Kantian sense (i.e., ideal objects), which are incapable of instantiation on the part of real, material things. It would be, therefore, a mistake to run these two conceptions together as Joseph J. Kockelmans does in his exposition of Husserl's concept of the mathematization of nature. There he states that pure mathematics is interested "only in the abstract forms of spatio-temporal reality which furthermore are to be taken as pure and ideal limit-poles."[23] Robert Sokolowski makes a similar error when he refers to the products of idealization as "exact essences," and then speaks of things as instances of exact essences.[24] As I have endeavored to make clear, if the objects of pure mathematics are the forms of real objects in space and time, they cannot be ideal limit-poles, or Ideas in the Kantian sense. And if they are ideal objects, then they cannot be the essences or forms of real things. For Kantian Ideas cannot be instantiated in the real world. They can only be approximated. And for precisely that reason, they will never be the forms of real physical objects in space and time.

3. GEOMETRY AND PHYSICAL SCIENCE

The putative object of physical science is the physical world. And yet, the later Husserl claims, to the degree that physical science is a mathematical science it is not about the physical world, but about an idealized world of its own device. This could be taken as a devastating immanent critique of modern mathematical physics: while physics aims at objective knowledge about the real physical world, the methods it has adopted in order to achieve such knowledge mean that it can never be about the real physical world. Alternatively, this could be taken as an indication that there is something desperately amiss in Husserl's understanding of physical science. For the physical sciences are, quite obviously, about the physical world. Any position that is led to deny this point should reexamine its premises.

In this section I will show that we need not adopt either conclusion. For Husserl, physical science is, indeed, about the real world. According to its original bestowal of sense, its method "has the sense of achieving knowledge about the world" (C, 47 / H VI, 46–47). Yet it does so indirectly and by way of approximation. It approaches the real by way of the ideal. The ideal gas laws hold for ideal, not real, gases. But such laws can be modified to approximate the behavior of real gases through the incorporation of empirical constants. In this way physical science retains its exact character and at the same time counts as knowledge of the real world. But such knowledge, as long as it is exact, will only be approximate. In the mathematical physical sciences, the real world, to use Husserl's metaphor, is measured for a "well-fitting garb of ideas" (C, 51 / H VI, 51). This garb of ideas is not itself the real world, but it fits the real world to a greater or lesser degree. It is therefore informative. One can tell the height and proportions of a man by examining his suit. Something similar holds for nature's suit.

On this point Husserl's phenomenological assessment of physical science, circa 1935, resembles and anticipates Frederick Suppe's semantic conception of the structure of scientific theories, developed during the 1970s in reaction to the epistemological oversights of the logical positivist philosophy of science. Rejecting the notion that scientific theories are tested against the results of direct observation, and that the theoretical language of science can be reduced to and expressed in a language of pure observation, Suppe contends that science tests its theories not against a directly observable phenomenal system, but against a highly abstract, theoretically defined "physical system." The physical system is abstract because it is constructed of only a few selected elements to be found in the phenomenal system. "A science does not deal with phenomena in all their complexity, but rather is concerned with certain kinds of phenomena only insofar as their behavior is determined by or characteristic of a small number of parameters abstracted from those phenomena."[25] In the science of classical mechanics, for instance, falling bodies will be treated solely in terms of mass, velocity, distance over time, and the like. Their color, taste, texture, value, and beauty, or the lack of it, are systematically ignored.

Not only is a physical system highly abstract, it is also idealized. For "the process of abstraction from the phenomena goes one step further—we are not concerned with actual velocities, etc., but rather with velocity under idealized conditions, (e.g. in a frictionless environment, with the mass one object would have if it were concentrated at an extensionless point, etc.). Thus, for example, classical particle mechanics is concerned with the behavior of isolated systems of extentionless point-masses which interact in a vacuum, where the behavior of the point-masses depends on their position and momenta at a given time."[26] The laws of classical mechanics, then, directly characterize the behavior of the physical system. But they do not directly characterize the system of actually observed phenomena. Being highly abstract and idealized, the physical system only represents "how the phenomena *would have* behaved *had* the idealized conditions been met."[27] "Thus," Suppe points out, "in classical particle mechanics our data do not represent, e.g. the velocity with which the milk bottle actually fell, but rather the velocity with which it *would have* fallen *had* it fallen in a vacuum, had it been a point mass, etc."[28] For this reason the laws of an empirical science, if true of the physical system within its scope, are only counterfactually true of the observed phenomenal system. The gas laws, as a case in point, "describe the behavior of ideal gases, not real gases; yet they are used to work with actual gases."[29]

Suppe's semantics for scientific theories bears a close resemblance to the "simulacrum" account more recently developed by Nancy Cartwright.[30] Cartwright claims that a proper analysis of scientific theories will involve not just two elements—theories and reality—but three: theories, models, and reality. Theories are not true of reality; rather, they are true of abstract and idealized models of reality.[31] "My basic view," she writes, "is that fundamental equations [of a theory] do not govern objects in reality; they govern only objects in models."[32] Models, however, do bear a likeness to reality, and can be applied to reality by way of ceteris paribus clauses, the composition of causes, and a series of approximations.[33] Alternatively, reality can be made to approximate a model by way of experimental control over various complicating factors, for instance, by eliminating the resistance of the medium for falling bodies through the artificial creation of a vacuum.[34] Thus models and reality can be made to meet halfway either through the de-idealization of the model or through the idealization of reality. But, "in general, nature does not prepare situations to fit the kinds of mathematical theories we hanker for. We construct both the theories and the objects to which they apply, then match them piecemeal onto real situations, deriving—sometimes with great precision—a bit of what happens, but generally not getting all the facts straight at once."[35] No Cartesian rational geometer, God—Cartwright asserts—possesses the untidy mind of the English. He created not the exact universe portrayed in the physical sciences, but rather the "dappled world" celebrated in the poetry of Gerard Manley Hopkins.[36] Our mathematical theories, then, can at best only capture a highly reduced and schematized version of reality, not the "blousy situations" of reality itself.[37]

To point to the disparity between model and reality, however, is not the same as to make an antirealist case for the interpretation of scientific theories. Here, Cartwright cautions, we must distinguish between the laws formulated within a theory and its causal principles. Granted, the laws, couched in the exact language of mathematics, falsify reality; granted, the objects they describe are ideal constructs. But the causal principles proposed by a theory make basic claims about the way reality is put together. If we have reason to believe the claims are true, then we have reason to believe that the theoretical entities they posit exist—even if we can only construct models of such entities when we try to capture their behavior by way of exact formulations.[38] Causal principles are informal ideas about the basic constituents of the world and how they relate to one another. If such principles are to be accepted, we must have reason to believe they are true. The laws of the physical sciences, on the other hand, are almost always false, but acceptable if they yield predictions that are "close enough."[39] Causal principles proposed by theories demand the falsehood of principles incompatible with them; models projected by laws are more tolerant, allowing for the use of alternate models for specific purposes. In the case of quantum damping, where atoms de-excite and emit photons describing a spread of line frequencies, Cartwright identifies six distinct mathematical treatments. Although they yield the same results, they make use of different laws and equations. Yet all are acceptable.[40] Cartwright is an instrumentalist when it comes to scientific laws, but a realist when it comes to scientific theories.

In essential agreement with the thrust of recent Anglo-American model-theoretic accounts of scientific theories, the burden of Husserl's critique was to expose nature as conceived by the physical sciences as a highly abstract and idealized construct by recourse to its phenomenological origins in the mental processes of abstraction and idealization, which take their point of departure from the perceptually given lifeworld. If we follow Husserl's account to this point, however, we might wonder why modern physics has chosen to know the real world only indirectly and by way of approximation. Would not direct methods be preferable? Not for the kind of knowledge science seeks to establish. For knowledge of the real world on the basis of perception, without passage to the ideal, would not achieve the status of objective knowledge. Such knowledge would remain "subjectively relative." As we saw in section 1 of this chapter, the physical sciences must, in their pursuit of objectivity, abstract from all subject-relative properties of the real object in order to determine the object as it is "in-itself." But even the quantitative shape characteristics of the real object are not exact, but only typical, and therefore cannot be determined with an exactness that excludes all subjective interpretation. It is here that Galileo, the founder of modern mathematical physics, took his cue for the already well-established science of geometry (C, 29 / H VI, 27). Through the process of idealization, geometry has produced exact ideal objects that admit of univocal determination. They can therefore be known objectively.

But the science of geometry not only makes objective knowledge of ideal objects possible. In its applied form, it also makes objective knowledge of real objects possible through the application of the ideal to the real by way of approximation. Pure geometry affords objective (and exact) knowledge of ideal objects; applied geometry affords objective (but approximate) knowledge of real objects. That is, applied geometry represents a method whereby the real can be known (C, 33 / H VI, 31). Ideal objects, which do not exist in reality, then, can serve as the means by which real objects can be objectively known.

In its imitation of the methods of pure and applied geometry, modern mathematical physics will generally follow a two-step process in preparing the natural world for representation through the exact formulae of empirical laws. First: the step of idealization, which produces an ideal case. Unlike real cases, the ideal cases will admit of an exact and uniform determination. Second: the ideal case will be applied to real cases through a process of successive approximation. As an example of this method as practiced in the early period of modern physics, we can take Galileo's paradigmatic treatment of free-falling bodies in the *Two New Sciences*.[41] In our common, everyday experience of falling bodies, we see that the rate of fall varies with respect to a number of real factors—the weight and shape of the falling body, the density of the medium, and so on. A bowling ball falls faster through the air than a feather. A stone falls faster through the air than in does through water. With respect to real, observed cases of falling bodies, Galileo notes that "the inequality of speeds is always greater in the more resistant mediums of different resistances."[42] This suggests a convergent series: "Movables of different weight differ less and less in speed as they are situated in more and more yielding mediums; and that finally, despite extreme difference in weight, their diversity of speed in the most tenuous medium of all . . . is found to be very small and almost unobservable."[43] On the horizon of such a series there then arises the ideal limit, where the resistance of the medium is reduced to zero: "In the void all speeds would be entirely equal."[44] As a void exists nowhere in nature, there are, strictly speaking, no free-falling bodies. The free fall is an ideal case. But precisely because it is an ideal case, where the rate of acceleration is uniform, it can be expressed in terms of an exact empirical law that holds irrespective of the variations that inevitably crop up in real cases. This law can, in turn, be applied to real cases of falling bodies through successive complication (i.e., adding in the resistance of the medium and the like).

As Ernst Mach pointed out in *The Science of Mechanics*, Galileo's thought experiments with inclined planes led to the law of inertia in the same way: by abstracting from real factors that were considered to be accidental—in this case, by reducing friction and the resistance of the medium to zero. Pressing real cases of physical processes on to the limiting case draws upon what Mach calls the "principle of continuity."[45] The same kind of analysis holds for other idealized objects for which the empirical laws of the physical sciences hold—incompressible fluids, perfectly elastic bodies, ideal heat reservoirs, and the like. In each case they are the constructs brought about by mental processes of idealization performed on real cases converging on a limit. They themselves are not real objects, but they are used in the exact scientific determination of real objects.

This, briefly, is Husserl's conception of the basic method of the empirical component of modern mathematical physics: first the generation of an idealized object that admits of exact—and therefore objective—determination; then the application of the ideal case to the real by way of successive approximation. This method affords knowledge of the real that is exact, objective—and approximate. Idealized objects are posited as means by which real objects receive an exact determination. Given this understanding of the method of modern physics, Husserl's chief concern in the *Crisis* is the ontological interpretation that typically accompanies it.

Following the Platonistic interpretation of Galileo,[46] Husserl holds that modern physics tends to identify the correlate of objective knowledge as that which exists objectively (C, 29 / H VI, 27). The ideal objects take on a sense of independent existence, while the real, apparent objects of straightforward perception are demoted to the status of "mere appearances," appearances that are subject-relative. This ontological position is not entailed by the method. But, nonetheless, "some were misled into taking these formulae and their formula meaning for the true being of nature itself" (C, 43–44 / H VI, 43). The "essential principle" of Galilean physics, insofar as it takes itself to be directly about nature, is that nature is, in itself, mathematical (C, 53 / H VI, 53). Mathematical physics gets at the true being of nature. Of this Platonizing tendency Nancy Cartwright says, "It would be wrong to say, as a first easy description might have it, that these philosophers are not interested in what the world is like. Rather they are interested in a world that is not our world, not the world of appearances but rather a purer, more orderly world, a world which is thought to be represented 'directly' by the theory's equations."[47] Yet both Cartwright and Husserl could contend that the purer and more orderly world is but a reified product of mathematical method. "As early as Galileo himself," Husserl contends, there was already a "surreptitious substitution of the mathematically substructed world of idealities for the only real world, the one that is actually given through perception, that is ever experienced and experienceable—our everyday life-world" (C, 48–49 / H VI, 48–49). The product of the method of idealization was substituted for that which "is given immediately and presupposed in all idealization" (C, 50 / H VI, 51).[48] Thus, under the Platonizing interpretation, mathematical physics not only outfits the world (*einkleiden*) in a cloak of intelligbility, but disguises it (*verkleiden*). "Mathematics and mathematical science, as a garb of ideas, or the garb of symbols of the symbolic mathematical theories, encompasses everything which, for scientists and the educated generally, represents the life-world, dresses it up as 'objectively actual and true' nature. It is through the garb of ideas that we take for true being what is actually a method—a method which is designed for the purpose of progressively improving, *in infinitum*, through 'scientific' predictions the rough predictions which are the only ones originally possible within the sphere of what is actually experienced and experienceable in the life-world" (C, 51–52 / H VI, 52).

Although this ontological interpretation is not forced by the method itself, it holds sway over the general understanding of the epistemic aims of physical science. For if nature itself is taken to be an ideal mathematical manifold, it would follow that this manifold would no longer be construed as the means of scientific knowledge, but rather as the object of scientific knowledge.[49] Thus,

Husserl says, the idealized natural world has become the center of interest in all natural scientific inquiry (C, 48 / H VI, 48). As a result, modern physics has lost sight of what he took to be its original purpose, which was to provide predictive knowledge of the actual world as given in intuition. "All knowledge of laws could be knowledge only of predictions, grasped as lawful, about occurrences of actual or possible experiential phenomena " (C, 50 / H VI, 50). The ontological reversal represents to Husserl a "dangerous shift of meaning," which will obscure the original sense of the method of modern physics, the sense of "achieving knowledge about the world" (C, 47 / H VI, 47).

Husserl's critique of modern mathematical physics, then, is a rejection not of its method, nor of its results, but of the platonistic ontology often attached to it. This ontology is rejected as a category mistake: the ideal is taken to be the real. While the method involves only the application of the ideal to the real, the mistaken ontology suggests that the ideal is the real. Here the real is idealized, and nature is forthwith converted into a "mathematical manifold" (C, 23 / H VI, 20).

Husserl's phenomenological critique of modern mathematical physics was directed at the foundations of what he characterized in the *Crisis* as "physicalistic rationalism," or "scientific objectivism" (C, 65–70 / H VI, 66–71). Physicalistic rationalism represented one side of a dualistic tension in modern philosophy, which, since Descartes, took modern mathematical physics as its epistemological model. Its undergirding ontological assumption was that the world was "in itself a rational systematic unity," and that insofar as its rational structure was mathematical in nature, it could be known through the a priori insights of the human mind (C, 65 / H VI, 66). Thus rationalistic philosophy took itself to be on the road to an infinite extension of its knowledge of the world as it is in itself through the deductive extension of its a priori principles and the inductive subsumption of all empirical data under the relevant categories (C, 65–66 / H VI, 66–67).

To claim that modern philosophical rationalism was epistemologically modeled on mathematical physics is to presuppose, however, a certain interpretation of mathematical physics. We find this interpretation in Husserl's Galileo analysis in section 9 of the *Crisis*. It is not unlikely that Husserl based his Galileo analysis, which at the same time represents his critical statement on modern mathematical physics, on the historical work of Alexandre Koyré. A former student of Husserl at Göttingen, Koyré went on to make outstanding contributions to the history of science, not the least of which was his justly famous *Etudes Galiléennes*, published in 1940. Koyré kept in touch with

Husserl throughout his career. In fact, David Carr notes that Koyré paid an extended visit to Husserl in the mid-1930s at the time Husserl was composing the material we now find in the *Crisis*. Given the similarity in Koyré's and Husserl's assessment of Galileo, David Carr writes that "it is interesting to speculate that the Galileo section might have resulted from a reported visit during this period by Husserl's friend and former student Alexandre Koyré."[50]

In the figure and work of Galileo, Koyré sees the victory of the Platonic approach to the science of nature over the Aristotelian. During the Renaissance there was much debate over the applicability of mathematics within the domain of natural science. The Aristotelian tradition had eschewed the use of mathematics, since, in its view, the proper object of physics is motion, while mathematical entities are incorrigibly static. Aristotelian natural science was therefore quantitatively inexact, relying on qualitatively differentiated natures in order to account for the diverse phenomena of motion and change within the physical universe. The burden of Galileo's project was to convince the predominantly Aristotelian scientific world that the proper approach to the science of nature was exact and quantitative in nature. Physics ought to be conducted in the language of mathematics.

According to Koyré, Galileo's methodological conviction was predicated on the underlying ontological assumption of the Platonic tradition that nature was in itself mathematically structured. The mathematical approach to nature was entirely appropriate because nature was itself mathematical in essence.[51] "The grand book of the universe," Galileo himself once wrote, "is written in the language of mathematics, and its characters are triangles, circles, and other geometric figures without which it is humanly impossible to understand a single word of it."[52] Thus the mathematical style of Galileo's science was more than just a theoretically interesting way to represent physical phenomena. It converted physics into "a *real* science, a science of the *real* world."[53] For Galileo, Koyré claims, mathematical physics "is a matter of truth about nature and knowledge of the real world. This is the knowledge, the truly 'philosophical' knowledge, knowledge concerning the very essence of reality, about which the true Platonist, consciously Platonist, Galileo speaks."[54]

The fact that observable phenomena never quite accord with the demands of mathematical treatment, that experimental results do not turn out exactly as mathematical laws predict, does not reflect negatively upon the new physics of Galileo. On the contrary, it is perfectly consistent with the Platonic ontology of Galilean science. It reinforces the Platonic notion that what is perceivable by the senses is but an imperfect visible manifestation of the ideal forms, where true being makes its home. Thus the lack of perfect fit between mathematical theory and observed phenomena serves to indicate to Galileo that sensuously intuited objects only "'imitate' and 'approximate' geometrical entities."[55] The inexact relation between theory and phenomena, then, presents no insurmountable problem to the Platonist, who "accepts that the real is ultimately mathematical in essence."[56] Thus the mathematicization of physical science at the hands of Galileo represents to Koyré a "return to Plato" and the Platonic ontology that identifies true being with the ideal and relegates the perceived world to the status of mere imperfect appearance.[57]

Koyré's interpretation of Galileo provides the foundation of his critique of Galilean science. For he holds, contrary to Galileo's Platonism, that "in the real world, the physical world, there are no straight lines, nor planes, nor triangles, nor spheres. The bodies of the material world do not have regular geometrical forms. Therefore geometrical laws cannot be applied to them."[58] Galilean physics applies not to real material bodies existing in real physical space, but only to idealized mathematical objects in mathematical space. "The bodies of Galilean physics, the bodies of his dynamics, are not real bodies."[59] Clearly, "these bodies moving in straight lines in infinite empty space are not *real* bodies moving in *real* space, but *mathematical* bodies moving in *mathematical* space."[60] Hence, "Galilean dynamics only holds for the abstract bodies located in geometrical space."[61] For this reason Koyré will claim that modern mathematical physics does not deal directly with the real material world, but with an idealized construct of its own device. "The process which gave rise to classical physics consisted in an attempt to rationalise, in other words to geometricise, space, and to mathematicise the laws of nature."[62]

Koyré's Platonic interpretation of Galileo has not gone uncontested.[63] But for our purposes it is important to note that the Platonic interpretation of Galileo, and, by extension, of the sense of modern mathematical physics in general, is what defines the polemic context for Husserl's phenomenological critique of science. Convinced that the Platonizing ontological assumptions underlying the method of modern physics represent a reversal in the order of being, Husserl sought to expose nature as conceived and projected in the physical sciences as an idealized abstraction by rehearsing the course of its constitution within modern scientific consciousness. In so doing, Husserl takes himself to be challenging the epistemological hegemony of modern physical science together with its pretension to possess exclusive access to the world as it is in itself—all other approaches being summarily dismissed as unscientific or merely subjective.

Although Husserl faults modern physics if it thinks that the objects it posits for purely methodological purposes really exist, his critique is not instrumentalist in the standard sense. For his critique is entirely confined to issues that pertain to the conditions of the possibility of exact laws. What he denies really exist are the idealized objects posited in the course of an exact determination of the real. He is not denying that certain entities posited in theories as real do not, in fact, exist. His critique is primarily categorial, not existential. What he faults modern physics for is taking ideal objects, products of the methods of physics, as if they were original constituents of the physical world.

In this way Husserl's critique of physics is similar to Kant's critique of metaphysics. Kant holds that the chief error of traditional metaphysics is to take the subjective conditions of the systematic empirical knowledge of objects as if they were themselves objects. Thus, for example, in traditional metaphysics, the ideal of reason, the idea of the perfect reality, which is a necessary regulatory idea guiding the complete determination of any empirical object, is itself assigned objective status and subsequently determined by the unschematized categories of the understanding.[64] So with Husserl, the ideal objects posited by physics in the course of—and as the condition for—the exact determination of the empirical objects are themselves given real standing and hence made into objects of physical inquiry. The very method of modern physics generates a "transcendental illusion" that must be guarded against by the constant reminder of the constitutive origins and methodological purpose of idealized objects.

In his major statement on the physical sciences, then, the existence that Husserl seeks to deny is not that of theoretical entities as they are understood in the contemporary realist-instrumentalist debates in the Anglo-American philosophy of science. As entities postulated by theories in order to explain the lawlike regularities in the behavior of empirical objects, they are not the target of his remarks. Rather, he denies only that the ideal objects that serve as the basis of exact formulation of empirical laws of the physical sciences are real. As I will show in the conclusion, the major deficiency in previous work on the question of Husserl's instrumentalism, his scientific antirealism, stems from drawing Husserl into the contemporary debate without first ascertaining the specific sense of his claims. His instrumentalism is then asserted or denied with respect to the question of the existence of theoretical entities. But, as we have seen, Husserl did not directly address himself to this question. His instrumentalism is an instrumentalism of scientific laws, not scientific theories. Furthermore, his instrumentalist interpretation of scientific laws is compatible with a realist interpretation of scientific theories. For by claiming that idealized objects are not real, but only posited for the sake of an exact determination of the real, one has not yet determined the possible extent of the real. As Mario Bunge points out, one can hold, as he does, that the representations of the world in the science of physics "are not portraits of reality but that they involve brutal simplifications leading to ideal schemas, or object models, such as those of homogenous field or free particle." But, he says, "none of this turns physics into a mere fiction."[65]

There are, however, other aspects of Husserl's phenomenology that may have a direct bearing on the question of theoretical existence. In *Ideas* I, for instance, Husserl claims that the extent of the real is coextensive with the domain of the perceivable (*ID* I, 106 / *H* III 1, 100). If theoretical entities are defined as imperceptible, it would appear that, on Husserl's account, they cannot really exist. We will take up this issue, together with the larger question of Husserl's idealism, in the next chapter.

CHAPTER SIX

CONSCIOUSNESS, PERCEPTION, AND EXISTENCE

In the preceding chapter I argued that Husserl's instrumentalism, being an instrumentalism of scientific laws, is entirely consistent with a realistic interpretation of scientific theories. It was not Husserl's intent in the *Crisis* to deny that theoretical entities exist, but rather to deny that idealized objects are real. At the conclusion of that chapter, I claimed that Husserl's law-instrumentalism did not—and could not, in itself—decide the ontological question pertaining to the extent of the real. It merely claims that those ideal objects whereby the real is determined with exactness and objectivity are not genuine members of the physical world. They are not causal players in the material world of space and time. Conceptually, the question of the extent of real existence—given the bounds of human sense perception—is left open.

There are, however, other aspects of Husserl's phenomenology that speak directly to this question. In the *Logical Investigations*, Husserl maintains that "the sphere of real objects . . . is in fact no other than the sphere of possible sense-perception." For "we define a real object as the possible object of a straightforward percept" (*LI* II, 791 / *H* XIX 2, B2 151). Hence, "nothing exists that cannot be perceived" (*LI* II, 822 / *H* XIX 2, B2 188). This position is reinforced in *Ideas* I where Husserl writes, "It must always be borne in mind here that whatever physical things are . . . they are as experienceable physical things" (*ID* I, 106 / *H III* 1, 100). Moreover, "it is inherent in the essence that anything whatever which exists in reality but is not yet actually experienced can become given and that this means that the thing in question belongs to the undetermined but determinable horizon of my experiential actuality at the particular time" (*ID* I, 107 / *H III* 1, 101). Such a reference to experience is inherent, Husserl claims, in the meaning of existence claims: "That the unperceived physical thing 'is there' means that, from my actually present perception, with the actually appearing background field, possible, and, moreover, continuously harmoniously motivated perception-sequences, with ever new fields of physical things (as unheeded backgrounds), lead to those concatenations of perceptions in which the physical thing in question would make its appearance and become seized upon" (ID I, 99 / H III 1, 96). "Thus," he concludes, "a transcendency which lacked the above-described connection by harmonious motivational concatenations with my current sphere of actually present perceptions would be a completely groundless assumption; a transcendency which lacked such concatenations essentially would be nonsensical" (ID I 100 / H III 1, 96).

It would seem, then, that although Husserl's instrumentalism is compatible with a realist construal of scientific theories, there is at least strong prima facie textual evidence for the position that Husserl's phenomenology is not. For clearly Husserl holds to the following two theses: (a) that real existence is restricted to that which is perceivable; and (b) that it is irrational to assert that something exists if it is not, in fact, perceivable. If theoretical entities are defined as imperceptible, or unobservable, entities, then it would seem that they are, on Husserl's account, in deep existential trouble: they cannot exist, and it would be irrational to assert that they do.

Edward G. Ballard takes this position and runs with it. According to Husserl, he claims, "the authenticity of any belief about an object is determinable only through immediate or mediate reference to that which perception presents.... Phenomenology thus is a radical empiricism. Any object that is not originally given in perception or is not derived in a determined manner from something originally given in my experience must be suspect."[1] For that reason, Ballard takes it that Husserl's phenomenology is incompatible with a realist interpretation of the theories of the physical sciences. In fact, he thinks this is one of Husserl's major shortcomings and suggests that phenomenology be enriched with the concept of "structural evidence," which would allow for the rationality of positing things beyond what is, or could be, given in perceptual experience.[2]

In addition, there is the matter of Husserl's idealism. When Husserl's idealism is interpreted as a metaphysical idealism,[3] it is usually represented in terms of two interrelated core claims. First, the claim that the existence of things is dependent upon, or relative to, consciousness. Such an interpretation gains much plausibility from section 49 of *Ideas* I, where Husserl apparently takes himself to have shown, on the basis of eidetic considerations alone, that consciousness is an absolute, self-contained sphere of being and that the physical world in space and time is secondary and exists only for a consciousness (ID I, 112 / H III 1, 106). "Reality, the reality of the physical thing," Husserl there proclaims, "taken singly and the reality of the whole world, lacks self-sufficiency in virtue of its essence" (*ID* I, 113 / *H* III 1, 106). Consciousness, in its existence, is not dependent upon the real world; rather, the existence of the real world is dependent upon consciousness. "Thus," in phenomenology, Husserl claims, "the sense commonly expressed in speaking of being is reversed" (*ID* I, 112 / *H* III 1, 106). "Everything outside," as Husserl restates his idealist position in *Formal and Transcendental Logic*, "is what it is in this inside [my ego, my life of consciousness], and gets its true being from the givings of itself, and from the verifications, within this inside" (*FTL*, 250 / *H* XVII, 221). In short, "all objective being has in transcendental subjectivity the grounds for its being" (*FTL*, 274 / *H* XVII, 242).

Second, the metaphysical idealist interpretation will typically ascribe to Husserl the claim that things are nothing other or more than intentional formations of transcendental consciousness. The second claim, in a sense, explains the first. The existence of objective being is grounded in transcendental subjectivity because "something objective is nothing more than the synthetic unity of actual and potential intentionality, a unity belonging to the proper essence of transcendental subjectivity" (*FTL*, 274 / *H* XVII, 242). It is a "pole of unity in my ... actual and possible multiplicities" (*FTL*, 250 / *H* XVII, 221). Reality is not self-sufficient in its existence because it is "only intentional, only an object of consciousness" (*ID* I, 113 / *H* III 1, 106). In *Cartesian Meditations*, Husserl asks himself, "What are others, what is the world, for me?" He answers, "Constituted phenomena, merely something produced within me. Never can I reach the point of ascribing being in the absolute sense to others, any more than to the physical things of nature, which exist only as transcendentally produced formations [*Gebilde*]" (*CM*, 52 / *H* I, 238; translation modified). A physical thing is an identity intuited and determined in and through the multiplicities of appearances in consciousness. Beyond that, Husserl asserts, "it is nothing" (*ID* I, 112 / *H* III 1, 106).

The first claim, although idealist in tenor, is not inconsistent with a realist interpretation of scientific theories. For it does not deny that physical things in general or theoretical entities in particular exist. It claims only that their existence is dependent upon consciousness. It does not limit the scope of real existence. It specifies only the grounds of real existence. But the second claim seems to limit the scope of real existence to that which appears, or can appear, to perceptual consciousness. If physical things are nothing more than identities constituted within a coherent multiplicity of appearances, then it would seem that theoretical entities cannot be physical things. They cannot appear; therefore, they cannot exist as an identity of appearances.

In this chapter I will endeavor to show that the aforementioned prima facie evidence for the incompatibility of Husserl's phenomenology and a realist construal of scientific theories fails to stand up under careful scrutiny of the sense of Husserl's claims together with the riders that attach to them by virtue of the phenomenological method.

1. PERCEPTIONS AND EXISTENCE

Let us first turn to Husserl's claim that the extent of the real is limited to the domain of the perceivable. We will construe this claim as an existence condition (EC) for real objects:

> EC: For any real object x, x exists if and only if it is possible that x be perceived.

Above, we indicated that theoretical entities are posited as real objects—real yet imperceptible. It would seem, then, that such entities fail to meet Husserl's existence condition. In this section I will argue that once the sense of the modal operator in the existence condition is made explicit and properly specified, the existential status of theoretical entities remains intact.

Husserl's phenomenology is an eidetic discipline. All claims Husserl puts forth in the name of phenomenology are to be taken as assertions of necessary and universal truth. Their universal validity is grounded in methodically achieved insight into the essence of things as experienced together with the essence of the experience of things. For this very reason the claims Husserl makes about the possibility of perception should not be taken as factual statements about what happens to be possible for human perceivers. For such claims would then be tied to the contingent constitution of the perceptual apparatus of the human species. To claim, then, that any existing physical thing must be perceivable, must be experienceable, is not to claim that human beings must be able to perceive or experience it, but only that it be perceivable or experienceable by some possible consciousness. "Obviously," Husserl writes in *Ideas* I, "there are physical things and worlds of physical things which do not admit of being definitely demonstrated in any human experience; but that has purely factual grounds which lie within the limits of such experience" (*ID* I, 109 / *H* III 1, 103). When Husserl posits perceivability as an existence condition for real objects, he is not restricting the extent of real existence to what is humanly perceivable. Thus, when he says that "if there are any worlds, any real physical things whatever, then the experienced motivations constituting them must be able to extend into my experience" (*ID* I, 109 / *H* III 1, 103), the ego functioning as the subject of this projected series of possible experiences must be taken as an ego independent of any particular empirical limitations. The ability of the motivations to extend into this ego's experience must not be inhibited by contingent circumstances. The kind of possibility Husserl has in mind, then, in the formulation of the existence condition for real existence is, again, an ideal possibility, not real possibility. As Karl Ameriks points out in his article on Husserl's brand of realism, when Husserl ties the existence of things to the possibility of perception, he is asserting nothing more than that "any meaningful claim that a thing exists presumes that it is logically [i.e., ideally] possible for that thing to be in some way perceived."[4] He is not claiming "that things are relative to the physical [i.e., real] possibility of being perceived."[5] When the modal status of the condition has thus been made explicit, it reads:

> EC*: For any real object x, x exists if and only if it is ideally possible that x be perceived.

Husserl is not tying the possibility of real existence to the real possibility of human perception.

This interpretation is corroborated by Husserl's self-explication in connection with the above-cited claim in the Sixth Logical Investigation. There he asserts that "nothing exists that cannot be perceived" (*LI* II, 822 / *H* XIX 2, B2 188). But again, the "cannot" here should not be construed in terms of real possibilities for the human species. Rather, expanding on the sense of his claim, Husserl says, "This means that the actual performance of actual acts on the ground of just these straightforward intuitions is *in the ideal sense* possible" (*LI* II, 822 / *H* XIX 2, B2 188; my emphasis). In the same passage, he refers to these possibilities as "ideal possibilities" governed by "ideal laws" (*LI* II, 822 / *H* XIX 2, B2 188). Again, the perceivability condition does not restrict the domain of real existence to that which is perceivable on the part of human beings. It simply states, in an ontologically generous way, that anything that exists must be perceivable by some possible consciousness.

Theoretical entities, we have claimed, are by definition imperceptible. They cannot be observed—which is precisely why they are called "theoretical." They are posited as existing not because they have been observed, but because a theory designed to explain the lawlike behavior of what is observed has been to some degree confirmed. But the impossibility of their perception does not count against their existence on Husserl's real existence condition. For here the impossibility of their perception is not an ideal impossibility. Rather, it is a real impossibility tied to the factual limitations of human perception. Theoretical entities cannot be observed by us. Thus there is no conflict between Husserl's contention that only perceivable things exist and the claim on the part of the theoretical component of the physical sciences that there are imperceptible things. Husserl's statement concerns the ideal possibility of perception, while the claim of theoretical science concerns the real impossibility of perception for human beings. It is entirely possible that an existing thing be imperceivable by a particular species of percipients—or any existing species of percipients—and yet be perceivable in the ideal sense. Such is the case with theoretical entities.

2. CONSCIOUSNESS AND EXISTENCE

We now turn to Husserl's idealism. I will begin with the first of the two core claims that together constitute Husserl's idealism, namely, the claim that the existence of things is somehow dependent upon consciousness. Although, as I pointed out earlier, this claim is not technically incompatible with the existence of theoretical entities, it does bear upon a thesis usually associated with a realist construal of scientific theories, namely, that the existence of theoretical entities is independent of our consciousness of them.[6] Furthermore, Husserl's idealism may be taken to be incompatible with realism in general, insofar as realism with respect to a certain range of entities holds that those entities exist independently of our consciousness of them.

It must be emphasized at the very outset of this section that phenomenology is a reflective discipline. It is not about the objects of consciousness. Rather, it is about the consciousness of objects. If it directs its attention to objects, it does so with respect to the manner in which objects are intended by consciousness. For this reason, the claims that Husserl advances in the name of phenomenology must not be taken as straightforward claims about objects—about either their existence or their properties:

> In the phenomenology of the consciousness of physical things the question is not how physical things in general are, or what in truth

belongs to them as such; but rather how the consciousness of physical things is qualified, what sorts of consciousness of physical things are to be distinguished, or what manner and with what correlates a physical thing as such presents and manifests itself in the manner peculiar to consciousness . . . to make assertions about what belongs eidetically to these sorts of physical-thing-intentions as such—that is not to explore physical things, physical things as such. A "physical thing" as correlate is not a physical thing; therefore the quotation marks. (*ID* III, 72 / *H* V, 84; typography corrected)

In *Phenomenological Psychology*, Husserl repeats the point with the same typographical gesture. In the phenomenological reduction, interest is restricted exclusively to the domain of experience. "The external object belongs there, but purely as that which is meant in the external perception itself, as its transcendent meaning. In phenomenology we say: the object in parentheses or quotation marks, not the object unqualifiedly" (*PP*, 145 / *H* IX, 190). Husserl's use of quotation marks signals the phenomenological shift in attention from object to sense, from the thing of straightforward perception to the noema by which that thing is intended.

This point has not been lost on some of the more perceptive of Husserl's commentators. "Given the nature of such a phenomenology," Aron Gurwitsch writes, "no ontological inquiry [into the question of existence] is to be pursued directly; the inquiry must proceed, so to speak, in an oblique manner."[7] "Raising the ontological problems," he explains, "therefore, means, on phenomenological grounds, embarking upon investigations of acts of consciousness . . . through which the object in question presents itself as existing and from which it derives the specific meaning of its existence."[8] He continues: "With respect to the notions of existence and being this demands . . . inquiry into the intertexture of acts of consciousness through which an object presents itself as existing in a certain mode."[9] Indeed, I will argue that Husserl does not approach the question of existence in a straightforward sense, but that his phenomenological inquiry is directed toward the question of how and under what conditions an object is given and therefore rationally posited as existing. Phenomenology, then, does not deal directly with the question of what exists, but rather with the question of how an object acquires the sense of existing in and through the course of conscious experience (cf. *C*, 145 / *H* VI, 148). In short, what depends upon consciousness is not the existence of things, but rather the justification with which we posit the existence of things.[10] Under this heading Husserl claims that within the phenomenological account, "the object of perception gains its sense of existence by the sense-bestowal which takes place in the series of appearances, in their motivations; that is, intentionally as sense-bestowal" (*PP*, 141 / *H* IX, 184).

This point bears directly on the nature of Husserl's idealism. On the interpretation I am advancing, an object could acquire the sense of actually existing and yet fail to exist actually; similarly, an object could actually exist and yet fail to have acquired the sense of actually existing.[11] Of course it would be irrational to deny the existence of that which has acquired the sense of existing, just as it would be irrational to assert the existence of that which has not acquired the sense of existing. But the conditions for the existence of an object and the conditions for the justification with which we posit the existence of an object are distinct. The metaphysical idealist interpretation of Husserl tends to conflate these conditions, claiming that, for Husserl, an object exists if and only if it is given to consciousness as existing. I will argue that the account of existence in Husserl's phenomenology deals exclusively with the question of how an object is given as existing and, therefore, the conditions under which we are justified in positing it as existing. I will also contend that Husserl himself recognized the distinction between the conditions of existence and the conditions of givenness and justification. Thus Husserl's idealism is not a metaphysical idealism.[12] It does not posit a real dependence of things upon consciousness. In this section I will contend that Husserl's idealism—his "transcendental idealism"—is wholly compatible with realism in general and a realistic construal of scientific theories in particular. I will argue that this is the case because of the rider that attaches itself to all of Husserl's prima facie idealistic claims by virtue of the method and specific subject matter of transcendental phenomenology.

In the light of the above, let us turn to the locus classicus of Husserl's idealism: part 2 of *Ideas* I. There, in section 49, Husserl apparently argues for two interrelated theses: first, that the existence of consciousness is not dependent upon the existence of the world of physical things; and second, that the world of physical things is dependent in its existence upon consciousness (*ID* I, 110 / *H* III 1, 103–4). The being of consciousness is thus "absolute" in the sense that it depends upon nothing else for its existence; moreover, the existence of everything else is relative to consciousness and, thus, dependent upon it.

Here I will conduct an examination of his argument for these two theses with an eye to the way these theses must be qualified in the light of the proper force of the argument together with its methodological context. In the course of the examination, it should become clear that what first appears as a straightforward claim about the existence of things is in fact a claim about the conditions under which we are justified in believing in the existence of things. That is, what depends upon consciousness is not the existence of things *simpliciter*, but the justification with which we posit their existence. Moreover, what initially appears as a denial of the independent existence of things with respect to consciousness is nothing of the sort. Rather, it is an affirmation of the necessary dependence of the rational positing of the existence of things upon the consciousness in which those things are given as existing.

But first a word in defense of my approach. It has sometimes been said that in phenomenology "nothing follows"—a striking claim designed not only to shock an audience, but to emphasize that fact that phenomenology is a purely descriptive discipline. As such, phenomenology does not seek to argue for certain conclusions, but only to uncover and exhibit certain states of affairs that are, in principle, open to intersubjective examination and validation. Is it not inappropriate, then, to embark upon an examination of this text as if it were a stretch of argumentative discourse? Is that not to impose upon it standards essentially foreign to its nature? Not at all. For although it is the case that phenomenology is a descriptive discipline and, therefore, that phenomenological claims can properly be criticized only by going back to the "matters themselves," not everything that Husserl wrote is phenomenology. The better part of *Ideas*, in fact, is not an exercise in phenomenological research into the "matters themselves." Rather, it is an introduction to the idea of phenomenology. More specifically, it is a treatise on the nature of consciousness such that phenomenology as a new discipline can be both conceived and pursued. Insofar as this is the case, it is not phenomenology—it is about phenomenology. It is, to use a popular prefix, metaphenomenological.

In the passage we are about to consider, Husserl wants to establish certain claims about the being of consciousness on the basis of inference and argument.[13] The results of preceding eidetic findings, in which a number of essential distinctions were made pertaining to the differences in the consciousness of ontologically distinct types of objects, are now to function as "premises" from which certain conclusions follow (*ID* I, 103–4 / H III 1, 99). What I propose to do is ascertain the sense of the conclusions on the basis of the arguments given for them together with their methodological context.

Let us turn, then, to Husserl's own formulation of the first thesis: "No real being, no being which is presented and legitimated in consciousness by appearances, is necessary to the being of consciousness itself" (*ID* I, 110 / *H* III 1, 104; emphasis deleted). A second formulation immediately follows the first as, evidently, a direct consequence: "Immanental being [the being of consciousness] is therefore indubitably absolute being in the sense that by essential necessity immanental being *nulla 're' indiget ad existendum* [needs no thing in order to exist]" (*ID* I, 110 / *H* III 1, 104; emphasis deleted).

To convince us of the truth of this first thesis, Husserl asks us to perform a simple thought experiment. Imagine a stream of consciousness in which the course of experience is so chaotic, reduced perhaps to nothing more than an amorphous mass of sensations, that physical objects could never become presented, or constituted, within it as transcendent. Clearly the subject of such a consciousness would never be motivated to posit the existence of transcendent physical objects. Such a course of experience is indeed possible, for there is nothing included in the essence of consciousness that makes it necessary that consciousness be so organized as to consistently and harmoniously present a world of enduring physical objects (*ID* I, 109 / *H* III 1, 103). But even if experience were such that it did not motivate the positing of the existence of physical things transcendent to consciousness, there would still be consciousness, albeit in a sorry, preintentional state. Consciousness can exist, evidently, even if it presents no objects.[14] "Consequently," Husserl states, "no real being, no being which is presented and legitimated in consciousness by appearances, is necessary to the being of consciousness itself" (*ID* I, 109 / *H* III,1, 103; emphasis deleted).

These considerations support the first formulation of the first thesis if they are construed as making the following, relatively weak claim: consciousness, in the broadest sense, need not be intentional. That is, consciousness need not be so organized as to present objects transcendent to it in order to exist and count as consciousness. This weak interpretation of the first thesis is based upon the subordinate clause of the first formulation, which is here construed as limiting those objects from which consciousness is independent to those which might have become constituted within consciousness were it differently organized. This is in fact the only interpretation sustained by the thought experiment. Thus the second formulation, which states that consciousness needs no other thing in order to exist, must be interpreted as claiming only that consciousness need *present* no other thing in order to exist. Husserl is not claiming that the existence of consciousness is independent of physical things in general. For even if consciousness could exist without presenting physical objects, it does not follow that consciousness does not require a physical substrate for its existence—a physical substrate that perhaps never could, in any straightforward sense, become an object for that consciousness were it differently organized.

Perhaps an analogy would help to clarify the point. Imagine a series of photographs taken while a camera was seriously out of focus. Photographs taken under more congenial circumstances usually present physical objects with more or less clarity. These photographs represent no objects, yet they still count as photographs, however disappointing. Reflecting on this case, we might be led to claim that photographs need not represent physical objects in order to exist. But we would not then be entitled to the conclusion that photographs need no physical objects in order to exist. For they regularly require cameras, sensors, storage devices, displays, and batteries in order to exist—all objects that do not usually appear in the photographs themselves, but nonetheless form the material conditions for the existence of photographs as such.

It may be objected here that there are sufficient disanalogies between photographs and perceptual consciousness to make the example both irrelevant and uninstructive. Surely there are many differences between photographs and consciousness: one is itself a physical object, while the other is a temporal stream of mental processes; one represents things by way of images, the other has the capacity to present the things themselves. But there is enough of a similarity in their representational function to make the point. Just as it does not follow that because photographs need not represent objects in order to exist and count as photographs their existence is independent of physical objects in general, so it does not follow that because consciousness need not present physical objects that its existence is independent of all physical reality. Consciousness may indeed exist independently of all real being, but its existential independence does not follow as a consequence of the proposed thought experiment.

Let us now turn to the second thesis. Husserl gives it the following formulation: "The world of transcendent '*res*' is entirely dependent upon consciousness " (*ID* I, 109 / *H* III 1, 103; my translation).[15] To demonstrate the dependence of the physical world upon consciousness, Husserl proposes another thought experiment, in many ways the reverse of the preceding thought experiment used to establish the first thesis. We are asked to imagine a person who is able to bring about, presumably at will, a regular organization of conscious experience such that it consistently and harmoniously presents a world of physical objects, where "nothing is lacking which is requisite for the appearance of a unitary world." Husserl then asks the rhetorical question "Is it still conceivable and not rather a countersense [*widersinnig*] that the corresponding world does not exist?" (*ID* I, 111 / *H* III 1, 105). Obviously he expects the reader to reply that it would not be conceivable that such a world would not exist.

It would seem, then, that Husserl's claim amounts to the following: if a physical world is constituted within consciousness as existing, then, necessarily, it exists. But such is not the case. For Husserl himself admits that it is logically possible that a world other than the one presently constituted within consciousness actually exists (*ID* I, 108 / *H* III 1, 102). But, he continues, such a world would be, materially, a "countersense" (i.e., absurd):

> The hypothetical assumption of something real outside this world is, of course, "logically" possible; obviously it involves no formal contradiction. But when we ask about the essential conditions on which its [the hypothetical assumption's] validity would depend, about the mode of demonstration demanded by its sense, when we ask the mode of demonstration taken universally, essentially determined by the positing of something transcendent . . . we recognize that something transcendent necessarily must be experienceable, not merely by an Ego conceived as a empty possibility but by an actual Ego as a demonstrable unity relative to its concatenations of experience. (*ID* I, 108 / *H* III 1, 102)

From this passage it is evident that the absurdity of a world failing to exist even though it has been constituted within consciousness as existing, or the absurdity of the world existing otherwise than it has been constituted within consciousness, must be understood in a justification-theoretic context. For experience is not brought in as a desideratum with respect to the question of existence in the straightforward sense, but rather with respect to the question of the validity of existence-claims. As Karl Ameriks pointed out in commenting on this passage, "the idea [of the world constituted in consciousness failing to exist] is not self-contradictory but it is 'absurd' in that it involves a positing which has no justification in experience."[16] Thus, "for Husserl, full harmonious experience does not entail the existence of things, although it does make absurd the denial of their being."[17] Conversely, "were one's mind suitably impoverished the assertion of transcendent items would be unjustified and without motivation."[18] Again, what depends upon consciousness and the harmonious course of its experiences is not the existence of the physical world per se, but the justification with which we posit the existence of the physical world. It is logically possible that the world is otherwise than it is constituted within consciousness; but we would be unjustified in believing that it was.

To claim that the question of existence in Husserl's phenomenology must be posed within a justification-theoretic context is to insist that the concept of existence is always a matter of existence "for us." That is, it is always a question of existence insofar as it could be rationally posited by us. As Wesley Morriston points out, the "for us" qualification, which Husserl does not always append to the terms "being" and "existence," is "all important."[19] With the phenomenological shift of attention from the object *simpliciter* to the way in which objects are given in and through the synthesis of consciousness, there is the concomitant disclosure of the "universal accomplishing life in which the world comes to be," Husserl says, "as existing *for us*" (C, 145 / H VI, 148; my emphasis). Within this methodologically induced context, it is perfectly consistent with a realist position to claim, as Husserl does in *Formal and Transcendental Logic*, that "anything that can exist, and be this or that, *for him* (accordingly, that can have sense for him and be accepted by him as existent and as being this or that) must be something of which he has consciousness in the shape of an appurtenant intentional performance, which corresponds to the particularity of that existent" (FTL, 244 / H XVII, 216; my emphasis). Shifting to the first person singular, Husserl makes the same point in *Ideas* II. Through phenomenological reflection I attain the essence of a sphere of self-enclosed experience. "To this essence pertains all actual and possible experience by means of which the Objective world is there *for me* with all the experiential verifications in which it has for me ontological validity, one that is verified even if never scientifically examined" (ID II, 416 / H V, 149, my emphasis). "My phenomenologically self-enclosed proper essence can be posited absolutely, as the Ego (and I am this Ego) that bestows ontological validity on the being of the world of which I speak at any time. It is *for me* and is what it is *for me* only insofar as it acquires sense and self-confirming validity from my own pure life and from that of the others who are disclosed to me in my own life" (ID II, 416–17 / H V, 149, my emphasis). Furthermore, in this context, it is perfectly consistent with a realistic position to claim that consciousness "precedes the being of the world." For the precedence and priority of consciousness holds only "from the standpoint of cognition" (FTL, 228 / H XVII, 202). The priority of consciousness is a priority that is indexed to "everything which conceivably has being *for me*" (*C*, 78 / *H* VI, 79–80; my emphasis). It is the "primitive basis" not of everything that exists, but of "everything *I accept as existent*" (*FTL*, 239 / *H* XVII, 212; my emphasis).

In transcendental phenomenology, existence is always a question of how objects are given as existing such that they have the sense of existing for me. For that very reason, all existence will be referred back to those intentional experiences in which something comes to be constituted as existing. "Whatever I encounter as an existing object," Husserl writes in *Formal and Transcendental Logic*, "is something that . . . has received its whole being sense *for me* from my effective intentionality, not a shadow of that sense remains excluded from my effective intentionality" (*FTL*, 234 / *H* XVII, 207; my emphasis). Again, in *Cartesian Meditations*, he states that "this world, with all its Objects . . . derives its whole sense and its existential status, which it has *for me*, from me myself, from me as the transcendental Ego, the Ego who comes to the fore only with the transcendental-phenomenological *epoché*" (*CM*, 26 / *H* I, 65; my emphasis).[20] In the intersubjective context, "an experienced object holds for us as an actuality of experience, as an existing real thing, which we designate afterwards as a member of the real and actually existing world, insofar as it holds for us as something harmoniously experienceable by ever new experience—one's own and others', actual or to be made possible—as what is continuously confirmed *for us*, or possibly, what could have been consistently confirmed" (*PP*, 71–72 / *H* IX, 95; my emphasis). Formulations such as these clearly do not entail the claim that objects are metaphysically dependent upon consciousness for their existence.

In his entry on Husserl's transcendental idealism for *The Cambridge Companion to Husserl*, however, Herman Philipse argues that Husserl's transcendental idealism was in fact an idealism of the metaphysical sort. In his analysis of the world destruction passage in section 49 of *Ideas* I, he claims that Husserl's argument for idealism can be rendered valid only if one assumes what he calls the "principle of immanence," the notion that all perceived objects and their properties are nothing but internal mental contents, images on the inner screen of consciousness. Therefore, he argues, this principle must have been Husserl's assumption. The principle of immanence, however, cannot be read off the face of experience; it is not simply there waiting for theoretically innocent phenomenological description. It was in fact established in the early modern period on the basis of the causal explanations of the relationship between the mind and the world offered by the new physics of Galileo and company. Here Husserl's "descriptivist ideology" kept him from realizing that he was philosophically dependent on the very tradition from which he thought he had attained critical distance.[21]

Philipse's Husserl interpretation deserves a few comments. It is impressively detailed and documented; it is no doubt influential, but it is also completely wrongheaded. To assign the principle of immanence to Husserl is to ignore the distinction Husserl repeatedly and explicitly drew between the immanent contents of consciousness and the transcendent object of consciousness, more specifically, between sensations and perceived physical objects.

Philipse develops his case by enacting a series of reductions on Husserl's behalf: the putative transcendent object of our awareness is an intended object of consciousness; the intended object is an intentional correlate of transcendental consciousness; the intentional correlate of transcendental consciousness is constituted by way of adumbrations (a series of profiles, of appearances); and adumbrations are to be identified with sensations, immanent components of consciousness, which in the act of perception are simply—and somewhat deceptively—interpreted objectively.[22] Hence, Philipse argues, if the transcendent object of our awareness is always an intentional correlate of consciousness, and the intentional correlate is always immanent in consciousness as a collection of sensations, then the "transcendent object" is really immanent in consciousness: "The transcendent 'thing itself' is nothing but a complex of *objectified sensations*."[23] The physical thing is in this way reduced to the contents of consciousness, in which case, of course, it follows that consciousness exists independently of an external physical world (since there is none), and the physical world depends upon consciousness for its existence (since it is part of the contents of consciousness). Thus does Philipse convert Husserl's position into a kind of transcendental version of Berkeley's idealism.[24]

Philipse's contention that for Husserl physical objects are just objectified sensations is based upon the theory of perception he claims to find in the *Logical Investigations* (especially the first edition). But it is in fact wholly contrary to Husserl's emphases in both editions of the *Logical Investigations* on the distinction between sensations and the physical objects presented by their means. Granted, on Husserl's account, physical objects and their properties are presented in perception on the basis of an objective interpretation (*Auffassung*) of sensations; but this is not to make sensations the objects of perception. "Sensations, animated by interpretations, present objective determinations [i.e., objective properties] in corresponding percepts of things, but they are not themselves," Husserl notes, "these objective determinations. The apparent object, as it appears in the appearance, transcends the appearance as a phenomenon" (*LI* I, 356 / *H* XIX 1, B 129). Take the example of the objective determination of the color of a red ball. Typically, that color is perceived as uniform, while the sensations by which this objective color is presented are varied in hue and tone. One will have to recognize, as a descriptive feature of the perceptual experience, "the difference between the red of the ball, objectively seen as uniform, and the indubitable, unavoidable projective differences among the subjective color-sensations in our percept" (*LI* II, 538 / *H* XIX 1, B 349). Thus, turning a critical remark toward Berkeley and all who would follow him, "it is the fundamental defect of phenomenalistic theories that they draw no distinction between appearance as intentional experience, and the apparent object (the subject of objective predicates), and therefore identify the experienced complex of sensation with the complex of objective features" (*LI* II, 546 / *H* XIX 1, A 338). Again Husserl explicitly states that "sensational content differs from that of the perceived object presented by it, which is not a reality in consciousness" (*LI* II, 565 / *H* XIX 1, B 382). For that reason, "it is phenomenologically false to say that the difference between a conscious content in perception, and the external object perceived (or perceptually intended) in it, is a mere difference in mode of treatment, the same appearance being at one time dealt with in a subjective connection . . . and at another time in an objective connection" (*LI* II, 538 / *H* XIX 1, B 349). In a warning that readers of Philipse's interpretation should take to heart, Husserl issues this statement: "We should not be led astray by the fact that we make an equivocal use of the same words to refer to the sensuously apparent determinations of things, and to the presentative aspects of our percepts, and that we at one time speak of 'color,' 'smoothness,' 'shape,' etc., in the sense of objective properties, and at another time in the sense of sensations" (*LI* I, 356 / *H* XIX 1, B 129). The equivocation of which Husserl speaks would not be possible unless sensations, the "presentative aspects of our percepts," and the perceived properties of objects were two different things. Clearly, if Husserl is an idealist in the metaphysical sense, it is not because he collapses the distinction between sensations and physical objects.

I have been developing a case for the position that Husserl's transcendental idealism is consistent with the basic claims of realism, that is, that things exist apart from consciousness, and that the existence of such things is not dependent upon consciousness. Of course one would be rationally unjustified in positing the existence of a thing apart from some consciousness of it.

But here what depends upon consciousness is not the existence of the thing posited, but the justification with which we posit its existence. Up to this point, my case has been based upon two considerations: (1) The specific methodological context of Husserl's claims concerning the relation between consciousness and reality. In the phenomenological turn from things to the consciousness of things, from things to how things are given to consciousness, the question of existence *simpliciter* (*Sein*) is transmuted into the question of the sense of existence (*Seinssinn*). What is necessarily correlated to consciousness and dependent upon it is not existence per se, but the sense of existence. This follows directly from the fact that while the object of consciousness is not a part of consciousness, the sense is—it is an intentional component of consciousness by which the act achieves a direction to its object under a certain description. The sense of existence that an object acquires is that intentional component of the act in which the object is intended as existing. The specific justification-theoretic methodological context for phenomenological claims about existence is signaled, as we pointed out, by the "for us" locution often—but not always—employed by Husserl. What is of interest, what is within the proper competence of phenomenology, is the question of the existence of things insofar as their existence achieves validity for us in and through the course of conscious experience—that is, insofar as an object acquires the sense of existence for us. (2) The specific arguments Husserl sets forth for the prima facie idealist claim that the existence of the physical world is dependent upon consciousness demonstrate only that the justification with which we posit the existence of the physical world is dependent upon a consciousness in which the physical world is given as existing.

But our case for the compatibility of Husserl's phenomenological idealism and the core claims of realism need not be limited to such circumspection. We find corroboration from Husserl himself. In his "*Nachwort*" to *Ideas* I, published in 1931, Husserl himself states, "Above all: phenomenological idealism does not deny the actual existence of the real world (in the first place, that means nature), as if it maintained that the world were mere semblance, to which natural thinking and the positive sciences would be subject, though unwittingly." For phenomenology's "sole task and accomplishment is to clarify the *sense* of this world, precisely the *sense* in which everyone accepts it—and rightly so—as actually existing" (*ID* II 420 / *H* V, 152; my emphasis). That the world exists, and that the world is given as existing in experience, is, Husserl claims, completely indubitable ("*vollkomen zweifellos*"), even though it is always possible ("*immerfort denkbar*") that the world does not exist despite the fact that it has been given as existing (*ID* II 420 / *H* V, 153). For, "of course, experience does not exclude the possibility that it be annulled by future experience or even that the real be not at all, though it had been given in a concordant way" (*ID* II, 81 / *H* IV, 76). With respect to the dependency relation between consciousness and the world, the "relativity" of the real world to transcendental subjectivity, the results of the phenomenological clarification of the manner of existence of the real world show only that the real world can acquire its sense as existing (*Sinn als seiende*) only as an intentional sense-formation of transcendental subjectivity (*ID* II, 420 / *H* V, 153). Again, Husserl's claim is not that the existence of the physical world is dependent upon consciousness, but rather its sense as existing. That existence and the sense of existence are not equivalent is evidenced by Husserl's contention that it is logically possible that the world acquire the sense of existence in the course of conscious experience and at the same time fail to exist.

3. THE "EXISTENCE-INDEPENDENCE" OF INTENTIONAL RELATIONS

There is a deeper reason for the fact that, in Husserl's phenomenology, there is no necessary connection between an object's existence and its being constituted within consciousness as existing. It stems from what David Woodruff Smith and Ronald McIntyre have called the "existence-independence" of intentional relations—a property of intentional relations that Husserl recognized and enunciated already in the *Logical Investigations*.[25] The existence-independence of intentional relations, once recognized, makes possible the phenomenological reduction in which the question of the actual existence of objects intended is set in abeyance, while at the same time retaining the objects as intended for phenomenological description. It also eliminates any metaphysical idealist implications from Husserl statements concerning the necessary correlation of experience and being qua experienced.

Intentionality, as we have already noted, designates a basic and distinguishing property of consciousness: consciousness is always consciousness of something. This is not to say that all processes occurring in the stream of consciousness are intentional. Sensations are generally taken to be nonintentional mental processes. Sensations are not of an object, even if they were caused by one. But if sensations are taken up into perceptual consciousness, that perceptual consciousness will be of an object. This would seem to suggest that there is something like an "intentional relation," a relation that holds between consciousness and the object of which it is conscious. Husserl says as much in *Ideas* I, section 36: "Insofar as they [intentional experiences] are conscious of something, they are said to be 'intentionally related' to ['*intentional bezogen' auf*] this something" (ID I, 73 / H III 1, 74; my translation). But here Husserl emphasizes that by "intentional relation" he does not have in mind a specie of real relations, that is, a contingent relation between a real psychological event and a real object. Rather, an intentional relation is essential to the act itself. An act of consciousness is intrinsically related to the object of which it is conscious. And this relation is evidently other than and distinct from whatever real relation may obtain between that act and an actual object (ID I, 73 / H III 1, 74).

If the intentional act is not necessarily related to an actual object, then what is it related to? It would seem that if the intentional relation is like other dyadic relations, it requires the existence of both terms in order to obtain. Both the act and the object must be actual. If I am smaller than the private detective who has been stalking me for the last five months, then presumably there must be a private detective such that I am smaller than him. Otherwise, the relation of "being smaller than" would not hold between me and the private detective. On the other hand, the detective need not exist in order for me to have a fear of a detective. The feared detective may be the product of my paranoia. Nonetheless, my fear has an object—and necessarily so, Husserl would add—namely, the private detective feared. This would be the case even if he did not exist. To what, then, is my intentional act of fear related, if not to an existing object?

One response to this question, construing intentional relations to be like real relations with respect to their existence-dependence, would have it that the direct object of my fear is an "intentional object," which exists, if nowhere else, in the mind. If the intentional relation is to hold, both terms of the relation must exist. If consciousness is consciousness of an object, then there must be an object of which it is conscious. If this object does not enjoy real existence, then it must at least have an intentional existence, an existence in the mind, an "inexistence." An object of this unique ontological type would then be the direct and immediate object of all mistaken perceptions and hallucinations, where the objects that the intentional act takes itself to be about fail to exist in reality. The postulation of such entities would also account for the possibility of thinking about or imagining nonexistent external objects, such as fictional characters or mythical beings. All such intentional acts of consciousness would be duly supplied with their own objects, which exist—but only intentionally.

For the sake of consistency, this response generally holds that intentional objects are the direct and immediate objects of all intentional experience, veridical or not. Hence the difference between veridical and nonveridical cases of perception is not that the former have the actual external thing as their direct object, while the latter have nothing but the internal intentional object. Rather, they both have intentional objects as their direct objects. In the case of veridical perception, it just so happens that there is an actual thing in the neighborhood that corresponds to the intentional object. This actual thing, however, is not the immediate object of the perception. Perception of an "external" object is actually a perception of an "internal" object—the intentional object—accompanied by a belief that an external object corresponding to the internal object exists or is determined in a certain way. Such a belief is the result of an instinctual inference procedure, a procedure taught to us by nature, as Descartes would have it, that takes place within us with such ease and with such rapidity that we are rarely aware of its occurrence. For this reason we are inclined to think that the direct and immediate object of our perception is the external object itself. But, as Hume states in his *Enquiry*, even the smallest dose of philosophical reflection would disabuse us of such a mistake (*Enquiry*, section 12, part 1). It is also typical of this response to the question of the object of intentional experience to hold that the direct intentional object has the function of representing the putative actual thing. It may do so as either an image, as in Descartes, or a sign, as in Locke.

There are a number of reasons for thinking that Husserl himself does not make this typically modern, representational account of intentional relations his own. One is his explicit rejection of the representational theory of the intentional object. In an act of perception, what is perceived, according to Husserl, is not an ontologically novel type of internal object that serves as an image or a sign of an external object, but rather the external object itself—if, indeed, it exists. When I perceive, in a furtive backward glance, the private detective, it is the private detective himself that I perceive—provided he actually exists—and not an image or a sign of the private detective existing in my mind. Husserl contends in section 90 of *Ideas* I that it would be tempting to separate the intentional object from the actual object in order to account for cases of being intentionally related to what would otherwise be a nonexistent object. But then, he objects, all cases of perception would involve two existing objects, two "realities," when in fact there is only one, namely, the actual external thing perceived and not some hypothetically interpolated mental surrogate. "I perceive the physical thing, the Object belonging to Nature, the tree out there in the garden; and that and nothing else is the actual Object of the perceptual 'intention'" (*ID* I, 219 / *H* III 1, 207–8). One finds a similar, and equally emphatic statement to the same effect in the appendix to sections 11 and 20 of the Fifth Logical Investigation:

> It is a serious error to draw a real distinction between "merely immanent" or "intentional" objects, on the one hand, and "transcendent," "actual" objects, which may correspond to them on the other. It is an error whether one makes the distinction between a sign or image really present in consciousness and the thing it stands for, or whether one substitutes for the "immanent" object some other real datum of consciousness, a content, e.g. as a sense-giving factor. . . . It need only be said to be acknowledged that the intentional object [here the object that is intended] of a presentation is the same as its actual object, and on occasion as its external object, and that it is absurd to distinguish between them. (*LI* II, 595 / *H* XIX 1, 439; emphasis deleted translation corrected)

Another reason for thinking that Husserl has no truck with the account of the intentional object outlined above is that the postulation of an ontologically unique intentional object as the direct and immediate object of consciousness is altogether unmotivated by his theory of intentional relations. According to Husserl, the intentional relation is unlike real relations in that it does not require the actual existence of its object term in order to obtain. In section 11 of the Fifth Logical Investigation, he states, "Intentional experiences have the peculiarity of directing themselves in varying fashion to presented objects, but they do so in an intentional sense. An object is 'referred to' [*gemeint*] or 'aimed at' [*abgezielt*] in them, and in presentative or judging or other fashion. . . . If this experience is presentation, *eo ipso* and through its own essence (we must insist), the intentional 'relation' to an object is achieved, and an object is 'intentionally present'; these two phrases mean precisely the same" (*LI* II, 558 / *H* XIX 1, 386). Later on in the Fifth Logical Investigation Husserl writes,

> If I represent God to myself, or an angel, or an intelligible thing-in-itself, or a physical thing or a round square etc., I mean the transcendent object named in each case, in other words my intentional object: it makes no difference whether this object exists or is

> imaginary or absurd. "The object is merely intentional" does not mean, of course, that it exists, but only in an intention, of which it is a real part, or that some shadow of it exists. It means rather that the intention, the reference to an object so qualified, exists, but not that the object does. If the intentional object exists, the intention, the reference, does not exist alone, but the thing referred to exists also. (*LI* II, 596 / *H* XIX 2, 439)

The intentional act refers to its object, whether that object exists or not. "Relating-itself-to-something-transcendent, to refer to it in one way or another, is an inner characteristic" of the act (*IP*, 10 / *H* II, 46). For this reason, Husserl says, "it makes no difference what sort of being we give our object . . . the act remains 'directed upon' its object" (*LI* II, 587 / *H* XIX 2, 427).[26]

In *Ideas* I Husserl claims that "the perceived as perceived stands over against the perceiving in a way excluding the question of whether the perceived truly exists" (*ID* I, 232 / *H* III 1, 221). Although any act of perceiving, or thinking, or remembering will necessarily have its object, this does not mean that there is an object that is perceived, thought, or remembered. Perhaps the private detective referred to above is a mere figment of my troubled imagination. This does not prevent my fear from having its object, namely, the private detective, feared. If I fear a private detective, then my fear has an object, and has it necessarily. Intentional relations, then, have the property of being "existence-independent." As Roderick M. Chisholm puts it, it appears that "one can be 'intentionally related' to something which does not exist."[27] If this is the case, it is not necessary to invent objects of some novel ontological type that could stand in for the intended object just in case the intended object fails to exist in reality.[28] It is possible for an act to be intentionally related to a nonexistent object. No tertium quid, no special intermediate intentional object, need be introduced to guarantee that the intentional relation always have an existing object.

Nevertheless, Husserl does make use of the term "intentional object." At the beginning of section 90 of *Ideas* I, for instance, he states, "Like perception, every intentive mental process—just this makes up the fundamental part of intentionality—has its 'intentional object'" (*ID* I, 217 / *H* III 1, 221). Here everything hangs on precisely what Husserl means by "intentional object." Fortunately, we do not have to look far to discover what he means, for in the very sentence just quoted, Husserl adds, "i.e. its objective sense" to the phrase "intentional object." Now the objective sense of an intentional act is not its direct object, but that component of the act whereby it refers to an object (see *IP*, 17 / *H* II, 20). As such the objective sense, the central core of the "noema" in Husserl's later terminology, is, as Smith and McIntyre put it, an abstract intentional entity that can be objectified only in a special act of phenomenological reflection.[29] The sense, or intentional object here, of an act, then, is not the object of the act, but that component of an act by which it refers to its object. In straightforward experience it is hidden.

The upshot of Husserl's position on the existence-independence of intentional relations is that intentional acts have the capacity to present objects in a way that does not presuppose a real relation to the object presented. Smith and McIntyre make this clear when they point out that

> even if the intention is unsuccessful—i.e., even if there exists no object as that which the content prescribes—the "prescribing," or "pointing" character of the content is unaffected; for the act's being intentional in virtue of having this content is independent of the existence or non-existence of an intended object—indeed, it is independent of the existence of anything not found among the phenomenological, or transcendental, feature of the experience. Accordingly, this "pointing" character of an act's content must be an intrinsic feature of the content, due to its very own nature alone; and it is therefore not properly analyzable in terms of any natural, or empirical, relations that might happen to obtain between the content (or act) and object.[30]

It is for this reason that the transcendental reduction can be put into effect with no net phenomenological loss. Even though the question of the existence of the object has been set aside, everything within the intentional act remains the same, but is now open for description with respect to precisely how it intends objects. Thus it is the very existence-independence of intentional relations that makes the key methodological step in phenomenology possible. By the same token, it prevents any metaphysical idealist inference from the consciousness of things to the actual existence of things. For as the intentional relation is independent of the existence of the object intended, so the existence of the object intended is independent of the intentional relation. An object can be constituted within consciousness as existing, and yet fail to exist. Again, what depends upon consciousness is the givenness of the object as existing and hence the justification with which the object is posited as existing.

Since the transcendental reduction represents a radicalization of the internalist standpoint, a deliberate restriction to what is in fact given in experience together with the manners of givenness, the mere possibility of things being otherwise than they are constituted, while a formal possibility, provides neither grounds for doubt in any specific case nor grounds for a global skepticism. The mere possibility of being otherwise than constituted represents no epistemological threat with respect to the justification of a belief. For any rational assertion or denial of existence must be based upon some form of evidence, some form of givenness within consciousness (*FTL*, 201 / *H* XVII, 179). Mere possibility provides no rational grounds for assertoric claims, be they affirmations or denials. Thus, all that anyone could ask for by way of an internalist theory of justified belief is already available in transcendentally reduced consciousness. Descartes's attempt to guarantee the epistemic reliability of consciousness by going outside consciousness, beyond all "egological validities," by way of an argument for the existence and veracity of God represents a failure, Husserl says, to appreciate this crucial point. For already within the intentional acts of the transcendental ego, "the world has all the ontic meaning it can ever have for him" (*C*, 82 / *H* VI, 84).

4. THE ONTOLOGICAL STATUS OF THE NOEMA

We move now to what I characterized at the beginning of this chapter as the second core claim ascribed to Husserl in the metaphysical idealistic interpretation of his phenomenology: the claim that real objects are nothing more than intentional formations of consciousness. In section 2 I considered the claim that for Husserl physical objects are nothing more than objectified sensations. Here I will consider the claim that physical objects are nothing more than unified systems of noemata (unlike Philipse, I do not identify noemata with sensations). On this interpretation of phenomenological ontology, things have no existence independently of consciousness. Indeed, how can they, since they are nothing but intentional components of consciousness? Furthermore, such an interpretation is incompatible with a realistic construal of scientific theories, if we include in this construal the claim that theoretical entities exist independently of consciousness.

In this section I will reject such idealistic interpretations of Husserl as predicated on a misreading of the ontological status and semantic function of the noema. Much philosophical ink has been spilled of late over the question of Husserl's concept of the noema. I cannot not adequately review and assess all the relevant secondary literature here. But given that I am arguing for the thesis that Husserl's phenomenology is compatible not only with a realistic construal of scientific theory, but with the general realist claim that things exist independently of consciousness, I am at least obligated to mark out my position with respect to that literature. Here I will argue that in Husserl's phenomenology, there is no ontological reduction of real objects to systems of noemata. Rather, what one finds is a methodological correlation of real objects that are intended with the systems of noemata by which they are intended.

The idealistic interpretation of Husserl has no lack of proponents. In his work on Husserl's philosophy of science, Christopher Prendergast claims that "animated by various acts, the object, by virtue of the fundamental achievement of intentionality, ceases to be something 'transcendent' to consciousness. It becomes an immanent meaning, a noema."[31] Similarly, Louis Dupré holds that "the object belongs to the act of consciousness itself; it is not outside it. It is not even an independent reality within consciousness itself. Rather it is a moment of consciousness which is constituted as soon as consciousness itself is constituted."[32] Although Aron Gurwitsch distinguishes between the thing as perceived (the perceptual noema) and the thing that is perceived, the relation between the two is one of part to whole. The thing that is perceived is nothing other than the entire system of possible noemata by which it is presented: "The thing cannot be perceived except in one or the other manner of adumbrational presentation. It is nothing besides, or in addition to, the multiplicity of those presentations through all of which it appears in its identity. Consequently, the thing perceived proves to be the group, more precisely put, the systematically organized totality of adumbrational presentations. Both the difference and the relationship between the thing perceived and a particular perceptual noema can now be defined in terms of a noematic system as a whole and one member of that system."[33]

A number of Husserl commentators believe that Husserl's ontological reduction of what is naively taken to be the external thing to an intentionally immanent system of noemata is motivated by the epistemological problem of transcendence. As we already indicated in chapter 2, Husserl took the problem of transcendence—the problem of how subjective acts of cognition can make contact with and correspond to an external object—as the key problem for critical epistemology. Edward G. Ballard formulates this problem as the problem of "how the cognitive subject can possibly get outside itself to gain access to the object."³⁴ Husserl's transcendental idealism is then understood as the phenomenological solution to this problem. This solution, as Ballard represents it, amounts to reducing being to consciousness, or, more specifically, to the intentional components of consciousness, the noemata. "Object-noemata," Ballard explains, "are within the sphere of consciousness—although they are quite naturally assumed to be external to consciousness; consequently, the sphere of conscious being includes all that is; thus the natural world is not separate from subjectivity; and thus, finally, the playing rules of consciousness apply within the natural world."³⁵ Idealistic phenomenological ontology, then, serves as Husserl's transcendental deduction of the categories of the understanding. There is a guaranteed fit between consciousness and being because being just is a component of consciousness. There is no being outside consciousness. To make contact with the natural world, consciousness need not reach out beyond itself. Thus the epistemological problem of transcendence is not so much solved as it is eliminated, exposed as a pseudo-problem.

Theodore De Boer takes the same approach. The problem of transcendence as formulated in Husserl's pretranscendental works, he contends, was "insoluble."³⁶ Husserl's turn to transcendental idealism represents a "radical" solution to the problem in that it does not seek to solve the problem on its own level, but to expose it as ill-formulated:

> As to the epistemological difficulty, [Husserl's] idealism amounts to a radical solution of the problem of transcendence, because it undermines the foundations of the presuppositions that defined the problem in the [*Logical*] *Investigations*. In the Fundamental Meditation of Phenomenology [section 49 of *Ideas* I] Husserl shows that the material thing and material nature as a whole do not enjoy an independent existence. They exist as a dependent correlate of consciousness. This means that the presupposition of a naturalistic ontology—i.e. the (hypo)thesis of the natural attitude—has no phenomenological foundation. It is an illusion. The true presupposition (=ground) of the world is consciousness. This is the Copernican revolution in ontology which Husserl desires to bring about by the transcendental reduction.³⁷

As a solution to the epistemological problem of transcendence, the transcendental reduction is, on this view, at the same time an ontological reduction.

The object that, in the natural attitude, appeared to exist independently of consciousness, is reduced to an intentional component within consciousness. The object is now, De Boer writes, "the central point of unity in a series of noemata; it is not something behind the noema but an intrinsic feature of it."[38]

This reductive claim on the part of the idealistic interpretation of Husserl, as articulated above by its several representatives, is to be rejected for its failure to grasp the nature of the noema in two respects. First, it misconstrues the ontological status of the noema. If I perceive a real object, say, a tree, the object that I perceive is not a noema. Nor is it a system of noemata. Nor does the tree become a noema or a system of noemata within the act of phenomenological reflection. For real objects and noemata, as Husserl repeatedly emphasizes, belong to ontologically distinct categories. The former are real entities; the latter are ideal entities. "The tree *simpliciter*," says Husserl, "can burn up, be resolved into its chemical elements, etc. But the sense [i.e., the noematic correlate]—the sense of this perception, something belonging necessarily to its essence—cannot burn up; it has no chemical elements, no forces, no real properties" (*ID* I, 216 / *H* III 1, 205). Noema and object have different kinds of properties because they belong to distinct realms of being: "While objects *simpliciter* (understood in the unmodified sense) stand under fundamentally different highest genera, all object-sense and all noemas taken completely, no matter how different they may be otherwise, are of essential necessity of one single highest genus" (*ID* I, 307 / *H* III 1, 295–96). Just as a whole cannot be composed of parts that belong to a fundamentally different ontological realm, so a real object cannot be a whole composed of noemata as its parts. "The tree *simpliciter*, the physical thing belonging to Nature, is anything but this perceived tree as perceived which, as perceptual sense, belongs inseparably to the perception" (*ID* I, 216 / *H* III 1, 205; my translation).[39]

Yet Husserl does refer to the noema of an act of perception as the "perceived object as perceived." This would seem to indicate that the noema is indeed the object of the perceptual act, albeit the object under a certain aspect, namely, "as perceived." But what Husserl actually means by the "perceived as perceived" is something quite different. In section 88 of *Ideas* I, he speaks of the "perceived as perceived" as the noema of a perception, and then immediately proceeds to identify its core with the "perceptual sense" of the perceptual act. The "perceptual sense," as the noematic *Sinn* of the act of perception, is not the object of the act, but the intentional component of the act whereby it refers to its object. When Husserl refers to the "object as perceived," he is not referring to a determination of the real object, but to the determining sense of the conscious act by which that object is intended. The noema, then, is not the object of a given act, nor even the object of an act under a certain aspect, but rather the sense of an act by which the act refers to its specific object. "Like the Fregean sense," writes Jitendramath N. Mohanty, "the noema of an act makes reference possible, i.e., makes it possible that the act be directed to this, and such an, object rather that to another."[40]

We should remind ourselves at this point that phenomenology is a reflective discipline; what it describes is not the object of consciousness, but the consciousness of the object. The difference is decisive for the very sense of phenomenological claims. As Husserl points out in *Ideas* III, "as phenomenologists we also execute positings [of existence], actual theoretical position-takings, but they are exclusively directed toward lived-processes and lived-process correlates [i.e., the noetic and noematic components of experience]. In ontology, on the other hand, we perform actual positings that are directed toward the objects pure and simple, instead of toward the correlates and objects in quotation marks . . . to posit physical things as actually present is not to posit something meant as a physical thing, it is not to posit something posited as a physical thing as such" (*ID* III, 76 / *H* V, 88–89). To emphasize the ontological difference between the noema and the object, Husserl underscores the semantic function of the noema by relating it to the linguistic notion of meaning or "signification" (*Bedeutung*). (Unlike Frege, Husserl thinks of *Bedeutung* not as the referent of an act but as the specifically linguistic version of *Sinn*, of sense.) As a speech act achieves reference to an object or state of affairs by virtue of its meaning (*Bedeutung*), so intentional acts in general achieve reference to objects or states of affairs by virtue of their sense (*Sinn*), which lies at the core of any noema (see also *ID* I, 309 / *H* III 1, 297). Moreover, just as the meaning of a straightforward speech act is not the object of that act, nor the object of that act under a special aspect, so the noema is not the object of a straightforward intentional act, nor the object of that act under a special aspect. The two cases are parallel because "the noema in general is, however, nothing more than the universalization of the idea of [linguistic] signification to the total province of the acts" (*ID* III, 76 / *H* V, 89; translation modified).

For any possible object of consciousness there is a system of noemata whereby it may be intended, but the object is not identical with that system. For any given act, the noema functions as its sense, not its referent. This noema can, of course, be objectified within an act of phenomenological reflection, but here the noema is not the object of the act reflected upon under a new aspect, but sense of the act reflected upon such that it refers to that object. The phenomenological reduction, which discloses the domain of transcendental consciousness with its noetic-noematic structure, then, does not involve or require the ontological reduction of the real object to a system of noemata. Rather, it sets up a methodological correlation between the two. For any intentional experience, phenomenology is in the position to describe how the object of that experience is presented in precisely the way that it is. The description rendered is not a description of the object. Rather, it is directed to the intentional component—the noematic correlate—of the act in which the object is intended. Noematic descriptions, which make use of the same terms employed in straightforward descriptions of the object, nonetheless undergo a radical transformation of sense. They no longer refer to properties of objects, but to components of the noema (*ID* I, 216 / *H* III 1, 205).[41]

5. SUMMARY

The major thesis of this study is that Husserl's phenomenology is wholly compatible with a realistic interpretation of scientific theories. There are, however, a number of claims Husserl is wont to make that provide prima facie evidence to the contrary. In each case, however, I have endeavored to show that the apparent incompatibility between Husserl's phenomenology and realism is in fact merely apparent. First, we examined the relation between perception and existence. Theoretical entities posited in the explanatory theories of the physical sciences are imperceptible. Husserl limits the extent of real existence to that which is perceivable. Yet we noted that what he meant by "perceivable" was not perceivable by human beings, but perceivable by some possible consciousness. Real existence is thus tied to the ideal possibility of perception, not to the real possibility of perception on the part of a particular species of percipients. The imperceptibility of theoretical entities, however, is a real, not an ideal imperceptibility. Thus the realistic construal of scientific theories and Husserl's phenomenology are compatible on this score.

Second, Husserl claims in *Ideas* I that the existence of things is dependent upon consciousness. It would then seem that those things that do not, or cannot, appear in consciousness cannot exist. That is, only those things that are, or can be, given within consciousness as existing can exist. Yet we pointed out that when such claims are considered in terms of the force of the arguments Husserl marshals for them together with their proper methodological context, it turns out that what is dependent upon consciousness is not the existence of things, but the justification with which we posit their existence. Thus it is possible that things exist apart from any consciousness of them, although it is not possible that asserting their existence is justified apart from some consciousness of them.

Third, Husserl will sometimes say that, from the phenomenological standpoint, an object just is the unity of a system of noemata. This would seem to indicate an ontological reduction of real objects to systems of intentional components within consciousness, a form of idealism incompatible with realism in general. Yet we noted that Husserl insists that real objects and noemata belong to radically different categories of being. Furthermore, the semantic function Husserl assigns to the noema means that the noema is not the object of a straightforward intentional act, but rather that component of the act by which the act refers to its object. Given phenomenology's exclusive direction to the real and intentional components of the acts of consciousness, it follows that what Husserl means by the "object" as a unity of noemata is not the real object, but the central point of the system of noemata whereby the act achieves its reference to a real object. The "noematic object" is not identified with the real object, but correlated with it.

In our examination of issues that pertain to the relation between perception, consciousness, and existence, I have shown that Husserl's phenomenology allows for the possibility of theoretical existence. It is thus compatible with a realist construal of scientific theories. This is not to say that the phenomenologist, qua phenomenologist, would, or should, participate in the positing of theoretical existence. For the transcendental reduction sets all positing of real existence out of action. But the positing of real existence is set out of action not in order to deny its validity within the natural attitude, which forms the basis for all our lifeworldly activities, both practical and scientific. Rather, it sets such positings out of action both in order to make them thematic and to show under what conditions they are justified without, at the same time, begging the question. Husserl claims that upon the direct and harmonious experience of a real object we, in the natural attitude, are justified in positing its existence. In fact, he says it is impossible not to do so (*ID* I, 111 / *H* III, 92).

Husserl also allows for the rationality of positing the existence of real objects that are not directly experienced, as long as such positing is "based" upon experience. In fact, he claims that "the *de facto* course of our human experiences is such that it constrains our reason to go beyond intuitionally given physical things . . . and base them on the 'truth of physics'" (*ID* I, 103 / *H* III 1, 99). Although Husserl does not specify the various forms of legitimate mediate positing of real existence in any detail, it is at least conceivable that he would have countenanced inference to the best explanation in the physical sciences as a legitimate inferential procedure within the scope of the natural attitude. The physical sciences move beyond the given in order to explain its behavior; phenomenology remains with the given in order to describe its manner of givenness. Although the two disciplines differ in object, goal, and method, they are nonetheless compatible. Any attempt to manufacture an antagonism between the two misconstrues the nature of one, the other, or both. In his 1924 essay on Kant and transcendental phenomenology, Husserl emphasizes precisely this point: in making an inquiry into the modes of objective givenness in the domain of consciousness, which natural life and the life of the sciences presuppose, "no damage of any kind is supposed to be done by that to the proper *legitimacy* of this life." Phenomenology is not to play the skeptic, not to cast doubt on the rationality of everyday life, or on the sciences; it is not to reduce the world to a fiction, or to mere subjective appearances, or deprive it of its sense of being actual. "It does not occur to it to deprive the objective truth of positive science of the least bit of the meaning that it really creates in the actual employment of its naturally evident methods and bears within itself as legitimately valid."[42] Phenomenology does not seek to deny or contradict science, but only to understand it (*C*, 66 / *H* VI, 67). In the *Crisis* Husserl delivered a phenomenological analysis of the physical sciences with respect to the development of exact empirical laws and the constitution of idealized objects. There is no reason why a phenomenology of science could not also proceed to give an intentional analysis of the formation of scientific theories and the constitution of theoretical entities.

CONCLUSION

Our study of Husserl's phenomenological philosophy of the physical sciences has been governed by two overriding considerations: the question concerning the epistemic status and existential import of scientific theories; and the reception of Husserl's philosophy of science in the anglophone secondary literature. Besides giving a general exposition of Husserl's phenomenology as it bears upon the question of science through a close examination of the primary texts, we have also addressed specific positions attributed to Husserl in the secondary literature. A number of those attributions to which we devoted most of our attention not only detract from the prima facie plausibility of Husserl's philosophy of science—they are also seriously mistaken. They were, in brief, that Husserl's philosophy of science is foundationalist and therefore represents science as a system of rigid dogmatic belief closed to future experience; that Husserl's philosophy of science is ambiguous with respect to the cognitive value of the scientific enterprise; and that Husserl's philosophy of science is committed to the instrumentalist interpretation of scientific theories and hence dismisses as mere fictions the entire array of theoretical entities that has been posited in the course of modern scientific explanation. By way of conclusion I will review these allegations and the reasons why they should be rejected.

1. HUSSERL'S "DOGMATISM"

A particularly pointed version of the charge of dogmatism comes from Christopher Prendergast's work titled "Phenomenology and the Problem of Foundations: A Critique of Edmund Husserl's Theory of Science."[1] There Prendergast held that Husserl's commitment to the strong foundationalist conception of scientific knowledge effectively prevented Husserl from grasping the central characteristics of systems of empirical scientific belief, namely, their methodological flexibility and their revisibility in the face of new evidence. Similar criticisms are made by Cornelius van Peursen and Herbert Marcuse.[2]

We found such charges to be unjustified on two counts. First, although Husserl was throughout his philosophical career an adherent of the strong foundationalist account of science, he limited the validity of that account to the purely deductive sciences. Such sciences display a deductive unity derived from their axioms. Being both self-evident and indemonstrable, axioms form their foundations. But in section 72 of the "Prolegomena to Pure Logic" in the *Logical Investigations*, Husserl clearly states that the empirical sciences, including the physical sciences, do not find their basis or unity in their deductive structure. Nor are they founded, once and for all, upon certain self-evident axioms. Rather, their unity is to be located in the idea of empirical explanation. Their laws are not certain, but only more or less probable on a given body of empirical evidence (*LI* I, 246 / *H* XVIII, B 255). The theories of the empirical sciences are thus "frequently modified in the course of scientific progress"; as the "process of knowledge progresses," we "progressively correct our conceptions" (*LI* I, 246 / *H* XVIII, B 255).

Moreover, the strong foundationalist idea of science was itself "idealized" as a direct consequence of the later Husserl's theory of evidence. Even the eidetic sciences could now no longer claim to have final insight into necessary states of affairs. For once the method of the eidetic sciences was developed as a form of induction over imagined possibilities, all de facto eidetic claims were relativized to future evidence. Furthermore, due to the ineluctably temporal structure of experience, even the reflective apprehension of mental processes within consciousness could no longer claim to lay hold of adequate evidence. Phenomenological claims, too, are relativized to the course of future evidence. This point has been persuasively argued by Elisabeth Ströker, as we noted in chapter 1.[3]

Husserl's "foundationalism"—if one can still speak of such—is thus functional rather than substantial. While priority relations in the order of cognition are still recognized, at each level the achievement of certainty through adequate evidence counts only as an Idea in the Kantian sense, as an ideal to be approached but never attained. The cognitions of the eidetic sciences still lie at the foundations of the empirical sciences; but this is not to say that such cognitions have been secured, or can be secured, once and for all. Similarly, the cognitions of phenomenology are intrinsically prior to those of the positive sciences; but this is not to say that they have been, or could be, secured once and for all.

2. THE "AMBIGUITY" OF HUSSERL'S PHILOSOPHY OF SCIENCE

The charge of ambiguity is leveled by Hans Wagner in his article titled, appropriately enough, "Husserl's Ambiguous Philosophy of Science."[4] Although Wagner considers the two major themes of Husserl's philosophy of science—lifeworld and subjectivity—to be worthy contributions to the discussion within the philosophy of science, he faults Husserl's approach for its ambiguity with respect to what he takes to be the most important issue in any philosophical reflection on science, namely, the cognitive value of science. On the one hand, Husserl states that the career and current status of the modern physical sciences is legitimate, and even necessary; on the other hand, he maintains that the physical sciences have replaced the real world, the world intuitively given in the everyday lifeworld, with the fiction of an idealized construct.

Wagner then suggests that Husserl's position is open to two divergent interpretations. One is that, on Husserl's account, the physical sciences should be taken only as a very complicated and sophisticated technical apparatus for calculating and predicting the future course of events in the intuitable lifeworld. Thus the physical sciences themselves are not about the "true being" of the world, and their truth claims are "negated."[5] This interpretation would have Husserl as an instrumentalist in the traditional sense. The other interpretation is that the truth claims of the physical sciences are somehow "derived" from the "truth of the life-world." What is meant by the "derivation" of the truth of sciences from the truth of the lifeworld is left unclear, as Wagner gives no explanation of it. At any rate, although the relevant textual evidence seems to point in the direction of the first interpretation, Wagner claims there is nothing in Husserl's writings that makes it possible to choose between these two interpretations. That Husserl should have left his philosophy of science ambiguous on this point, Wagner finds "utterly enigmatical."[6]

It is my contention that Husserl's philosophy of science is neither ambiguous nor enigmatic on this score. In chapter 5 we noted that, on Husserl's account, the methods of the physical sciences produce knowledge about the real world (C, 33 / H VI, 31). But they do so indirectly. In their attempt to establish exact and therefore objective knowledge about the lawful regularities of the real world, they are compelled to posit ideal objects that, unlike real objects, admit of exact determination. These objects are not real; they are not causal players in the world of space and time. If we were to leave the account at this point, we would have to admit that the physical sciences are not about the real world, nor about objects that really exist. But this is only half of the story. The other half is that the ideal objects posited by the physical sciences approximate real objects. They are regarded, as Gary G. Gutting points out, as "imperfect approximations of concrete phenomena."[7] Thus what is exactly true of these ideal objects is approximately true of real objects. The physical sciences may cast a garb of ideas around the real world—but the garb is well-fitting (C, 51 / H VI, 51). Granted, in the formulation of their laws, the physical sciences posit objects that do not really exist, and that serve only as means for the objective determination of what really exists. But this law-instrumentalism in no way negates the cognitive value of the sciences. It only seeks to account for the actual method and real cognitive value of the mathematical component of the physical sciences while at the same time reminding us that the objects they posit as means to achieve their end are devices that aid in the approximating representation of the real world.

3. HUSSERL'S "INSTRUMENTALISM"

Finally, there is the charge that Husserl's philosophy of science is committed to an instrumentalist interpretation of scientific theories. In chapter 5 I argued that Husserl's instrumentalism is restricted to an interpretation of scientific laws. His position in the *Crisis* is that the objects posited in the course of formulating exact empirical laws do not enjoy real, physical existence. This is because these objects are idealized, constructed through the process of idealization operating on real objects whereby variations caused by real factors are reduced to zero. His chief concern there was to counter the tendency of "physicalistic rationalism" to take the world of idealities posited by the physical sciences in this manner as the real, objective world, while the world as it is given in everyday intuition is demoted to the status of mere subjective appearance.

His instrumentalist thesis, however, does not apply to all objects of science, but only to those where exact mathematical laws are formulated. It is for precisely this reason that certain typical ways of representing Husserl's position on the ontological status of the world of science by some of Husserl's sympathetic expositors have only limited validity. Kockelmans, for instance, claims that for Husserl, "modern physics since Galileo's time has almost always overlooked the fact that 'real and objective nature,' which physics tries to bring to light (in contradistinction to nature as it manifests itself in our pre-scientific experience), is not more than an idea in the Kantian sense, toward which a set of human theoretical achievements converge."[8] Because Husserl explicitly addresses himself only to those objects posited by the mathematical component of the physical science in relation to empirical regularities, it is simply misleading to claim that the entirety of nature, on Husserl's account, is made up of nothing but "ideas." Evidence of this misunderstanding is also reflected in Ernan McMullin's claim that for Husserl, "the *theoretical* constructs of science are reached by a form of idealization."[9] We should remind ourselves that there are two kinds of unobservables: the ideal and the real. Ideal unobservables are in principle unobservable by virute of their ideality. They are not the kinds of things that can be seen, heard, or touched. Real unobservables are not unobservable in principle; they are unobservable in fact to the likes of us because they escape our sensory apparatus by virtue of their size, distance, speed, or physical nature. Husserl challenged only the real existence of the former.

Furthermore, I argued that there is nothing in Husserl's phenomenology in general that would preclude the possibility of real theoretical existence, of the existence of unobservables in the latter sense. Some might hold that according to Husserl's "evidence theory of truth," it could not be true that theoretical entities exist. For on the evidence theory of truth, only those propositions for which the corresponding state of affairs themselves could be given in expereince can be true. As theoretical entities cannot be given in experience, it cannot be true that they exist. In chapter 3 I maintained that the possibility of givenness Husserl has in mind is an ideal possibility. Hence, the domain of possibly true propositions is not restricted, on Husserl's account, by the empirical limitations of human perception. As there is no reason to believe that theoretical entities, to the extent that they are real, cannot be perceived by some possible consciousness, there is no reason to believe that it cannot be true that they exist. Furthermore, I argued that with respect to all occurrent cases of evidence, being inadequate by nature, the relevant correlate is not the truth of a proposition, but the justification with which one posits that proposition.

Granting this, however, some might hold that although on the phenomenological theory of truth it is possible that it is true that there are theoretical entities, on the phenomenological theory of rationality we could never be justified in asserting that there are. For phenomenology restricts justified belief to that which is given. As theoretical entities cannot be given, belief in the existence of such entities cannot be unjustified. In chapter 4 I argued that such an application of Husserl's stated rule of rationality is seriously mistaken. For the rule is meant as a rule of phenomenological rationality, not rationality in general. Only a person qua phenomenological philosopher is bound to the rule of phenomenological rationality. Qua person practically engaged in the world, that person is bound by other, less restricive, rules of rational belief. Similarly, the practicing scientist is bound not by the rules of phenomenological rationality, but by rules of scientific rationality—rules that allow for the rationality of explanatory inferences from what is given to what is not given. Thus, while a person living in the natural attitude may be justified in believing in the existence of transcendent objects that are not wholly given in perception, the phenomenologist abstains from such beliefs; likewise, while the scientist may be justified in believing in the existence of theoretical entities that are not given in perception at all, the phenomenologist abstains from such beliefs.

Although phenomenology does not participate in the positing of the natural attitude, it does not take such positing to be, in itself, invalid. Rather, it abstains from such positing in order to make it the theme of phenomenological description and analysis. Husserl's theory of rationality, then, is differentiated with respect to epistemic project. It is important not to confuse the theory of phenomenological rationality with the phenomenological theory of rationality. For the former is much more restrictive than the latter, and holds only for persons in their calling as philosophers in the strict science. A phenomenologist will not posit the existence of theoretical entities, but this does not mean, even from the phenomenological standpoint, that the positive scientist is not justified in doing so. The projects of phenomenology and empirical science are entirely consistent with each other. Potential tension arises, for the most part, only over the philosophical interpretation of the ontological status of the results of empirical science.

Still, there is Husserl's claim that the domain of the real is coextensive with the perceivable. Since theoretical entities are not perceivable, some might claim that, given Husserl's perceivability condition on real existence, theoretical entities cannot exist. In chapter 6 I argued that this is not the case. For what Husserl meant by "perceivable" is perceivable in the ideal sense. Theoretical entities are denominated as such because they are humanly imperceivable. That is, their being perceived is a real impossibility for human beings. But this does not mean that they are imperceivable in principle. Thus, on Husserl's account, it is possible that theoretical entities are real existents, even if it is not possible that human beings perceive them.

Again, there is Husserl's claim that the existence of the physical world is relative to and dependent upon the absolute existence of consciousness. Although he might grant that theoretical entities in the physical world exist, he claims, in classical idealist fashion, that they exist only in relation to consciousness, only as unified systems of mental contents. In chapter 6 I argue that what Husserl claims about the existential dependence of physical objects on consciousness must be understood in a justification-theoretic context; that what Husserl is in fact claiming is that the justification with which we posit the existence of physical objects depends upon consciousness, upon the coherent course of conscious experience. Consciousness here is absolute because, when it comes to the justification of belief, all existence claims must be funneled through it. This view is entirely consistent with realism—here the claim that physical things exist independently of consciousness. I also point out that Husserl repeatedly and explicitly denies that physical objects are identical to mental contents, either collections of sensations or collections of noemata. Sensations are real components of consciousness *through which* physical objects are presented in experience; noemata are ideal components of conscious experience *by which* physical objects are presented. But sensations and noemata themselves, the sensate matter and the intentional form of experience, are typically not the objects of experience—except in the experience of phenomenological reflection.

4. HUSSERL'S "PROVISIONAL INSTRUMENTALISM"

A kind of hybrid position has also been advanced regarding Husserl's philosophy of science and the question of theoretical existence. In an article published in *Syntheses*, Charles W. Harvey maintains that "there is a definite strain in his [Husserl's] thinking toward an instrumentalistic position in the philosophy of science."[10] But, he contends, Husserl's instrumentalism is only "moderate" and "provisional."[11] Harvey's central thesis is that the question of the existence of theoretical entities postulated in the physical sciences cannot be settled once and for all on the basis of a phenomenological analysis of the eidetic structure of consciousness. Husserl's instrumentalism is nondogmatic and provisional precisely because it is not based upon a priori principles, but upon the current state of human perceptual powers in conjunction with their technological augmentation.

I have already argued that there is no reason to think that Husserl's phenomenology was committed to an instrumentalist interpretation of scientific theories in any sense—dogmatic or provisional. Harvey will claim, however, that Husserl's instrumentalism is to be seen in his treatment of the question of the physical thing as the unknown cause of appearances in section 52 of *Ideas* I.[12] There Husserl holds that the imperceptible physical thing as determined by the physical sciences does not exist. Husserl's "instrumentalist tendencies" receive their impetus from the phenomenological critique of the representational theory of perceptual consciousness.

Harvey's Husserl interpretation on this point is flawed in a number of respects. Instrumentalist interpetations of scientific theories typically deny that the imperceptible microentities postulated in a scientific theory exist. But in section 52 of *Ideas* I, Husserl's attention is directed toward macro physical objects as they are determined by the empirical component of physical science. Furthermore, Husserl's thesis in section 52 is not that the physical thing as determined by the physical sciences does not exist, but rather that it is identical with the perceived object. There are not two objects—the perceived object and the physical thing—but one object that carries both sensuous and theoretical determinations. It is not as if behind the perceived object there were a physical thing bearing exclusively exact quantitative determinations that causes the appearance of the perceived object within our minds. And it is not as if the perceived object serves as a sign or image of an ontically distinct imperceptible physical thing that brings about its appearance. Rather, the thing as determined by the science of physics—and here Husserl has classical mechanics in mind—is no other than the perceived object. But then it follows that if the perceived thing exists, so does the physical thing.

Husserl holds that to think of the physical thing as distinct from and the cause of the perceived object is to commit oneself to the representational theory of perceptual consciousness, a theory that can be handily refuted by a phenomenological analysis of perceptual consciousness. This point, however, does not commit Husserl to an instrumentalist interpretation of scientific theories since, in the case before us, it is restricted to a consideration of the empirical scientific determination of macro physical objects. It does not show that the macro physical object is not composed of microtheoretical entities, nor does it show that microtheoretical entities are not involved in the appearance of the macro physical object, nor does it show that the physical sciences deal only with macro physical objects.

Harvey is correct, however, when he claims that the phenomenological analysis of sign consciousness, image consciousness, and sensuous thing consciousness does not, in itself, decide the issue of theoretical existence. To refute the sign or image theory of perceptual consciousness does not rule out the possibility of sign or image consciousness. A perceived physical thing can function, under the appropriate conditions, as a sign. As an indicative sign, a perceived physical thing can indicate the existence of another physical thing. That is, as Husserl has it in chapter 1 of the First Logical Investigation, a belief in the existence of a physical thing based on a perception of it can "motivate" the belief in the existence of something else (LI I, 270 / H XIX 1, B1 24). To a person acquainted with the relevant causal regularities, the perception of smoke can motivate the belief in the existence of fire. To that person the perceived smoke can thus serve as an "indicative sign" of fire. But the analysis of sign consciousness does not, in itself, tell us whether what is indicated must itself be a sign, an image, or a physical thing. Neither does it tell us, in those cases where the thing signified is imperceptible, whether the thing signified is imperceptible in fact or imperceptible in principle.

The reference Harvey makes to indicative signs is especially relevant to the discussion of theoretical science and the question of Husserl's instrumentalism. In physical experiments, perceived objects and events will typically serve as indicative signs of theoretical states of affairs. In Ernest Rutherford's alpha particle scattering experiment at the beginning of the last century, for instance, the distribution of scintillations on a zinc sulfide screen serves to indicate the mass structure of the gold atom. Against the background of a theory pertaining to the causal interaction of alpha particles, gold atoms, and the screen, the perception and measurement of the distribution of scintillations on the screen motivates beliefs pertaining to the existence and properties of certain theoretical entities.

But there is a significant difference between the perception of smoke motivating the belief in the existence of fire and the perception of scintillations motivating the belief about the mass structure of a gold atom. The fire is itself a humanly perceivable object, whereas the gold atom is not. The gold atom may interact with instruments in an experimental context, yielding perceived results on the basis of which we may "see that" the atom has a certain mass structure. But we never see the gold atom itself. It is imperceivable. Does it follow, then, on Husserl's perceivability condition for real existence mentioned above, that the gold atom cannot exist?

To answer this question, Harvey turns to a passage in section 52 of *Ideas* I. There Husserl states that we must make a distinction between those entities that are postulated by a theory and in fact imperceivable, and those that are posited by a theory and are in principle imperceivable. Husserl then gives the following example. On the basis of the perturbations in the orbits of the perceived planets, the existence of the unperceived planet, Neptune, is postulated. Although this planet is not perceivable by us, it is perceivable by "other Egos who see better and further" (*ID* I, 119 / *H* III 1, 98). As such, Neptune is to be contrasted with atoms and ions, which Husserl takes to be imperceptible in principle. It follows from Husserl's perceivability condition that atoms, ions, and the like, do not exist.

Here Harvey claims that Husserl "was victim to the historical contingencies surrounding the vision of egos."[13] For with the invention of scientific instruments such as cloud chambers, it is now possible to perceive what were once posited as mere theoretical entities. Husserl's instrumentalism is in fact provisional because the perceivability condition on real existence is tied to the empirical question of the current scope of the instrumentally mediated powers of human perception. Thus Husserl's phenomenology is consistent with a realistic construal of a scientific theory, just in case it is possible to gain perceptual access to the theoretical entities postulated by that theory by way of instrumentation. Since what can and what cannot be perceived by humans with the aid of instruments is an empirical question, and since the answer to this question will change with the development of technology, Husserl's instrumentalism is provisional and nondogmatic.

This interpretation of the sense of Husserl's instrumentalism is, however, wholly untenable. For even if Husserl were an instrumentalist, he would not be a provisional instrumentalist on the grounds adduced by Harvey. There are two reasons for this. First, Harvey takes it that what Husserl means by "perceivable in principle" as a real existence condition is "perceivable in principle by human beings." He states, for instance, that "just what is perceivable in principle is, in many cases, an empirical issue open to further developments in natural scientific investigation."[14] For what is perceivable in principle "is being constantly extended through the development of new instruments and new experiments."[15] But this is to convert what for Husserl was a question of ideal possibility into a question of real possibility. When Husserl claims that if it is "to be," an entity postulated by an explanatory theory must be perceivable, he is not claiming that it must be perceivable by us either now or in the technologically enhanced future. Rather, he is claiming that it must be perceivable by some possible ego. That is, a real thing exists if and only if it is possible that it be perceived by some possible consciousness. But here the possibility of real existence is not tied to a question of fact, or even to a question of what is within the realm of possibility for some factually existing egos. It is rather a statement of ideal possibility.

That Husserl appears, in the passage in question, to classify atoms and ions among those entities that are in principle imperceivable is based upon categorical, not contingent considerations. It is not as though he thinks that atoms and ions belong to the category of things, but casts them into the outer darkness of nonexistence under the mistaken impression that they could never be perceived by human beings. Rather, he considers them to be imperceivable in principle because he construes them as "physical determinations" of things rather than things. The contrast between the unperceived, hypothetically postulated planet Neptune and unperceived, hypothetically postulated entities such as atoms and ions is a contrast not between two kinds of "Dinglichkeiten," but between "Dinglichkeiten" and "physikalische Bestimmungen" (ID I, 119 / H III 1, 111). In *Ideas* I, Husserl takes atoms and ions to be of the same ontological order as the mechanical properties of mass, force, electrical resistance, and acceleration (see *ID* I, 121 / *H* III 1, 113). As Harvey points out, there is good reason to think that Husserl is mistaken here. And there is nothing in Husserl's phenomenology that forces such entities as atoms and ions into the category of physical determinations.[16] But it does show that Husserl takes such entities to be imperceptible in principle on categorial grounds rather than contingent considerations pertaining to the real present or future possibilities of instrumentally mediated human perception. The question of the in principle perceivablility of things is not an empirical question, it is a categorical one. If Husserl's phenomenology had compelled him to be an instrumentalist, he would have been a dogmatic one at that.

Second, Harvey evidently assumes that human perception would still count as a straightforward case of perception no matter how and to what degree it is augmented by way of instruments. New and sophisticated scientific instruments now make it possible for us to perceive what were previously imperceptible theoretical entities. Harvey mentions the cloud chamber as a case in point.[17] But in what sense does a cloud chamber make possible the perception of a theoretical entity, in this case, the perception of an ion? In the straightforward and direct sense, what one perceives in a cloud chamber is a line of condensation in a supersaturated atmosphere, that is, one perceives water droplets. It is only on atomic theory and the relevant correspondence rules that one is able to interpret what one sees as evidence for the existence and nature of ions. One by no means perceives the ion itself in Husserl's sense of perception. For by perception Husserl means the bodily presentation of the thing itself. What we are presented in the cloud chamber is not the ion itself, but a line of condensation, which, against a background of a theory, serves as an indicative sign of the ion's presence.[18] We don't see the ion, we "see that" the ion made its course through the chamber on the basis of seeing a line of condensation and embracing a whole host of causal/theoretical assumptions.

Commenting on the nature of observation in an experimental context, Bas C. van Fraassen makes the same point: "So while the particle is detected by means of the cloud chamber, and the detection is based on observation, it is clearly not a case of the particle's being observed."[19] Thus, in the relevant cases of instrumentally mediated "perception," we are actually dealing with indicative sign consciousness, not straightforward perceptual consciousness. With the advance of scientific instrumentation, the powers of human perception are, in most cases, advanced not one whit. Neither are new and different kinds of entities rendered perceivable in the phenomenological sense. They remain imperceivable (even if they are detected on the basis of what is perceivable). But this does not mean that, for Husserl, such entities cannot exist. For this direct imperceivability signifies only a real impossibility for the human species.

5. SUMMARY AND PROSPECT

It is likely that Peter Kosso expressed a consensus in the circles of contemporary philosophy of science when he wrote that instrumentalism "gives up what is most worth doing in science, namely, understanding what is happening behind the scenes in the realm of unobservables."[20] If Husserl's phenomenological philosophy of science is committed to instrumentalism in the standard sense, it is unlikely that it has much to contribute to an understanding of science as it is practiced today, a science that has ever since the turn of the last century been operating in a robust and impressive theoretical dimension. In this work I have argued that Husserl's phenomenology is wholly consistent with a realistic construal of scientific theories and that his "instrumentalism" is limited to an interpretation of scientific laws. What Husserl denies exist as real physical things are such entities as frictionless inclined planes, perfectly elastic bodies, extensionless point-masses, incompressible fluids, and the like. Such idealized objects are the proper objects of the exact and uniform laws of the physical sciences. Expressing the functional correlations between measurable physical quantities, these laws make the prediction of events in the lifeworld possible on a scale unknown to prescientific practical life. Husserl's phenomenological analysis of the meaning of such laws and the ontological status of their respective objects does not, however, touch upon the entities postulated by scientific theories designed to explain the functional correlations captured in scientific laws. Although the behavior of the entities postulated by theories may in turn be represented in exact mathematical laws, the theories themselves, as Ernan McMullin points out, are not purely mathematical. They possess real physical content, and the entities they postulate (e.g., atoms, ions, strong and weak nuclear forces, and the like), if they exist, exist as real physical entities.[21]

It is entirely possible that Husserl himself was not inclined to adopt a realistic view of theoretical science. There is some evidence for such a disinclination in section 52 of *Ideas* I, as we noted in chapter 5. Moreover, in his major works we find very little by way of a phenomenology of theoretical entities as we have defined them. In fact, Husserl's phenomenological critique of science, coupled with a lack of attention to the theoretical component of science, has led some Husserl commentators to declare that phenomenology is fundamentally opposed to modern theoretical science. Patrick A. Heelan, for instance, accuses Husserlian phenomenology of taking a "negative attitude" toward natural science.[22] Furthermore, he claims that "contemporary phenomenology cannot contribute much of value to the philosophy of science unless it is enlarged in some way."[23] Heelan then proceeds to "enlarge" phenomenology by developing a hermeneutically inspired theory of horizon intentionality. I, on the contrary, have maintained that Husserl's critique of science is not so much directed against science as a particular self-understanding that often accompanies science. That self-understanding mistakenly takes the idealized constructs of science for the real being of nature itself. Nonetheless, having made this point against the platonizers, Husserl continues to see in the physical sciences a method for gaining knowledge about the real world (C, 47 / H VI, 46–47). Furthermore, it is my belief that Husserlian phenomenology possesses within itself the resources for making a genuine contribution to the discussion of the nature of scientific theories in its concept of the indicative sign and the corresponding possibility of investigating indicative sign consciousness within a theoretical context. As such, Husserl's phenomenology of perception need not receive hermeneutical additions from the outside in order to deal with contemporary theoretical science. The resources are already there. In seed form, they lie in the first chapter of the first of the *Logical Investigations*.

NOTES

INTRODUCTION

1. Joseph Rouse, "Husserlian Phenomenology and Scientific Realism," *Philosophy of Science* 54, no. 2 (1987): 222.
2. Ernan McMullin, "Compton on the Philosophy of Nature," *Review of Metaphysics* 33, no. 1 (September 1979): 34.
3. Ibid., 31.
4. Gary G. Gutting, "Husserl and Scientific Realism," *Philosophy and Phenomenological Research* 39, no. 1 (September 1978): 43.
5. Patrick A. Heelan, "Husserl's Later Philosophy of Natural Science," *Philosophy of Science* 54, no. 3 (1987): 368.
6. Herman Philipse, "Transcendental Idealism," in *The Cambridge Companion to Husserl*, ed. Barry Smith and David Woodruff Smith (New York: Cambridge University Press, 1995), 287, 318.
7. Aurelio Rizzacasa, "The Epistemology of the Sciences of Nature in Relation to the Teleology of Research in the Thought of the Later Husserl," in *Analecta Husserliana* 9, ed. Anna-Teresa Tymieniecka (Dordrecht: Reidel, 1979), 78.
8. Theodore J. Kisiel, "On the Dimensions of a Phenomenology of Science in Husserl and the Young Dr. Heidegger," *Journal of the British Society for Phenomenology* 4 (October 1973): 222–23.
9. Heelan, "Husserl's Later Philosophy," 370.
10. Francis J. Zucker, "Phenomenological Evidence and the 'Idea' of Physics," in *Phenomenology: Dialogue and Bridges*, ed. Ronald Bruzina and Bruce Wilshire (Albany: State University of New York Press, 1982), 282–83.
11. Rouse, "Husserlian Phenomenology," 225.
12. Ibid., 231.
13. Gail Soffer, "Phenomenology and Scientific Realism: Husserl's Critique of Galileo," *Review of Metaphysics* 44 (September 1990): 68.
14. Charles W. Harvey, "Husserl and the Problem of Theoretical Entities," *Syntheses* 66 (February 1986): 301.
15. Ibid., 303.
16. Ibid., 304.
17. Frederick Suppe, "The Search for Philosophic Understanding of Scientific Theories," in *The Structure of Scientific Theories*, ed. Frederick Suppe, 2nd ed. (Urbana: University of Illinois Press, 1977), 3.

18. Ibid.

19. Of course, exact mathematical laws are also applied to the behavior of theoretical entities. Laws for mechanical determinations of empirical phenomena came first, however, and they are at the center of Husserl's concern.

20. Bas C. van Fraassen, *The Scientific Image* (Oxford: Oxford University Press, 1980), 29.

21. Richard N. Boyd, "Realism, Underdetermination, and a Causal Theory of Evidence," *Noûs* 7, no. 1 (March 1973): 1.

22. Peter Kosso, *Reading the Book of Nature: An Introduction to the Philosophy of Science* (Cambridge: Cambridge University Press, 1992), 15.

23. Stathis Psillos, *Scientific Realism: How Science Tracks Truth* (London: Routledge, 1999), 40.

24. Suppe, "Search," 29. Richard Boyd defines scientific realism with the following four theses: (1) that the theoretical terms of a scientific theory refer; (2) that well-confirmed scientific theories are approximately true; (3) that there is real continuity in the development of science; and (4) that the reality posited in scientific theories is largely independent of our concepts and commitments. Boyd, "On the Current Status of Scientific Realism," in *The Philosophy of Science*, ed. Richard N. Boyd, Philip Gasper, and J. D. Trout (Cambridge, MA: MIT Press, 1991), 195.

25. Van Fraassen, *Scientific Image*, 9.

26. Suppe, "Search," 9.

27. Van Fraassen, *Scientific Image*, 9.

28. For the classical statement of this position, see Rudolf Carnap, "The Methodological Character of Theoretical Concepts," in *The Foundations of Science and the Concepts of Psychology and Psychoanalysis*, ed. Herbert Feigl and Michael Scriven, vol. 1 of *Minnesota Studies in the Philosophy of Science* (Minneapolis: University of Minnesota Press, 1956), 38–76.

CHAPTER 1: THE IDEA OF SCIENCE IN HUSSERL AND THE TRADITION

1. Husserl takes it that there are such things as essences. He calls the sciences that study essential structures the "eidetic disciplines." Here he is drawing upon the Greek word *eidos*, usually translated into English as "idea" or "form." Phenomenology studies the essential structures of consciousness and therefore numbers among the eidetic disciplines.

2. This strong foundationalist demand is reflected as well in a manuscript written around 1923 and published as "Beilage VIII" in *Husserliana* VIII (*Erste Philosophie* [1923–24]): "Ohne eine absolut fundierte Erkenntnis ist jene Voraussetzung alles Erkenntnisstrebens nicht haltbar" (*H* VIII, 367). In achieving "absolute Wissenschaft," "absolute Gewißheit," we must see to it that "alle ihre Aussagen müssen aus solcher absoluter Erschauung stammen und an ihr als praktisch jederzeit wieder zugänglich ihre absolute Normgerechtigkeit schöpfen" (*H* VIII, 367).

3. Using the term "*Erschauung*" to denote the direct intuitive experience of both empirical objects and formal states of affairs, Husserl states that the justification of all scientific cognition draws on the absolute foundation of intuition: "Echte Wissenschaft ist ein systematischer Zusammenhang fortschreitender und in der Verflechtung einheitlicher Erkenntnisgebilde, die wir Theorien nennen, sprachlicher

Aussagenzusammenhänge, deren Gewißheit sich jederzeit und vor jedermann absolut rechtfertigen läßt. Absolute Rechtfertigung setzt also absolute Erschauung voraus" (H VIII, 367). This point is reinforced on the same and following pages: "Fragen wir nun: Wo sind jene zunächst postulierten echten oder absoluten Erschauungen, und wie kann diese Echtheit selbst erkannt werden?—so werden wir zunächst also zurückgeführt auf die Frage der unmittelbaren absoluten Erschauungen, also der absoluten Erfahrungen" (H VIII, 367–68).

4. In a manuscript from the 1932–33 manuscript series of convolute A IV 3, Husserl underscores the systematicity of scientific knowledge: "Sie [Wissenschaft] erhebt den Anspruch, von Anfang an und bis hinauf in die entlegensten Mittelbarkeiten der Theorie nichts aufzustellen, keinen Schritt der Erkenntnis zu vollziehen, der nicht vollkommen 'begründet' ist, unmittelbar order mittelbar, und der allen Feststellungen wirklich Festigkeit gibt" (A IV 3 / 3a).

5. Karl Schuhmann, *Husserl-Chronik: Denk- Und Lebensweg Edmund Husserls*, vol. 1 of *Husserliana* (The Hague: Martinus Nijhof, 1977), 25.

6. Ibid., 32.

7. Christopher Prendergast, "Phenomenology and the Problem of Foundations: A Critique of Edmund Husserl's Theory of Science" (PhD diss., Southern Illinois University, 1979), 71–83.

8. Cornelius van Peursen, "Creativity and the Method of the Sciences: A Problematic Issue in Husserl's Phenomenology," in *Analecta Husserliana* 14, ed. Anna-Teresa Tymieniecka (Dordrecht: Reidel, 1983), 380.

9. Prendergast, "Phenomenology," 116.

10. Ibid., 118.

11. Wilfrid Sellars, *Science, Perception and Reality* (London: Routledge and Kegan Paul, 1963), 170.

12. Elisabeth Ströker, "Husserls Evidenzprinzip: Sinn und Grenzen einer Methodischen Norm der Phänomenologie als Wissenschaft," *Zeitschrift für philosophische Forschung* 32 (1978): 23. English translation: "Husserl's Principle of Evidence: The Significance and Limitations of a Methodological Norm of Phenomenology as a Science," in *The Husserlian Foundations of Science*, ed. Lee Hardy (Lanham, MD: Center for Advanced Research in Phenomenology and University Press of America, 1987), 47.

13. Ströker, "Husserls Evidenzprinzip," 26 / "Husserl's Principle of Evidence," 50. Husserl makes the presumptive nature of all occurrent evidence clear in the late manuscript published as text No. 65 in *Husserliana* XXXIX:

Die getreue Auslegung dessen, was das ständig im wachen Weltleben vonstattengehende und sich vereinheitlichende Weltbewußtsein als "leere" Meinung und als Erfahrung leistet, führt zur Erkenntnis, dass im Fortgang des Lebens bislang geltende Meinungen durchgestrichen werden, ihre Fortgeltung einbüßend durch Widerstreit mit Erfahrungen (eventuell in Mittelbarkeit und im induktiven Zusammenhang), dass aber auch Erfahrungen nur so lange gelten, als sie sich zu einem einstimmigen Erfahrungszusammenhang, also zu der synthetischen Einheit einer einstimmigen Erfahrung zusammen fügen. Jede Durchstreichung greift zurück in die gesamte erinnerungsmäßig wieder zugängliche Erfahrung; und in jedem Moment des Lebens, der einzelnen oder vergemeinschafteten, in dem kein Widerspruch laut wird, ist als Welt in Geltung das, was aus der fortschreitenden und stets zurückwirkenden Seinskorrektur als seiend standhält. Letztlich stimmt, was jetzt als schlechthin seiend in Geltung ist, also aus der Einstimmigkeit der Erfahrung bis zum Jetzt, [die] eine Einstimmigkeit [ist], die zugleich einen Horizont künftiger Einstimmigkeit vorzeichnet mit allen Näherbestimmungen des Präsumierten, aber noch Unbestimmten (wie dergleichen auch für alle Vergangenheit als vergangene Gegenwart mit ihrer seienden Weltgegenwart schon gegolten hat). So ist *Seiendes immerzu bis jetzt und für uns Seiendes* und zugleich mit der *Präsumtion* behaftet, dass wie bisher Widerstreit, Widerstreit im eigenen Erfahren und Widerstreit im Zusammen-Erfahren bekannter und noch unbekannter (also selbst präsumierter) Anderer, sich durch Korrektur beseitigen und neue Einstimmigkeit sich herstellen wird. (*H* XXXIX, 725–26)

This is because, as he states in the same manuscript, the entire intersubjective stream of experience is always open to the future: "Der ganze Erfahrungsstrom in seinem anfangs- und endlosen intersubjektiven Gang ist ein Bewährungszusammenhang, immerfort bewährend, soweit einstimmig Konnex aktuell hergestellt ist, immerfort in Entwährung und wieder in Korrektur übergehend und so in ständiger Relativität" (*H* XXXIX, 728).

14. This may represent a form of self-critique on the part of Husserl. Compare the passage found in the *Logical Investigations* where Husserl claims that "in knowledge, however, we possess truth. In actual knowledge, to which we see ourselves ultimately referred back, we possess truth as the object of a correct judgment" (*LI* I, 60 / *H* XVIII, B 12).

15. The conversion of human knowledge from possession to goal is evidenced in the late unpublished manuscripts as well. In a manuscript from the convolute A IV 3 (1932–33), 34, Husserl speaks of the insurmountable limitations of our knowledge: "Zu dieser Vollendungsform gehörte die unvermeidliche Überzeugung, daß menschliche Erkenntnis eine unübersteigliche Schranke darin habe, dass sie die theoretische Bestimmung des an sich Seienden nur in fortgehender, aber unendlicher Approximation erstreben und erwirken kann" (A IV 3 / 19b–20a). And in the manuscript A VII 21 / 3–6 (1933), he speaks of omniscience as an accomplished fact in the divine mind, but as a regulative Idea for us below who seek complete scientific understanding:

Der Einstellung der positiven Wissenschaften, wenn sie als rein theoretische etabliert sind, ist, wie immer sie sich auf Gebiete und Einzelgegenstände beschränken, doch die Intention auf Allererkenntnis [eigen], obschon eine solche für kein einzelnes Subjekt, keine in der Zeit stehende Forschergemeinschaft wirklich zu erreichen ist. Eine solche Erkenntnis, als die eines Subjektes gedacht, wäre die göttliche Allwissenheit—sofern die Religion eben Gott als allwissende auf Grund des Allwissens allschaffende Persönlichkeit vorstellt. Aber das geht die Wissenschaft selbst nicht an als lebendiges Gebilde einer wissenschaftlichen Gemeinschaft. Ihr Ziel ist nicht die Herstellung einer menschlich fertigen, einer endlich abgeschlossenen Allerkenntnis, die wesensmäßig unmöglich ist, sondern Inswerksetzung und Durchführung eines unendlichen, in der Relativität von Vollkommenheitsstufen ins Unendliche fortschreitenden Gemeinschaftswerkes der wissenschaftlichen Erkenntnis auf das ideale Telos der Allheitserkenntnis hin, das eine "regulative Idee" ist und als Korrelat in sich trägt die unendliche Idee des wahren Seins der Welt. (A VII 21 / 3a)

CHAPTER 2: HUSSERL'S PHENOMENOLOGY AND THE FOUNDATIONS OF SCIENCE

1. Edmund Husserl, "The Method of Clarification," trans. Ted E. Klein and William E. Pohl, *Southwestern Journal of Philosophy* 5 (October 1974): 60.
2. Ibid.
3. Theodore De Boer, *The Development of Husserl's Thought* (The Hague: Martinus Nijhoff, 1978), 69.
4. Ibid., 63.
5. See Theodore J. Kisiel, "Phenomenology as the Science of Science," in *Phenomenology and the Natural Sciences*, ed. Joseph J. Kockelmans and Theodore J. Kisiel (Evanston, IL: Northwestern University Press, 1970), 5–44; Kisiel, "On the Dimensions of a Phenomenology of Science in Husserl and the Young Dr. Heidegger," *Journal of the British Society for Phenomenology* 4 (October 1973): 217–34; Elisabeth Ströker, "Husserl's Idea of Phenomenology as the Foundational Theory of Science," in *Husserlian Foundations of Science*, ed. Lee Hardy (Lanham, MD: Center for Advanced Research in Phenomenology and University Press of America, 1987), 1–14; and, more generally, Aron Gurwitsch, *Phenomenology and the Theory of Science*, ed. Lester E. Embree (Evanston, IL: Northwestern University Press, 1974).
6. This representation of Husserl's "*Denkweg*" is in line with Kisiel's construal of the development of phenomenology as a philosophy of science: "Thus Husserl's way to phenomenology through the critical effort to found the positive sciences laboriously wends its way from the empirical sciences to the formal *a priori* of mathematics and pure logic, then to the material ontologies of regions which culminate in the comprehensive ontology of the life-world, all of which receive their ultimate grounding in the transcendental subjectivity." Kisiel, "On the Dimensions," 218.
7. Husserl uses the term "*Wissenschaftslehre*" in the *Logical Investigations*, while the term "*Wissenschaftstheorie*" is used in *Formal and Transcendental Logic*. It appears that the two terms are interchangeable.
8. Hermann Weyl, *Space-Time-Matter*, trans. H. L. Browse (New York: Dover, 1952), 10.
9. In a manuscript from the convolute A IV 3 (1932–33), Husserl refers to the world as the general source of the specialized themes of the sciences: "Jeder Tatsachenwissenschaft ist ihr Gebiet vorgegeben durch Erfahrung, aber durch eine Erfahrung, die die universale Erfahrung, die der beständig für uns daseienden Welt, voraussetzt als Untergrund, aus dem sie ihr Sonderthema herausgreift als sozusagen abstrakt" (A IV 3 / 3b).
10. In a manuscript from the convolute A IV 3 (1932–33), Husserl states that the positive sciences will never, as such, achieve the goal of rigorous science: "Die allgemeinste Form aller wissenschaftlichen Methode ist damit bezeichnet: Erkenntnis aus dem 'Grunde.' Das in Sicht und Einsicht Gegebene ist Grund für fortschreitende Urteilsgeltung, die als wissenschaftliche nicht bloß subjektive Meinung, sondern Wahrheit, Endgültigkeit ist. Dies ist das Ideal, und jede strenge Wissenschaft erkennt es an und beansprucht, danach zu verfahren. Aber in diesem Sinn ist keine positive Wissenschaft, wie sie es stets vermeinte, wirklich echte [Wissenschaft], und das aus prinzipiellen, also unabänderlichen Gründen—solange sie in der Positivität verbleibt" (A IV 3 / 3a).
11. Husserl makes this point with respect to transcendental subjectivity in a short manuscript titled "Überwindung der Relativität als Aufgabe" (probably from 1930): "Durch diese Änderung der Urteilseinstellung [die transzendentale Reduktion] werden alle Erfahrungen und Urteile und alles in ihnen als seiend oder nicht-seiend,

als relativ oder irrelativ Geltende relativ auf die transzendentale Subjektivität und ihr transzendentales Leben. Die unter Voraussetzung der natürlichen Generalthesis als objektiv Seiendes in Wahrheiten an sich herauszustellende präsumierte Welt wird zu einem transzendental-intentionalem 'Gebilde'der transzendentalem Subjektivität, die faktisch unter einer entsprechend universalen Regel fortgehender transzendentaler Konstitution steht" (A VII 20 / 65b).

12. Everything we hold to be true and valid must be referred back to some form of givenness in cognitive experience. See manuscript A IV 2 / 9–16 (1926): "Alles, was ich erkenne und je erkennen konnte und erkennen werde, ist mir—ist uns—prinzipiell in subjektiven Modis gegeben, in passiven Erscheinungsweisen oder aktiv von mir—von uns—erzeugten Gebilden. Alles Erkannte ist Erkanntes im Erkennen, in den in ihm geworden Erkenntnisgestalten."

13. In this passage the German word *Leisten* is translated as "producing." This is probably too strong, too amenable to an idealistic interpretation of Husserl. *Leisten* is better translated as "accomplishing," as we find in the translation of the *Crisis* text.

14. Joseph J. Kockelmans, "Gurwitsch's Phenomenological Theory of Natural Science," *Research in Phenomenology* 5 (1975): 32. All of the positive sciences, Husserl writes in his manuscripts, are channeled through experience: "Alle historisch gewordenen Wissenschaften fußten auf der universalen Erfahrung, bezogen sich auf die ihnen durch Erfahrung vorgegebene Welt. Sie waren in diesem Sinne positive Wissenschaften und waren geradehin gerichtet auf die objektiv-wissenschaftliche Bestimmung der Welt, bezw. der verschiedenen Weltgebiete" (A IV 2 / 2a; probably 1926).

15. Edmund Husserl, "Die Frage nach dem Ursprung der Geometrie als intentional-historisches Problem," *Revue Internationale de Philosophie* 1, no. 2 (1938–39): 203–25.

16. In the Fourth Set of Objections to Descartes's *Meditations on First Philosophy*. See *The Philosophical Writings of Descartes*, trans. and ed. John Cottingham, Robert Stoothoff, and Dugald Murdoch (Cambridge: University of Cambridge Press, 1985), 2:150.

17. Edmund Husserl, "Rapport entre la phénoménologie et les sciences," *Les Etudes philosophiques* 4 (1949): 3.

CHAPTER 3: TRUTH, EVIDENCE, AND EXISTENCE IN HUSSERL'S PHENOMENOLOGY

1. Stathis Psillos, *Scientific Realism: How Science Tracks Truth* (London: Routledge, 1999), 40.

2. Dallas Willard, *Logic and the Objectivity of Knowledge: A Study in Husserl's Early Philosophy* (Athens: Ohio University Press, 1984), 237.

3. Günther Patzig, "Kritische Bemerkungen zu Husserl's Thesen über das Verhältnis von Wahrheit und Evidenz," *Neue Hefte Philosophie* 1 (1973): 12; my translation.

4. Donn Welton, *The Origins of Meaning: A Critical Study of the Thresholds of Husserlian Phenomenology* (The Hague: Martinus Nijhoff, 1983), 139.

5. Louis Dupré, "The Concept of Truth in Husserl's *Logical Investigations*," *Philosophy and Phenomenological Research* 24 (1964): 347.

6. Henry Pietersma, "Husserl's Views on the Evident and the True," in *Husserl: Expositions and Appraisals*, ed. Frederick A. Elliston and Peter McCormick (Notre Dame, IN: University of Notre Dame Press, 1977), 43.

7. Henry Pietersma, *Phenomenological Epistemology* (Oxford: Oxford University Press, 2000), 38.
8. Patzig, "Kritische Bemerkungen," 12.
9. Dupré, "Concept of Truth," 354.
10. Pietersma, "Husserl's Views," 39.
11. This is not to say that all mental processes are intentional. Sensations, for instance, as actual or potential components of full-fledged acts, are preintentional.
12. Here I am making use of a distinction that has been made in analytic meta-epistemological research between internalist and externalist epistemologies. Alvin I. Goldman characterizes this distinction in terms of differing conceptions of the task of epistemology: the regulatory and the evaluative. The internalist takes epistemology to be a regulatory discipline. The task is to provide rules for the direction of the mind (i.e., "doxastic decision principles"), which would enable the cognitive subject to tell, in each case, if he or she was justified in holding a certain belief or not. Hence the internalist will demand that the conditions for justified belief (e.g., evidence) be accessible to the cognitive subject. The externalist, on the other hand, takes epistemology to be an evaluative discipline. It seeks only to specify the conditions under which a belief is justified; those conditions, however, may not be accessible to the cognitive subject. See Goldman, "The Internalist Conception of Justification," in *Midwest Studies in Philosophy* 5, ed. Peter A. French, Theodore E. Uehling Jr., and Howard K. Wettstein (Minneapolis: University of Minnesota Press, 1980), 27–51.
13. Husserl not only speaks of evidence as an act of consciousness, but of the "evident" as what is given in an act of evidence. The concept of evidence has a noetic and noematic side to it. This twofold sense of the concept of evidence is, Husserl claims, "universal and necessary" (*ID* I, 328–29 / *H* III 1, 316). He also speaks of the "evident logical judgment, evident predicative proposition" (evidentes logisches Urteil, evidenter Aussagesatz) (*ID* I, 329 / *H* III 1, 317).
14. Ernst Tugendhat finds two concepts of evidence in Husserl. One represents evidence as a synthetic act of identification; the other represents evidence as a simple act, where the signitive act passes over into the intuitive act without the respective objects of the two acts being distinguished and then identified. While evidence as a synthetic act is always possible in reflection, most acts of evidence are in fact of the latter kind. It would therefore be phenomenologically inappropriate to designate the former concept of evidence as a general characterization of evidence. Tugendhat holds that precisely because of this *"Schwierigkeit,"* Husserl eventually abandoned that synthetic concept of evidence. By the time of the *Ideas*, the monothetic concept is predominant. See Ernst Tugendhat, *Der Wahrheitsbegriff bei Husserl und Heidegger* (Berlin: De Gruyter, 1967), 94.
15. In addition to this problem of the object side of the synthetic act of evidence, there is also the phenomenological fact that most cases of evidence do not consist of a synthetic act of identification. See *LI* II, 766 / *H* XIX 2, B2 123.
16. It is important to note that the existence of an object and the givenness of an object are two different matters. Elisabeth Ströker seems to take "givenness" and "existence" as equivalent concepts when she states, "Nur wenn der Sachverhalt besteht, 'gegeben' ist, kann der ihn behauptende Satz . . . wahr sein." See Ströker, "Husserls Evidenzprincip: Sinn and Grenzen einer Methodische Norm der Phänomenologie als Wissenschaft," *Zeitschrfit für Philosophische Forschung* 32, no. 1 (1978): 12. Here *"gegeben ist"* (given) is used in apposition to *"besteht"* (exists). But, according to

Husserl, it does not follow from the givenness of a state of affairs that the state of affairs exists (cf. *ID* I 102 / *H* III 1, 97).

17. Husserl sometimes speaks of truth as an agreement between a proposition and a state of affairs (*LI* I, 195 / *H* XVIII, B 189), and sometimes as an identity between states of affairs (*LI* II, 765 / *H* XIX 2, B2 122). These formulations are conceptually distinct.

18. "Allerdings läßt sich jeder Satz 'A ist wahr' umformen in den Satz 'es ist möglich, dass irgend jemand mit Evidenz urteilt, es sei A,' aber darin druckt sich nur ein *ideales* Bedingungsverhältnis aus, dass die *Möglichkeit* der Evidenz aller Urteile desselben Wesens betrifft, und daraus folgt nicht, dass jeder wahre Satz auch *realer* irgend jemandem evident sein muss." Tugendhat, *Der Wahrheitsbegriff*, 102.

19. Willard, *Logic*, 237–38.

20. Elisabeth Ströker, "Husserl's Principle of Evidence: The Significance and Limitations of a Methodological Norm of Phenomenology as a Science," in *Husserlian Foundations of Science*, ed. Lee Hardy (Lanham, MD: Center for Advanced Research in Phenomenology and University Press of America, 1987), 50.

21. Ibid.

22. "bliebe ... die adäquate Evidenz bei allem im weitesten Sinne sinnlich Gebbaren, bei allen konkreten Wirklichkeiten nur eine regulative Idee." Tugendhat, *Der Wahrheitsbegriff*, 105.

23. Ströker, "Husserl's Principle," 50.

24. At the end of his article on Husserl's concept of the relation between truth and evidence, Pietersma asks the question "Can what is really evident be false?" (Pietersma, "Husserl's Views," 51). He says, on Husserl's view, the answer must be negative. But what is meant by "really evident" here? Pietersma defines "really evident" as that which "stands up under all the evaluational procedures available to the transcendental subject" (51). But this definition, it seems, can be given an ideal or a real interpretation. If by "really evident" one means that which stands up to all possible evaluational procedures, then "really evident" is that which is given in an act of adequate evidence. But then the "really evident" is thereby converted into an ideal, which all real cases of the evidence can only approximate. For any real case of the evident, then, it does not follow that, necessarily, if p is evident, then p is true.

Husserl also speaks of cases of genuine evidence (*LI* II, 769 / *H* XIX 2, B2 127). Here he has in mind cases where the evidence in question is not illusory or deceptive. But that can only mean that, as a matter of definition, for any proposition p, p is evident = df p is evident and p is true. It follows quite trivially, then, that if p is genuinely evident, then p is true, since the consequent is built into the definition of the antecedent. The concept of genuine evidence can be of little use from the internal standpoint of the cognitive subject, however, since one can only tell whether p is true, and hence whether the corresponding evidence is genuine, on the basis of evidence. Cf. Christopher Prendergast, "Phenomenology and the Problem of Foundations: A Critique of Edmund Husserl's Theory of Science" (PhD diss., Southern Illinois University, 1979), 114; and David Michael Levin, *Reason and Evidence in Husserl's Phenomenology* (Evanston, IL: Northwestern University Press, 1970), 46–47.

25. Edward G. Ballard, "Objectivity and Rationality in Husserl's Philosophy," part 5 in *Philosophy at the Crossroads*, ed. Edward G. Ballard (Baton Rouge: Louisiana State University Press, 1971), 212.

26. Ströker, "Husserl's Principle," 115

27. Thomas Reid, *An Inquiry into the Human Mind on the Principles of Common Sense*, ed. Derek R. Brookes (University Park: Pennsylvania State University Press, 1997), 32.

28. Some twenty-five years after the publication of the *Logical Investigations*, Husserl makes the same point regarding the ultimacy of evidence in the manuscript published as Beilage VIII in *Husserliana* VIII. Here he uses the term *"Erschauung"* to cover the direct intuitive apprehension of empirical and ideal states of affairs. "Gäbe es nichts dergleichen wie echte Erschauungen, deren Echtheit wir selbst erfassen, uns ihrer—und wieder in Echtheit—erschauend versichern könnten, so wäre alles Erkenntnisstreben sinnlos. Warum strebte ich über meine 'blinden' Meinungen hinaus zu entsprechenden Erschauungen, warum glaubte ich, dieser Normierung zu bedürfen, wenn nicht in der Überzeugung, daß der Weg der Erfahrung und Einsicht Weg zur Neugestaltung meiner Überzeugungen im Sinne der Endgültigkeit wäre?" (*H* VIII, 365). "Wenn aber Einsicht, Erschauung jeder Art immer wieder Einsicht sozusagen auf Kündigung wäre, wenn jede schließlich doch modalisierbar wäre, jedes in ihr temporär als gewiß-seiend Erschaute hintennach doch durchstreichbar wäre, wenn ich keine Erschauung von einer besonderen Art haben könnte [als Einsicht] in ein [un] zerbrechliches Sein, das ich erschaute als ein für allemal unzerbrechlich, als apodiktisch 'absolut' gegeben, als absolut unbezweifelbar, als absolute Norm für alle entsprechend gerichteten Meinungen—so hätte all Rede von an sich gültiger Wahrheit und alles Wahrheitsstreben seinen Sinn verloren" (*H* VIII, 366).

CHAPTER 4: EVIDENCE, RATIONALITY, AND EXISTENCE IN HUSSERL'S PHENOMENOLOGY

1. Dorion Cairns, "An Approach to Phenomenology," in *Philosophical Essays in Memory of Edmund Husserl*, ed. Marvin Faber (Cambridge, MA: Harvard University Press, 1940), 4; my emphasis.

2. In a manuscript from 1931 in the convolute A IV 7, Husserl recognizes this as well: "Aber höchste Besinnung [die der Phänomenologie] gibt schließlich die Naivität auf und gibt andererseits die Möglichkeiten . . . der Klärung des Rechts der Naivitäten, die ursprünglich vorausgesetzt und empirisch leitend waren. Dieses Recht aber hat selbst seine Rationalität" (A IV 7 / 22b).

3. Husserl makes reference to the strong form of rationality as a specifically philosophical epistemic project in a manuscript from convolute A IV 8 (which contains manuscripts up to 1926): "Letzte Selbstverantwortung freilich kann nur eine solche Wissenschaft üben, die ihre Methode in jeder Hinsicht und bis ins Letzte aus Prinzipien rechtfertigen kann; aber das ist bisher nur ein philosophisches Postulat, oder das Postulat, dessen Erfüllung der Wissenschaft die letzte, die 'philosophische' Wissenschaftlichkeit geben würde" (A IV 8 / 31a).

4. René Descartes, "Meditations on First Philosophy," in *The Philosophical Writings of Descartes*, trans. and ed. John Cottingham, Robert Stoothof, and Dugald Murdoch (Cambridge: Cambridge University Press, 1984), 2:12.

5. René Descartes, "Letter to Hyperaspistes, August, 1641," in *Descartes: Philosophical Letters*, trans. and ed. Anthony Kenny (Minneapolis: University of Minnesota Press, 1970), 110.

6. Descartes, *Philosophical Writings*, 2:12; my emphasis.

7. Ibid.

8. Descartes, *Philosophical Writings*, 1:193.
9. Descartes, *Philosophical Writings*, 1:289–90.
10. In manuscript B I 7/2–20 (1926), Husserl sketches out the contours of a finite rationality:

In der Endlichkeit bewegt sich das Handeln, auch das erkennende Handeln. Als das in der Endlichkeit vollzogene greift es doch beständig über die Endlichkeit hinaus, antizipiert die Fernen und zieht sie in die Nähen hinein. Es sorgt vor, es antizipiert das, was künftige Erfahrung erst geben kann, und die Antizipation ist keine Willkür, obschon sie durch Willkür aus schon geweckter, lebendiger Antizipation heraus "geschlossen" werden kann. So, wie sie es da wird, hat sie ihre Notwendigkeit, hat sie ihre Bewährung, Bestätigung vor der wirklichen Erfahrung. Das was in der Erfahrung ist und war, zeichnet nicht nur im Nahhorizont die Zukunft vor und je weiter die Erfahrung aufgeschlossen wird, um so mehr erschließt sich durch sie, was sie in Notwendigkeit ihrem präsumtiven Stile gemäß vorzeichnet. Die Voraussetzung des konstanten Einheitsstils der bisherigen Erfahrung als eines Stils der Einstimmigkeit zeichnet als eine synthetische und in sich bestätigte Erfahrung der Zukunft eine Form vor. (B I 7 / 8b)

11. Gary G. Gutting, "Husserl and Logical Empiricism," *Metaphilosophy* 2, no. 3 (1971): 204.
12. In manuscript A VII 11 / 39–43, under the title "Seiendes, das An-sich der Welt" (probably from 1932), Husserl once again recognizes the epistemic dignity of unscientific knowledge, here called "situational knowledge": "Diese *unwissenschaftliche Erkenntnis* [im Alltag] ist in der Tat Erkenntnis der *Wahrheit* und sie hat den Charakter einer durch Bewährung zu rechtfertigenden, einer Entscheidung ihrer Meinungen nach Wahr und Falsch, zwischen denen es kein Drittes gibt. Die unwissenschaftliche Erkenntnis nennen wir Situationserkenntnis, die Wahrheit Situationswahrheit.... Aber Situationswahrheit ist eben wirkliche Wahrheit, wenn auch nicht wissenschaftliche" (A VII 11 / 41a).
13. In commenting on Husserl's phenomenology as a "science of science," Theodore J. Kisiel makes the same point: "It is apparently not necessary for a working scientist to possess this intrinsic rationality [provided through the phenomenological clarification of the foundations of science]. It is even a fortunate situation that not essential insight but a certain 'scientific instinct' coupled with method is what makes scientific research possible. The typical working scientist is like an artist who creates without being particularly aware of the theory behind his performances. This one-sided brilliance is even to a certain degree necessary for the advance of science. He who goes forward cannot look over his shoulder for long." Kisiel, "Phenomenology as the Science of Science," in *Phenomenology and the Natural Sciences*, ed. Joseph J. Kockelmans and Theodore J. Kisiel (Evanston, IL: Northwestern University Press, 1970), 10.
14. On page 3a of the convolute A IV 3 (1932–33), Husserl recognizes the social aspect, the epistemic interdependence, involved in the acquisition of scientific knowledge. At the same time he speaks of the modern will to epistemic autonomy. Clearly if one were to be seized by the will to autonomous belief, one has at that point decided to become a philosopher engaged in the critical reconstruction of knowledge, not its positive scientific elaboration on the basis of inherited belief:

Zu jeder Wissenschaft gehört der ideell offene unendliche Umkreis der wirklichen und möglichen Sachverständigen—die als solche einstimmig anerkennen, was notwendig anerkennt werden muß, die jedes wirklich wissenschaftliche Ergebnis in sich nacherzeugen können in zusammenstimmender Einsicht. Sachverständigkeit ist durch Lehren und Belehrung prinzipiell für jedermann zu erreichen. Der Student gewinnt sie durch unsere Vorlesungen, unsere Seminarien, unsere Institute und Institutsübungen; mitbringen muß er nur den Willen zur autonomischen Urteils- und Erkenntnisbildung, d.h. den zum Sinn neuzeitlicher Wissenschaft gehörigen Habitus, nichts gelten zu lassen, was nicht ‚rational' durch eigene Einsicht Geltung gewinnt, mag diese Einsicht auch durch Nacherzeugung früherer fremder Einsichten erwachsen und miterwachsen müssen. (A IV 3 / 3a)

15. In a manuscript from 1931 in convolute A IV 7, Husserl speaks of the construction of ideal mathematical correlates for empirical states of affairs, and the subsequent subsumption of the empirical under the mathematical: "Selbstverständlich ist, wenn die allgemeine Methode der Idealisierung der anschaulichen Welt geklärt und so verständlich ist, daß jeder empirisch-typischen Komponente der empirischen Weltstruktur sein entsprechender Ideales zugehört, der empirischen Geraden die reine Gerade, der empirischen Größe die exakte Größe, usw. So macht also auch die 'Subsumption' des Empirisch-Faktischen, dieser empirischen Größe hier unter ihre Idee, kein Problem" (A IV 7 / 29a).

16. Moritz Schlick, "Positivism and Realism," in *The Philosophy of Science*, ed. Richard N. Boyd, Philip Gasper, and J. D. Trout (Cambridge, MA: MIT Press, 1991), 37–55.

17. Hans Wagner, "Husserl's Ambiguous Philosophy of Science," *Southwestern Journal of Philosophy* 5, no. 2 (1974): 175.

CHAPTER 5: PHYSICAL THINGS, IDEALIZED OBJECTS, AND THEORETICAL ENTITIES

1. Henry Pietersma, "Husserl's Views on the Evident and the True," in *Husserl: Expositions and Appraisals*, ed. Frederick A. Elliston and Peter McCormick (Notre Dame, IN: University of Notre Dame Press, 1977), 38.

2. Frederick Suppe, "The Search for Philosophic Understanding of Scientific Theories," in *The Structure of Scientific Theories*, ed. Frederick Suppe (Urbana: University of Illinois Press, 1977), 3–241.

3. Suppe, "Search," 3. Stathis Psillos characterizes the generally received view of instrumentalism as the view that takes theories as "mere instruments for the systematization and prediction of observable phenomena, without attributing reality to the invisible entities they posit." Psillos, *Scientific Realism: How Science Tracks Truth* (London: Routledge, 1999), xvii.

4. Suppe, "Search," 3. Michael Devitt has a similar formulation: "According to instrumentalism, a theory is a partially interpreted formal system. It is a mere computational device or instrument to take us from observation statement to observation statement.... Hence, for the instrumentalist, theoretical statements are not (correspondence-) true or false." Devitt, *Realism and Truth* (Princeton, NJ: Princeton University Press, 1997), 128.

5. Suppe, "Search," 23; see also Mario Bunge, *Philosophy of Physics* (Dordrecht: Reidel, 1973), 2.
6. Stephen Toulmin, *The Philosophy of Science: An Introduction* (New York: Harper and Row, 1953).
7. Gary G. Gutting, "Husserl and Scientific Realism," *Philosophy and Phenomenological Research* 39, no. 1 (September 1978): 44–45.
8. See Alexandre Koyré, *Galileo Studies* (Atlantic Highlands, NJ: Humanities Press, 1978), 203. Koyré contends that because the exact formulation of empirical laws is predicated on the process of idealization, such laws are not about real objects.
9. Hans Wagner, "Husserl's Ambiguous Philosophy of Science," *Southwestern Journal of Philosophy* 5 (1974): 169–85.
10. Bunge, *Philosophy*, 86. In a manuscript from the convolute A IV 8, Husserl writes of the approximate determination of empirical facts with reference to the apriori of pure ideas: "Und hier bedarf es einer eigenen Methodik, um das Faktum dem Apriori der rein objektiven Begriffe sozusagen gefügiger zu machen, da ja das Faktum nicht im eigentlichen Sinn unter diese 'kategorialen' Begriffe zu subsumieren ist und doch auf sie eine rationale, methodisch-apodiktische Beziehung haben muß. Es handelt sich natürlich um die Methode approximativer Bestimmung des Faktums gemäß der reinen Idee" (A IV 8 / 31b). In manuscript B I 7 / 2–20 (1926), he refers to the application of an ontology of nature produced by mathematics as a matter not of subsumption, but of approximation: "Ihr Resultat eine Ontologie der Natur. Das Zweite ist dann Anwendung dieser Ontologie, die nur das Formal-Allgemeine—die bloße reine Naturmathematik—herausgestellt hat. Die Anwendung ist nicht bloße Subsumption, sondern Methode, um diejenige ideale Form zu finden, die das hic et nunc in seinem Zusammenhang fordert. Das aber ist besondere Antizipation. Die Antizipation der besonderen idealen Gestalt geschieht in der Methode der Approximation und bezieht das Individuelle auf die faktische Stufe der Messmethoden und der naturwissenschaftlichen Erfahrungsweite" (B I 7 /15a). Again, in manuscript B I 7 / 21–33 (1930), Husserl speaks of

die Leistung der Substruktion von Ideen, denen sich die Anschauung approximieren kann, die Konzeption des mathematisch wahren Dinges und die Methoden der nicht in der Anschauung sich begrenzenden, sondern von Ideen und Approximationen geleiteten Messung und Zählung, und alles was damit zusammenhängt. Darin liegt die ursprüngliche Stiftung neuer Grundbegriffe, die auf die deskriptiven bezogen, aber in einer eigenen "Ideation" aus ihnen geschöpft sind. Das sind die naturontologischen Grundbegriffe, unter die man nicht einfach Anschauliches oder im anschaulichen Ding Erscheinendes subsumieren kann, da die Subsumption erst die methodisch exakte Bestimmung der "gegebenen" Dinges ist, eine nach einsichtigen Methoden approximative Bestimmung. (B I 7 / 28a)

11. Thus, according to Paul Janssen, "das Verhältnis der Ergebnisse der mathematischen Naturwissenschaften zur empirischen Realitäten beschreibt Husserl durch den Begriff eines Prozesses unendlichen Annäherung und Vervollkommnung an 'Ideen,' die für die Erfahrungswelt selber Charakter des Limes haben." (Husserl describes the relation between the results of the mathematical natural sciences to empirical realities through the concept of a process of infinite approximation and perfecting with respect to "Ideas," which in the world of experience have the character of limits.)

Janssen, "Ontologie, Wissenschaftstheorie und Geschichte im Spätwerk Husserls," in *Perspektiven transzendental-phänomenologischer Forschung*, ed. Ulrich Claesges and Klaus Held (The Hague: Martinus Nijhoff, 1972), 154–55; my translation.

12. Robert Sokolowski, "Exact Science and the World in Which We Live," in *Lebenswelt und Wissenschaft in der Philosophie Edmund Husserls*, ed. Elisabeth Ströker (Frankfurt am Main: Klostermann, 1979), 105.

13. As Aron Gurwitsch put it in his exposition of the *Crisis*, "Under the import of the growing prestige of the developing physics, a prestige stemming from its success, both theoretical and practical, that tissue of ideas which a closer philosophico-historical analysis reveals as a result and product of a special method and, hence, as correlate of specific mental operations, has come to be considered, by scientists and educated layman alike, as reality, as 'nature as it truly and objectively is' to the total disregard of the *Lebenswelt*." Gurwitsch, "The Last Work of Edmund Husserl," in *Studies in Phenomenology and Psychology* (Evanston, IL: Northwestern University Press, 1966), 411.

14. In a manuscript (written 1910–11) from the convolute D 13 I, Husserl makes a distinction between the appearances of a thing and the true thing, which physics seeks to determine:

Alle Physik gründet auf diesen Unterschieden. Es soll "aus den Erscheinungen das Wahre erkannt werden." Es ist immer angesetzt: Ein Ich, eine erfahrende, wahrnehmende Person und viele wahrnehmende Personen haben ihre Stellung im Raume, in dem Dinge sind, und eine Stellung in der Zeit, in der alle Vorgänge verlaufen. Das erfahrende Subjekt kann von einem und demselben Dinglichen verschiedene "Erscheinungen" haben, verschiedene Erfahrungen, in denen das Dingliche mit den und den Bestimmungen erfahren ist. Aber das Dingliche, das da erfahren ist, genommen mit den erfahrenen Bestimmungen, ist eine bloße "Erscheinung" von dem wahren Dinglichen (mit den wahren Vorkommnissen), und zwar so, dass man auch durch Vergleichung der Erscheinungen das Wahre herausfinden kann oder es erklären, dass ein so und so zu den wahren Dingen orientiertes Subjekt (ein normales) die und die Erscheinungen haben muss, die sich also aus dem Wahren, dem Sein des wahren Dinges, in Orientierung zu dem Subjekt erklären. (D 13 I / 114a)

In a manuscript (written probably 1918) from convolute D 13 II, properties independent of the perceiving subject are identified as objective in the physical sense: "Der Physiker nimmt alles Qualitative als bloß subjektiv, d.h. er sagt: Was daran zu den Sachen gehört unabhängig von der besonderen Leiblichkeit und psychischen Art der Erfahrenden und überhaupt von der 'zufälligen' . . . das ist das 'Objektive,' das Physikalische" (D 13 II / 28b). And in a short manuscript from the convolute A VII 20, written probably in 1930, he states that the true thing for physics exists beyond the relativities of secondary qualities: "Dazu die Bemerkung, daß das Wahre, das hier bestimmt ist, ein jederzeit und jedermann Zugängliches und Identisches ist, das unabhängig bleibt von der Subjektivität der sekundären Qualitäten in ihrer 'zufälligen' Relativität zu der Sinnlichkeit der Erfahrenden" (A VII 20 / 64b).

15. The idea of objectivity as anchored in the underlying identity of the object over against the variability of subject-relative appearances is picked up in another manuscript, written in 1923: "Genauer besehen, ist der Sinn dieses objektiven Daseins der, daß es erfahrbar und erfahrungsmäßig erkennbar ist so, daß es von jedermann als

dasselbe identifiziert werden kann als Substrat derselben Bestimmungen. Und als das soll es jederzeit und für jedermann ausweisbar sein" (*H* XI, 434).

16. In a manuscript (written probably in 1918) from convolute D 13 II, Husserl again emphasizes the importance of the elimination of all subjective elements in the construction of the objective world of physics: "Der Physiker nimmt alles Qualitative als bloß subjektiv, d.h. er sagt: Was daran zu den Sachen gehört unabhängig von der besonderen Leiblichkeit und psychischen Art der Erfahrenden und überhaupt von der 'zufälligen' . . . das ist das 'Objektive,' das Physikalische" (D 13 II / 28b).

17. In a manuscript from convolute A IV 8, Husserl emphasizes the independence of the scientific determination of the world from all sensibility:

> Idee der Wissenschaft. 1) Sätze der Wissenschaft, die für sie unter dem Gegensatz Wahrheit und Falschheit stehen und befähigt sind, diese Prädikate—im Sinn der Wissenschaft—anzunehmen: Objektive Sätze, Sätze im Sinn der "Logik." Sätze, die frei sind von okkasionellem Sinn, die das aussagende Subjekt jederzeit im selben Sinn aussagen könnte, aber auch, im Fall strengster objektiver Wissensschaft, die jedes wirkliche und erdenkliche andere Subjekt in identischen Sinn verstehen bzw. aussagen könnte. Dazu müssen die Sätze nicht nur nicht okkasionell sein, sie dürfen auch keinen Sinngehalt haben, der wie ein bestimmter hyletischer nur faktisch, also zufällig in den Urteilsbereich einer einzelnen Subjekts gehört oder einer besonderen Subjektgemeinschaft. Freilich haben wir dabei "Wissenschaft" in einem besonderen Sinn genommen—den der rein objektiven, vollkommen logifizierten Wissenschaft. (A IV 8 / 23a)

18. In the manuscripts stemming from the period of the *Ideas*, Husserl claims that the object of the physical sciences is also the perceived object. See the manuscript, written in 1910–11, from the convolute D 13 I, where Husserl writes,

> Richtig ist ferner, dass das Objekt der begrifflichen Bestimmung, das wahre Objekt, eben das Objekt ist, das erfahren wird und erfahren werden kann: die Wahrheit richtet sich nach ihrem Erfahrungsgrund. Was ich wissenschaftlich bestimmen will, ist ja der Gegenstand der Erfahrung, und so ist er derselbe; er ist gegebenenfalls erfahren und zugleich Subjekt der logischen Prädikate, die in der Begründung in der Erfahrung evidente Gründe haben; erscheinen tun aber nicht mehrere Objekte, sondern nur eines; und es gibt hier auch nicht mehrere, sondern nur eines, aber eines, das einmal bloß erfahren und das andere Mal gedacht und durch Wahrheit begriffen ist. Das physikalische Objekt ist also nichts neues [Objekt], sondern besagt nur den wahren Begriff vom Erfahrungsobjekte. Dem physikalischen Begriff können wir als dem wahren Objekt ein unbekanntes Objekt unterlegen, da eine höhere Anschauung, etwa ein göttlicher Intellekt, sehen könnte, wie es ist, während wir nur einen mathematischen Begriff haben, der darauf hinweist, und während wir mit unseren Erfahrungserscheinungen einen bloßen geregelten Schein haben, aufgrund dessen wir das wahre Sein indirekt erschließen, ohne über Indizes hinauszukommen für eine uns versagte adäquate Anschauung, —das alles ist Mythologie. (D 13 I / 116a–b)

19. In a short manuscript written in 1910–11 under the title "Die naturwissenschaftliche Begriffsbildung," from the convolute D 13 I, Husserl speaks of the development of physics as an enrichment of our empirical experience of the world:

Die exakten Begriffe und Feststellungen der Physik, sagte ich, ... könnten auch als Indizes für gewisse rein phänomenale Zusammenhänge in der Sphäre der schlichten Erfahrung angesehen werden. Das darf nicht missverstanden werden. Im Laufe der wissenschaftlichen Erfahrung, der absichtlich geordneten, experimentellen und beobachtenden Erfahrung des Naturforschers, gewinnen die Dinge der vorwissenschaftlichen Erfahrung oder der schon wissenschaftlich anderweitig bearbeiteten Erfahrung, immer neue Motivationsbeziehungen, besser gesprochen, sie haben einen reicheren Bestimmungsgehalt, in dem sie sich in universaler empirischer Auffassung darbieten. Jedem neuen Begriff, jedem neuen Naturgesetz entspricht eine Erweiterung der empirischen Auffassung, deren Bereicherung mit der Begründung des Gesetzes zusammenfällt. (D 13 I / 105a)

20. Interestingly, in a short manuscript written in 1910–11 under the title "Die naturwissenschaftliche Begriffsbildung," from the convolute D 13 I, Husserl makes a clear distinction between mechanical properties and theoretical entities, and claims that experience often justifies inferences to the latter:

Es gibt nun Begriffe, die gar nichts weiter sein wollen (zunächst wenigstens) als solche Indices für Erfahrungen: z.B. Gewicht, Beschleunigung etc., elektrische Zustände, magnetische Zustände. Andererseits aber, wie steht es mit Begriffen wie Atom, Molekül, Ion etc.? Auch mit all den supponierten Schwingungen, Schwingungen der Luft, unsichtbaren und direkt nicht beschreibaren und erfahrbaren Bewegungsarten? Ebenso Unterschiede der Stoffe, die auf Unterschiede der Atomlagerungen und molekularen Konstellation zurückgeführt werden.
  Natürlich kann aufgrund der Erfahrung Nichterfahrenes interpoliert werden. Das tun wir beständig und mit dem Recht, das Erfahrung uns selbst hier gibt. Fast beständig ist Fortgang der Erfahrung zugleich Interpolation vorgängiger Erfahrungen nach dem, was sie unbestimmt lassen, und offen zu halten ist das Wesen der dinglichen Erfahrung.
  Die Interpolation ist offenbar gebunden an die Bedingungen möglicher Erfahrung, und sie hat genau so weit Recht, als sie motiviert ist. Darüber kann nur durch Kritik der einzelnen Interpolationbegriffe und inhaltlich entschieden werden.
  Eine besondere Frage ist aber die der "Anschaulichkeit" der verwendeten Begriffe und der "Verständlichkeit" welche durch die Anschaulichkeit vermittelt ist. Die Natur des naiven Menschen ist ein ihm verständlicher Zusammenhang.... Auch der Naturforscher macht sich "Bilder" von der Materie, die das Letztseiende im physikalischen Sinne für ihn ist, Bilder in den Gebieten der verschiedenen Energieformen. Er will sich nicht damit begnügen, eine "unanschauliche" Differenzialgleichung zu besitzen, die ihm den Gang des Geschehens vorzeichnet, sondern [er] will diesen auch anschaulich sich "verbildlichen," wobei dann auch diese Verbildlichung ihren Wert als Instrument der Entdeckung. (D 13 I / 105a–b)

21. And, in fact, Husserl asserts in a manuscript titled "Anschauliche Natur bzw. phänomenale Naturlehre und exakte physikalische Naturlehre" (written probably in 1910–11), from convolute D 13 I, that the physical determinations of things have no meaning apart from their intuitive "translation":

Das ist sicher, daß der Physiker die Dinge intuitiv vor Augen hat und in ihren intuitiven Übergängen, in ihrem intuitiven Verhalten die Motive für seine "exakten" Feststellungen findet, wie umgekehrt daß er seine physikalischen Begriffe und Sätze sich wieder übersetzt in die Anschauung. Er versteht seine Begriffe und Sätze erst, wenn er das Verhalten der anschaulichen Dinge, das sie ausdrücken, in sich intuitiv konstruieren kann. Über diese Konstruktion wird in den Lehrbüchern und ihren Theorien nicht gesprochen. Von dem Maße, aber, in dem der Naturforscher selbst diese Übersetzung vollzogen hat, indem er intuitives Verständnis des Exakten in sich erzeugen kann, hängt wesentlich seine Leistung als Forscher ab. Auf der einen Seite kommt es auf "Denken" an innerhalb der exakten Sphäre, auf 'logische' Arbeit, auf die anderen Seite aber [geht es] darum, in den intuitiven Zusammenhangen Motive für die Aufstellung von exakten Begriffen, von exakten physikalischen Hypothesen zu gewinnen, wie umgekehrt von den exakten Theorien zur Intuition zurückgehen zu können und an ihr ihren wahren Sinn verstehen zu können. Natürlich auch zu technischen Zwecken. Bloße Theorie ist nichts; sie hat nur Bedeutung für die intuitive Dinglichkeit, sie hat nur Bedeutung dadurch, daß sie Index ist für das geregelte Verhalten der intuitiven Gegebenheiten. (D 13 I / 106b)

22. In a manuscript in convolute A IV 3 (1932–33), Husserl speaks of geometry as a regional ontology, but not of the physical world, rather of the ideal world. The geometrical method is "die Schaffung oder Herausstellung der prinzipiellen Struktur dieser idealen Welt, also ihrer reinen Regionen (im Sinn der Reinheit der Idealität) und so weiter der vollen Grundlagen für regionale Wissenschaften, die eben idealontologische sein wollen" (A IV 3 / 23b).

23. Joseph J. Kockelmans, "The Mathematization of Nature in Husserl's Last Publication, *Krisis*," in *Phenomenology and the Natural Sciences*, ed. Joseph J. Kockelmans and Theodore J. Kisiel (Evanston, IL: Northwestern University press, 1970), 56.

24. Sokolowski, "Exact Science," 92–95.

25. Frederick Suppe, "What's Wrong with the Received View on the Structure of Scientific Theories?" *Philosophy of Science* 39, no. 1 (1972): 10.

26. Ibid.

27. Ibid.

28. Ibid., 13.

29. Ibid., 10.

30. Nancy Cartwright, *How the Laws of Physics Lie* (Oxford: Clarendon Press, 1983). Then later, with changes, in Cartwright, *The Dappled World: A Study of the Boundaries of Science* (Cambridge: Cambridge University Press, 1999).

31. Cartwright, *How the Laws*, 4 and 17.

32. Ibid., 129; see also 131.

33. Ibid., 3.

34. Cartwright, *Dappled World*, 83–89. Cartwright calls this "Galilean idealization." Models can serves as blueprints for the experimental construction of "nomological machines," which bring empirical phenomena close to the regularities specified by a scientific law.

35. Cartwright, *How the Laws*, 162.

36. Cartwright, *Dappled World*, 19 and 104; see also Cartwright, *How the Laws*, 19.

37. Cartwright, *How the Laws*, 160.

38. Ibid., 6.

39. Cartwright, *Dappled World*, 37 and 47. If the laws of the physical sciences do hold, it is only of situations we construct according to their dictates.

40. Nancy Cartwright, "The Reality of Causes in a World of Instrumental Laws," in *The Philosophy of Science*, ed. Richard N. Boyd, Philip Gasper, and J. D. Trout (Cambridge, MA: MIT Press, 1991), 382.

41. Galileo Galilei, *Two New Sciences*, trans. Stillman Drake (Madison: University of Wisconsin Press, 1974).

42. Ibid., 72.

43. Ibid., 76.

44. Ibid.

45. Ernst Mach, *The Science of Mechanics: A Critical and Historical Account of Its Development* (LaSalle: Open Court, 1960), 168–69.

46. See especially Koyré, *Galileo Studies*.

47. Cartwright, *Dappled World*, 189.

48. In commenting on the philosophical context of Galileo's work, Aron Gurwitsch states that the view that mathematical knowledge represents the ideal and norm of "true knowledge," "was perhaps the most fundamental presupposition of that metaphysics [of the sixteenth and seventeenth century].... Referred to this standard, the perceptual world as it is familiar in everyday experience came to be considered a mere subjective appearance concealing, or, at the most, pointing to an underlying 'true' reality to be conceived as a mathematical manifold." Gurwitsch, "The Problem of Existence in Constitutive Phenomenology," in *Studies in Phenomenology and Psychology* (Evanston, IL: Northwestern University Press, 1966), 120. "In this way," Kockelmans points out in his essay on the mathematicization of nature, "to an ever-growing degree, 'the' world becomes an artificial world projected by the sciences." Kockelmans, "Mathematization," 48.

49. "In den objectiven-mathematischen Weltwissenchaften," Paul Janssen writes in his article on the philosophy of science in Husserl's *Crisis*, "geschieht nach Husserl folgendes: Sie versuchen in ihren Erkenntnis prozessen das real-zeitlich Seinde mit den Möglichkeiten und Mitteln der 'Idealwissenschaften' zu erfassen, deren Gebilde ontologisch einen ganzlich anderen Status haben." (The objective-mathematical sciences proceed, according to Husserl, in the following manner: They seek in their knowing to grasp the processes of real-temporal existence by means of the possibilities and means of the "ideal sciences," whose formations have an ontological altogether different status.) To this basic procedure Husserl has no objection. But, "solange diese Wissenschaften glauben, auf diesem Weg an ein endgültiges Ziel gelangen und das Sein der Welt selber erfasen zu können, sind sie über ihr eigenes Wesen in unklaren. Solange sie das angestrebte objectiv exakte 'Sein' als Maßstab betrachten hinsichtlich dessen, was Sein der Welt besagen kann, verkennen sie das Rangverhältnis zwischen eigenlich sinnlich-realen Sein und 'seinsfeier' Idealität." (As long as these sciences believe that they have in this way arrived at their final goal and are now in a position to determine the being of the world itself, they are unclear about their own essence. As long as they think that the objectively exact "being" they have sought can serve as the measure of what the being of the world can mean, they have lost track of the priority relation between actual empirically real existence and "existence-free" ideality.) Janssen, "Ontologie," 155; my translation.

50. David Carr, Introduction to *The Crisis of the European Sciences and Transcendental Phenomenology* (Evanston, IL: Northwestern University Press, 1970), xix.

51. Alexandre Koyré, "Galileo and Plato," *Journal of the History of Ideas* 4 (1943): 421.
52. Galileo Galilei, "The Assayer," in *Discoveries and Opinions of Galileo*, trans. Stillman Drake (New York: Anchor, 1990), 237–38.
53. Koyré, "Galileo and Plato," 427.
54. Koyré, *Galileo Studies*, 206.
55. Ibid., 203.
56. Ibid.
57. Ibid., 202.
58. Ibid., 203.
59. Ibid., 37.
60. Koyré, "Galileo and Plato," 419.
61. Koyré, *Galileo Studies*, 38.
62. Ibid., 73.
63. See Thomas P. McTighe, "Galileo's 'Platonism': A Reconsideration," in *Galileo: Man of Science*, ed. Ernan McMullin (New York: Basic Books, 1967), 365–87; and Dudley Shapere, "Reason and Experience in Galileo's Thought," in *Galileo: A Philosophical Study* (Chicago: University of Chicago Press, 1974), 126–45.
64. Immanuel Kant, *Critique of Pure Reason*, ed. and trans. Paul Guyer and Allen W. Wood (Cambridge: Cambridge University Press, 1965). I have in mind the section on the Ideal of Pure Reason, 551–59 (A 567 / B 595–A 583 / B 661).
65. Bunge, *Philosophy*, 8.

CHAPTER 6: CONSCIOUSNESS, PERCEPTION, AND EXISTENCE

1. Edward G. Ballard, "Objectivity and Rationality in Husserl's Philosophy," part 5 in *Philosophy at the Crossroads*, ed. Edward G. Ballard (Baton Rouge: Louisiana State University Press, 1971), 179.
2. Ibid., 207.
3. See Harold I. Brown, "Idealism, Empiricism, and Materialism," *New Scholasticism* 47 (1973): 311–23. There Brown defines "metaphysical idealism" as the thesis that "the only things which exist are conscious beings and the objects that these beings are conscious of." Here I will assume that the objects of consciousness are mental representations of some sort.
4. Karl Ameriks, "Husserl's Realism," *Philosophical Review* 86, no. 4 (1977): 502.
5. Ibid.
6. Richard N. Boyd, "The Current Status of Scientific Realism," in *Scientific Realism*, ed. Jarrett Leplin (Berkeley: University of California Press, 1984), 42.
7. Aron Gurwitsch, "The Problem of Existence in Constitutive Phenomenology," in *Studies in Phenomenology and Psychology* (Evanston, IL: Northwestern University Press, 1966), 118.
8. Ibid., 117.
9. Ibid., 119.
10. Here I concur with Ameriks. See Ameriks, "Husserl's Realism," 503.
11. Ameriks claims that "just as existence does not entail experienceability by consciousness, although the assumption of things which are not at all experienceable is absurd, so also for Husserl full harmonious experience does not entail the existence

of things, although it does make absurd the denial of their being." Karl Ameriks, "Husserl's Realism," 507.

12. See Brown, "Idealism," 311; see also Richard H. Holmes, "Is Transcendental Phenomenology Committed to Idealism?" *Monist* 59, no. 1 (1975): 98, where Holmes claims that Husserl's idealism is "metaphysically neutral."

13. McKenna also holds that Husserl's "demonstration" of the transcendentality of consciousness in *Ideas* I is a matter of inference from premises established apart from the transcendental reduction. See William R. McKenna, *Husserl's "Introductions to Phenomenology": Interpretation and Critique* (The Hague: Martinus Nijhoff, 1982), 32.

14. On the other hand, if it is essential to consciousness, in the strict sense, to be intentional, to be about something, then the failure to present objects would at the same time signal the nonexistence of consciousness. Using Husserl's metaphysical language, consciousness would depend upon other things in order to exist. But, of course, the thought experiment shows only that consciousness depends upon the *presentation* of other things in order to exist. Without the presentation of objects there may be a stream of sensations, but no consciousness of something.

15. This statement of the second thesis is translated by Kersten as follows: "The world of transcendent '*res*' is entirely referred to consciousness." This word choice not only weakens the apparent ontological force of the thesis, but also is seriously mistaken. The German verbal phrase Husserl uses to express the relation between the world of physical things and consciousness is "*ist angewiesen auf*," which means "is dependent upon," or "relies entirely upon."

16. Ameriks, "Husserl's Realism," 506.

17. Ibid., 507.

18. Ibid., 504.

19. Wesley Morriston, "Intentionality and the Phenomenological Method: A Critique of Husserl's Transcendental Idealism," *Journal of the British Society for Phenomenology* 7, no. 1 (1976): 36.

20. This "for us," or "for me," qualification comes out clearly in Paul Janssen's statement of what existence comes to within the transcendental regard: "Everything that exists, is—transcendentally considered—synthetically constituted as a unity in the universal life of the ego. The synthetic accomplishments of consciousness, through which the sense and validity of every existence makes itself known *for me*, necessarily bear a reference back to the formal system of universal temporality." Janssen, "Ontologie, Wissenschaftstheorie und Geschichte im Spätwerk Husserls," in *Perspektiven transzendental-phänomenologischer Forschung*, ed. Ulrich Claesges and Klaus Held (The Hague: Martinus Nijhoff, 1972), 146–47; my translation; my emphasis.

21. Herman Philipse, "Transcendental Idealism," in *The Cambridge Companion to Husserl*, ed. Barry Smith and David Woodruff Smith (New York: Cambridge University Press, 1995), 261.

22. Ibid., 258.

23. Ibid., 265.

24. Ibid., 286–87.

25. See David Woodruff Smith and Ronald McIntyre, *Husserl and Intentionality: A Study of Mind, Meaning, and Language* (Dordrecht: Reidel, 1982).

26. Perhaps a conceptually cleaner way of representing this situation is to claim that intentional relations between an act and its object are actually intentional properties

of an act. An intentional act has the property of referring to an object under a certain description. The description is the sense of the act. One would then have no need to posit the existence of a unique species of two-place relations, ones that do not require the existence of both of their relata. On this analysis, all intentional acts have the property of referring to an object whether the object exists or not. If the object exists, then, as Husserl says, the act is not alone, it is related to that object.

27. Roderick M. Chisholm, *Perceiving: A Philosophical Study* (Ithaca, NY: Cornell University Press, 1957), 170.

28. Smith and McIntyre, *Husserl and Intentionality*, 11–13.

29. See *Ideas* I, sections 87, 89, and 150.

30. Smith and McIntyre, *Husserl and Intentionality*, 106.

31. Christopher Prendergast, "Phenomenology and the Problem of Foundations: A Critique of Edmund Husserl's Theory of Science" (PhD diss., Southern Illinois University, 1979), 88.

32. Louis Dupré, "The Concept of Truth in Husserl's *Logical Investigations*," *Philosophy and Phenomenological Research* 24 (1964): 354.

33. Aron Gurwitsch, "Husserl's Theory of the Intentionality of Consciousness in Historical Perspective," in *Phenomenology and Existentialism*, ed. Edward N. Lee and Maurice H. Mandelbaum (Baltimore: Johns Hopkins Press, 1967), 53.

34. Ballard, "Objectivity," 176.

35. Ibid., 177.

36. Theodore De Boer, "The Meaning of Husserl's Idealism in the Light of His Development," in *Analecta Husserliana* 2, ed. Anna-Teresa Tymieniecka (Dordrecht: Reidel, 1972), 329.

37. Ibid.

38. Ibid.

39. In German this passage reads "Der Baum schlechthin . . . ist nichts weniger als dieses Baumwahrgenomenes als solches." Kersten translates this passage as "The *tree simpliciter* . . . is nothing less than this *perceived* tree as perceived." Here he takes the phrase "*nichts weniger als*" to mean, quite literally, "nothing less than," whereas the standard German idiomatic meaning is, in fact, "anything but" or "completely other than." This is an unfortunate error in translation, for it suggests an identity where Husserl wants to posit a difference.

40. Jitendramath N. Mohanty, *The Possibility of Transcendental Philosophy* (The Hague: Martinus Nijhoff, 1985), 16.

41. The best and most accessible treatment of Husserl's doctrine of the noema is to be found in David Woodruff Smith, *Husserl* (London: Routledge, 2007), chapter 6.

42. Edmund Husserl, "Kant and the Idea of Transcendental Phenomenology," trans. Ted E. Klein and William E. Pohl, *Southwestern Journal of Philosophy* 5 (October 1974): 22.

CONCLUSION

1. Christopher Prendergast, "Phenomenology and the Problem of Foundations: A Critique of Edmund Husserl's Theory of Science" (PhD diss., Southern Illinois University, 1979).

2. Cornelius van Peursen, "Creativity and the Method of the Sciences: A Problematic Issue in Husserl's Phenomenology," in *Analecta Husserliana* 14, ed. Anna-Teresa Tymieniecka (Dordrecht: Reidel, 1983); Herbert Marcuse, "On Science and Phenomenology," in *Boston Studies in the Philosophy of Science*, ed. Robert S. Cohen and Marx W. Wartofsky (New York: Humanities Press, 1965), 2:279-90.

3. Elisabeth Ströker, "Husserl's Principle of Evidence: The Significance and Limitations of a Methodological Norm of Phenomenology as a Science," in *The Husserlian Foundations of Science*, ed. Lee Hardy (Lanham, MD: Center for Advanced Research in Phenomenology and University Press of America, 1987), 31–53.

4. Hans Wagner, "Husserl's Ambiguous Philosophy of Science, *Southwestern Journal of Philosophy* 5, no. 2 (Fall 1974): 169–85.

5. Ibid., 175.

6. Ibid., 177.

7. Gary G. Gutting, "Husserl and Scientific Realism," *Philosophy and Phenomenological Research* 39, no. 1 (September 1978): 44.

8. Joseph Kockelmans, "Gurwitsch's Phenomenological Theory of Natural Science," *Research in Phenomenology* 5 (1975): 31.

9. Ernan McMullin, "Compton on the Philosophy of Nature," *Review of Metaphysics* 33, no. 1 (September 1979): 45; my emphasis.

10. Charles W. Harvey, "Husserl and the Problem of Theoretical Entities," *Syntheses* 66 (February 1986): 301; see also Harvey, *Husserl's Phenomenology and the Foundations of Natural Science* (Athens: Ohio University Press, 1989), 259–69.

11. Harvey, "Husserl and the Problem," 303.

12. Ibid., 297–98.

13. Ibid., 304.

14. Ibid., 303.

15. Ibid.

16. In fact, Husserl himself appears to make a distinction between physical determinations and theoretical entities in manuscript D 13 VIII (1910–11), pages 1–3. There he claims that there are some concepts in physical science like acceleration and electrical resistance that are nothing more than indices for experience. But he also claims that there are concepts of such things as atoms, molecules, and ions that cannot be experienced at all. How do things stand with them? he asks. He answers: "Natürlich kann aufgrund der Erfahrung Nichterfahrenes interpoliert werden. Das tun wir beständig und mit dem Recht, das Erfahrung uns hier selbst gibt." (Of course what cannot be experienced can be interpolated on the basis of experience. We do that constantly, and we do it with a justification that experience itself gives to us.) Husserl never explored in much depth and phenomenological detail the experience-based interpolation of theoretical entities; but here he claims that there is such a thing and that it has its own form of justification.

17. Ibid., 304.

18. Don Ihde makes the point that with the most technologically sophisticated forms of instrumentation, the instrument becomes opaque and delivers not the object itself, but a text that calls for informed interpretation. Thus, in the vast majority of experimental situations relevant to theoretical science, instruments establish a hermeneutic, not a perceptual, relation to the object. See Ihde, *Technics and Praxis* (Dordrecht: Reidel, 1979); see also Patrick A. Heelan, "Natural Science as a Hermeneutic

of Instrumentation," *Philosophy of Science* 50 (1983): 181–204; Heelan, however, takes it that all perception is essentially hermeneutical. See Heelan, "Husserl's Later Philosophy of Natural Science," *Philosophy of Science* 54, no. 3 (September 1987): 384. This is why he states that electrons can present themselves to "competent observers" (386). But again, this is only to confuse the distinction between observing and observing that.

19. Bas C. Van Fraasen, *The Scientific Image* (Oxford: Oxford University Press, 1989), 17.

20. Peter Kosso, *Reading the Book of Nature: An Introduction to the Philosophy of Science* (Cambridge: Cambridge University Press, 1992), 95.

21. McMullin, "Compton," 32.

22. Patrick A. Heelan, "Horizon, Objectivity and Reality in the Physical Sciences," *International Philosophical Quarterly* 7 (1967): 375.

23. Ibid., 376.

BIBLIOGRAPHY

Ameriks, Karl. "Husserl's Realism." *Philosophical Review* 86, no. 4 (1977): 498–519.
Angus, Ian. "Jacob Klein's Revision of Husserl's Crisis: A Contribution to the Transcendental History of Reification." *Philosophy Today* 49 (2005): 204–11.
Aristotle. "Posterior Analytics." In *The Complete Works of Aristotle.* Vol. 1, edited by Jonathan Barnes, 114–66. Princeton, NJ: Princeton University Press, 1984.
Bachelard, Suzanne. "Phenomenology and Mathematical Physics." In Kockelmans and Kisiel, *Phenomenology and the Natural Sciences*, 413–25.
———. *A Study of Husserl's Formal and Transcendental Logic.* Evanston, IL: Northwestern University Press, 1968.
Ballard, Edward G., ed. *Philosophy at the Crossroads.* Baton Rouge: Louisiana State University Press, 1971.
Belousek, Darrin W. "Husserl on Scientific Method and Conceptual Change: A Realist Appraisal." *Synthese* 115 (1998): 71–98.
Boehm, Rudolf. "Les sciences exact et l'ideal husserlien d'un savior rigoureux." *Archives de Philosophie* 27, nos. 3–4 (1964): 424–38.
———. "The Meaning of the Phenomenological Critique of Science." In Embree, *Essays in Memory of Aron Gurwitsch*, 375–90.
Boyd, Richard N. "The Current Status of Scientific Realism." In Leplin, *Scientific Realism*, 41–82.
———. "On the Current Status of Scientific Realism." In Boyd, Gasper, and Trout, *The Philosophy of Science*, 195–222.
———. "Realism, Underdetermination, and a Causal Theory of Evidence." *Noûs* 7, no. 1 (March 1973): 1–12.
Boyd, Richard N., Philip Gasper, and J. D. Trout. *The Philosophy of Science.* Cambridge, MA: MIT Press, 1991.
Brainard, Marcus. *Belief and Its Neutralization: Husserl's System of Phenomenology in "Ideas I."* Albany: State University of New York Press, 2002.
Brown, Harold I. "Idealism, Empiricism, and Materialism." *New Scholasticism* 47 (1973): 311–23.
———. *Perception, Theory and Commitment: The New Philosophy of Science.* Chicago: University of Chicago Press, 1977.
Bruzina, Ronald, and Bruce Wilshire, eds. *Phenomenology: Dialogues and Bridges.* Albany: State University of New York Press, 1982.
Buchdahl, Gerd. *Metaphysics and the Philosophy of Science: The Classical Origins; Descartes to Kant.* Cambridge, MA: MIT Press, 1969.

Bunge, Mario. *Philosophy of Physics*. Dordrecht: Reidel, 1973.
Cahoone, Lawrence E. "The Interpretation of Galilean Science: Cassirer Contrasted with Husserl and Heidegger." *Studies in the History and Philosophy of Science* 17, no. 1 (1986): 1–21.
Cairns, Dorion. "An Approach to Phenomenology." In Faber, *Philosophical Essays in Memory of Edmund Husserl*, 3–18
Carnap, Rudolf. "The Methodological Character of Theoretical Concepts." In *The Foundations of Science and the Concepts of Psychology and Psychoanalysis*, edited by Herbert Feigl and Michael Scriven, 38–76. Vol. 1 of *Minnesota Studies in the Philosophy of Science*. Minneapolis: University of Minnesota Press, 1956.
Carr, David. "Crisis and Reflection: An Essay on Husserl's *Crisis of the European Sciences*, by James Dodd." *Graduate Faculty Philosophy Journal* 27, no. 1 (2006): 195–205.
Cartwright, Nancy. *The Dappled World: A Study of the Boundaries of Science*. Cambridge: Cambridge University Press, 1999.
———. *How the Laws of Physics Lie*. Oxford: Clarendon Press, 1983.
———. "The Reality of Causes in a World of Instrumental Laws." In Boyd, Gasper, and Trout, *The Philosophy of Science*, 379–86.
Casey, Timothy. "Medieval Technology and the Husserlian Critique of Galilean Science." *American Catholic Philosophical Quarterly* 70 (1996): 219–27.
Cataldo, Peter J. "Husserl on Galileo's Intentionality." *Thomist* 51, no. 4 (1987): 680–98.
Cavaillès, Jean. "On Logic and the Theory of Science." In Kockelmans and Kisiel, *Phenomenology and the Natural Sciences*, 353–409.
Chisholm, Roderick M. *Perceiving: A Philosophical Study*. Ithaca, NY: Cornell University Press, 1957.
Cho, Kyung Kah, ed. *Philosophy and Science in Phenomenological Perspective*. The Hague: Martinus Nijhoff, 1984.
Churchland, Paul M., and Clifford A. Hooker, eds. *Images of Science*. Chicago: University of Chicago Press, 1985.
Claesges, Ulrich, and Klaus Held, eds. *Perspektiven transzendental-phänomenologischer Forschung*. The Hague: Martinus Nijhoff, 1972.
Cohen, Robert S., and Marx W. Wartofsky, eds. *Boston Studies in the Philosophy of Science*. Vol. 2. New York: Humanities Press, 1965.
Compton, John J. "Natural Science and the Experience of Nature." In *Phenomenology in America: Studies in the Philosophy of Experience*, edited by James M. Edie, 80–95. Chicago: Quadrangle Books, 1967.
———. "Reinventing the Philosophy of Nature." *Review of Metaphysics* 33, no. 1 (1979): 3–28.
———. "Some Contributions of Existential Phenomenology to the Philosophy of Natural Science." *American Philosophical Quarterly* 25, no. 2 (1988): 99–112.
De Boer, Theodore. *The Development of Husserl's Thought*. The Hague: Martinus Nijhoff, 1978.
———. "The Meaning of Husserl's Idealism in the Light of His Development." In Tymieniecka, *Analecta Husserliana* 2:322–32.
De Groot, Jean. "A Husserlian Perspective on Empirical Mathematics in Aristotle." *Proceedings of the American Catholic Philosophical Association* 80 (2006): 91–99.

Derrida, Jacques. "The 'World' of the Enlightenment to Come (Exception, Calculation, Sovereignty)." *Research in Phenomenology* 33 (2003): 9–52.
Descartes, René. *Philosophical Letters*. Translated and edited by Anthony Kenny. Minneapolis: University of Minnesota Press, 1970.
———. *The Philosophical Writings of Descartes*. Vols. 1–2. Translated and edited by John Cottingham, Robert Stoothoff, and Dugald Murdoch. Cambridge: Cambridge University Press, 1985.
Detmer, David. "Habermas and Husserl on Positivism and the Philosophy of Science." In *Perspectives on Habermas*, edited by Lewis E. Hahn, 515–30. Chicago: Open Court, 2000.
Devitt, Michael. *Realism and Truth*. Princeton, NJ: Princeton University Press, 1997.
Dijksterhuis, Eduard J. *The Mechanization of the World Picture*. Oxford: Oxford University Press, 1961.
Dreyfus, Hubert L., ed. *Husserl, Intentionality, and Cognitive Science*. Cambridge, MA: MIT Press, 1982.
Drummond, John J. "Indirect Mathematization in the Physical Sciences." In Hardy and Embree, *Phenomenology of Natural Science*, 71–92.
Dupré, Louis. "The Concept of Truth in Husserl's *Logical Investigations*." *Philosophy and Phenomenological Research* 24 (1964): 345–54.
Düsing, Klaus. "Das Problem der Denkökonomie bei Husserl und Mach." In Claesges and Held, *Perspektiven transzendental-phänomenologischer Forschung*, 225–55.
Elliston, Frederick A., and Peter McCormick, eds. *Husserl: Expositions and Appraisals*. Notre Dame, IN: University of Notre Dame Press, 1977.
Embree, Lester E., ed. *Essays in Memory of Aron Gurwitsch*. Washington, DC: Center for Advanced Research in Phenomenology and University Press of America, 1983.
———, ed. *Life-World and Consciousness: Essays for Aron Gurwitsch*. Evanston, IL: Northwestern University Press, 1972.
Farber, Martin, ed. *Philosophical Essays in Memory of Edmund Husserl*. Cambridge, MA: Harvard University Press, 1970.
Feist, Richard, ed. *Husserl and the Sciences: Selected Perspectives*. Ottawa: University of Ottawa Press, 2004.
———. "Husserl and Weyl: Phenomenology, Mathematics, and Physics." In Feist, *Husserl and the Sciences*, 153–72.
———. "Weyl's Appropriation of Husserl's and Poincaré's Thought." *Synthese* 132, no. 3 (2002): 273–301.
Fisette, Denis, ed. *Husserl's Logical Investigations Reconsidered*. Dordrecht: Kluwer, 2003.
Føllesdal, Dagfinn. "Husserl's Notion of Noema." *Journal of Philosophy* 66, no. 20 (1969): 680–87.
French, Peter A., Theodore E. Uehling Jr., and Howard K. Wettstein, eds. *Midwest Studies in Philosophy*. Vol. 5. Minneapolis: University of Minnesota Press, 1980.
French, Steven. "A Phenomenological Solution to the Measurement Problem? Husserl and the Foundations of Quantum Mechanics." *Studies in History and Philosophy of Modern Physics* 33 (2002): 467–91.
Funke, Gerhard. "Husserl's Phenomenology as the Foundational Science." *Southwestern Journal of Philosophy* 5 (1974): 187–201.

Gadamer, Hans Georg. "The Science of the Life-World." In Tymieniecka, *Analecta Husserliana* 2:173–85.
Galilei, Galileo. *Dialogue Concerning the Two Chief World Systems*. Translated by Stillman Drake. Berkeley: University of California Press, 1967.
———. *Discoveries and Opinions of Galileo*. Translated by Stillman Drake. Garden City, NY: Doubleday, 1957.
———. *Two New Sciences*. Translated by Stillman Drake. Madison: University of Wisconsin Press, 1974.
Gallagher, Shaun, and Dan Zahavi. *The Phenomenological Mind*. London: Routledge, 2008.
Garrison, James W. "Husserl, Galileo, and the Processes of Idealization." *Syntheses* 66 (1986): 329–38.
Gaukroger, Stephen. *Explanatory Structures: A Study of Concepts of Explanation in Early Physics and Philosophy*. Atlantic Highlands, NJ: Humanities Press, 1978.
Godfrey-Smith, Peter. *Theory and Reality: An Introduction to the Philosophy of Science*. Chicago: University of Chicago Press, 2003.
Goldman, Alvin I. "The Internalist Conception of Justification." In French, Uehling, and Wettstein, *Midwest Studies in Philosophy*, 27–51.
Grieder, Alfons. "Geometry and the Life-World in Husserl's Later Philosophy." *Journal of the British Society for Phenomenology* 8 (1977): 119–22..
Gurwitsch, Aron. "Comment on the Paper by H. Marcuse." In Cohen and Wartofsky, *Boston Studies in the Philosophy of Science*, 2:291–306.
———. "Husserl's Theory of the Intentionality of Consciousness in Historical Perspective." In Lee and Mandelbaum, *Phenomenology and Existentialism*, 25–57.
———. "The Last Work of Edmund Husserl." In *Studies in Phenomenology and Psychology*, 397–447.
———. *Phenomenology and the Theory of Science*. Edited by Lester E. Embree. Evanston, IL: Northwestern University Press, 1974.
———. "The Problem of Existence in Constitutive Phenomenology." In *Studies in Phenomenology and Psychology*, 116–23.
———. *Studies in Phenomenology and Psychology*. Evanston, IL: Northwestern University Press, 1966.
Gutting, Gary G., ed. *Continental Philosophy of Science*. Malden, MA: Blackwell, 2005.
———. "Continental Philosophy of Science." In Suppe and Asquith, *Current Research in Philosophy of Science*, 94–117.
———. "Husserl and Logical Empiricism." *Metaphilosophy* 2, no. 3 (1971): 197–226.
———. "Husserl and Scientific Realism." *Philosophy and Phenomenological Research* 39, no. 1 (September 1978): 42–56.
Hardy, Lee, ed. *Husserlian Foundations of Science*. Lanham, MD: Center for Advanced Research in Phenomenology and University Press of America, 1987.
———. "The Idea of Science in Husserl and the Tradition." In Hardy and Embree, *Phenomenology of Natural Science*, 1–27.
Hardy, Lee, and Lester E. Embree, eds. *Phenomenology of Natural Science*. Dordrecht: Kluwer, 1992.
Harman, Gilbert H. "The Inference to the Best Explanation." *Philosophical Review* 74, no. 1 (1965): 88–95.

Harré, Rom. "An Interpretation of the Philosophy of Niels Bohr in the Light of the Philosophies of Kant and Husserl." *Nordic Journal of Philosophy* 5, no. 2 (2004): 5–13.
Hartmann, Klaus. "Abstraction and Existence in Husserl's Phenomenological Reduction." *Journal of the British Society for Phenomenology* 2, no. 1 (1971): 10–18.
Harvey, Charles W. "Husserl and the Problem of Theoretical Entities." *Syntheses* 66 (February 1986): 291–309.
———. *Husserl's Phenomenology and the Foundations of Natural Science*. Athens: Ohio University Press, 1989.
Harvey, Charles W., and Jim D. Shelton. "Husserl's Phenomenology and the Ontology of the Natural Sciences." In Hardy and Embree, *Phenomenology of Natural Science*, 119–33.
Hauser, Kai. "Lotze and Husserl." *Archiv für Geschichte for Philosophie* 85, no. 2 (2003): 152–78.
Heelan, Patrick A. "Continental Philosophy and the Philosophy of Science." In Suppe and Asquith, *Current Research in Philosophy of Science*, 84–93.
———. "Galileo, Luther, and the Hermeneutics of Natural Science." In *The Question of Hermeneutics: Essays in Honor of Joseph J. Kockelmans*, edited by Timothy J. Stapleton, 363–75.Dordrecht: Kluwer, 1994.
———. "Horizon, Objectivity and Reality in the Physical Sciences." *International Philosophical Quarterly* 7 (1967): 375–412.
———. "Husserl's Later Philosophy of Natural Science." *Philosophy of Science* 54, no. 3 (September 1987): 368–90.
———. "Natural Science as a Hermeneutic of Instrumentation." *Philosophy of Science* 50 (1983): 181–204.
———. "Phenomenology and the Philosophy of the Natural Sciences." In *Analecta Husserliana* 80, edited by Anna-Teresa Tymieniecka, 631–41. Dordrecht: Kluwer, 2002.
———. "Toward a Hermeneutic of Natural Science." *Journal of the British Society for Phenomenology* 3 (1972): 252–60.
Heffner, John. "Husserl's Critique of Traditional Empiricism." *Journal of the British Society for Phenomenology* 5 (1974): 159–62.
Hein, K. F. "Husserl's Criterion of Truth." *Journal of Critical Analysis* 3 (1971): 125–36.
Hemmendinger, David. "Husserl's Concepts of Evidence and Science." *Monist* 59, no. 1 (1975): 81–97.
Hempel, Carl G. "On the 'Standard Conception' of Scientific Theories." In *Analyses of Theories and Methods of Physics and Psychology*, edited by Michael Radner and Stephen Winokur, 142–63. Vol. 4 of *Minnesota Studies in the Philosophy of Science*. Minneapolis: University of Minnesota Press, 1970.
———. *Philosophy of Natural Science*. Englewood Cliffs, NJ: Prentice-Hall, 1966.
Hindess, Barry. "Transcendentalism and History: The Problem of the History of Philosophy and the Sciences in the Later Philosophy of Husserl." *Economy and Society* 2, no. 3 (1973): 309–42.
Holmes, Richard H. "Is Transcendental Phenomenology Committed to Idealism?" *Monist* 59, no. 1 (1975): 98–114.
Howell, Russell W., and W. James Bradley, eds. *Mathematics in a Postmodern Age: A Christian Perspective*. Grand Rapids: Eerdmans, 2001.

Hume, David. *An Enquiry Concerning Human Understanding*. Edited by Eric Steinberg. Indianapolis: Hackett, 1977.
Husserl, Edmund. *Cartesian Meditations*. Translated by Dorion Cairns. The Hague: Martinus Nijhoff, 1969. Originally published as *Cartesianische Meditationen und Pariser Vorträge*. Vol. I of *Husserliana*, edited by Stephan Strasser (The Hague: Martinus Nijhoff, 1950).
——. *The Crisis of European Sciences and Transcendental Phenomenology: An Introduction to Phenomenological Philosophy*. Translated by David Carr. Evanston, IL: Northwestern University Press, 1970. Originally published as *Die Krisis der europäischen Wissenschaften und die transzendentalen Phänomenologie: Eine Einleitung in die phänomenologische Philosophie*. Vol. VI of *Husserliana*, edited by Walter Biemel (The Hague: Martinus Nijhoff, 1954).
——. "Die Frage nach dem Ursprung der Geometrie als intentional-historisches Problem." *Revue Internationale de Philosophie* 1, no. 2 (1938–39): 203–25.
——. *Erste Philosophie*. Vol. VII and VIII of *Husserliana*, edited by Rudolf Boehm. The Hague: Martinus Nijhoff, 1956.
——. *Experience and Judgment*. Translated by James S. Churchill and Karl Ameriks. Evanston, IL: Northwestern University Press, 1973. Originally published as *Erfahrung und Urteil: Untersuchungen zur Genealogie der Logik*, edited by Ludwig Landgrebe (Hamburg: Claassen and Goverts, 1948).
——. *Formal and Transcendental Logic*. Translated by Dorion Cairns. The Hague: Martinus Nijhoff, 1978. Originally published as *Formale und Transzendentale Logik*. Vol. XVII of *Husserliana*, edited by Paul Janssen (The Hague: Martinus Nijhoff, 1974).
——. *The Idea of Phenomenology*. Translated by Lee Hardy. Dordrecht: Kluwer, 1993. Originally published as *Die Idee der Phänomenologie*: Fünf Vorlesungen. Vol. II of *Husserliana*, edited by Walter Biemel (The Hague: Martinus Nijhoff, 1950).
——. *Ideas Pertaining to a Pure Phenomenology and to a Phenomenological Philosophy*. First Book: *General Introduction to a Pure Phenomenology*. Translated by Fred Kersten. The Hague: Martinus Nijhoff, 1983. Originally published as *Ideen zu einer reinen Phänomenologie und phänomenologische Philosophie. Erste Buch: Allgemeine Einfuhrung in die reine Phänomenologie*. Vol. III, bk. 1 of *Husserliana*, edited by Karl Schuhmann (The Hague: Martinus Nijhoff, 1976).
——. *Ideas Pertaining to a Pure Phenomenology and to a Phenomenological Philosophy*. Second Book: *Studies in the Phenomenology of Constitution*. Translated by R. Rojcewicz and Andre Schuwer. Dordrecht: Kluwer, 1989. Originally published as *Ideen zu einer reinen Phänomenologie und phänomenologische Philosophie. Zweites Buch: Phänomenologische Untersuchungen zur Konstitution*. Vol. IV of *Husserliana*, edited by Marly Biemel (The Hague: Martinus Nijhoff, 1952).
——. *Ideas Pertaining to a Pure Phenomenology and to a Phenomenological Philosophy*. Third Book: *Phenomenology and the Foundation of the Sciences*. Translated by Ted E. Klein and William E. Pohl. The Hague: Martinus Nijhoff, 1980. Originally published as *Ideen zu einer reinen Phänomenologie und phänomenologische Philosophie. Drittes Buch: Die Phänomenologie und*

die Fundamente der Wissenschaften. Vol. V of *Husserliana*, edited by Marly Biemel (The Hague: Martinus Nijhoff, 1952).

———. "Kant and the Idea of Transcendental Phenomenology." Translated by Ted E. Klein and William E. Pohl. *Southwestern Journal of Philosophy* 5 (October 1974): 9–56.

———. *Logical Investigations*. Vol. I. Translated by J. N. Findlay. London: Routledge and Kegan Paul, 1970. Originally published as *Logische Untersuchungen, Erste Band: Prolegomena zur reinen Logik*. Vol. XVIII of *Husserliana*, edited by Elmar Holenstein (The Hague: Martinus Nijhoff, 1975); and *Logische Untersuchungen, Zweiter Band, Erster Teil*. Vol. XIX, bk. 1 of *Husserliana*, edited by Ursula Panzer (The Hague: Martinus Nijhoff, 1984).

———. *Logical Investigations*. Vol. II. Translated by J. N. Findlay. London: Routledge and Kegan Paul, 1970. Originally published as *Logische Untersuchungen, Zweiter Band, Zweiter Teil*. Vol. XIX, bk. 2 of *Husserliana*, edited by Ursula Panzer (The Hague: Martinus Nijhoff, 1984).

———. "The Method of Clarification." Translated by Ted E. Klein and William E. Pohl. *Southwestern Journal of Philosophy* 5 (October 1974): 57–67.

———. *The Paris Lectures*. Translated by Peter Koestenbaum. The Hague: Martinus Nijhoff, 1964. Originally published as *Cartesianische Meditationen und Pariser Vorträge*. Vol. I of *Husserliana*, edited by Stephan Strasser (The Hague: Martinus Nijhoff, 1950).

———. *Phenomenological Psychology*. Translated by John Scanlon. The Hague: Martinus Nijhoff, 1977. Originally published as *Phänomenologische Psychologie*. Vol. IX of *Husserliana*, edited by Walter Biemel (The Hague: Martinus Nijhoff, 1961).

———. *Philosophie als Strenge Wissenschaft*. Edited by Rudolph Berlinger. Frankfurt am Main: Klostermann, 1965. Originally published as "Philosophie als Strenge Wissenschaft," *Logos* 1 (1910–11): 289–341.

———. "Philosophy as a Strict Science." Translated by Dorion Cairns. Unpublished manuscript. Originally published as "Philosophie als Strenge Wissenschaft," *Logos* 1 (1910–11): 289–341.

———. "Philosophy as a Rigorous Science." Translated by Quentin Lauer. In *Phenomenology and the Crisis of Philosophy*, translated and edited by Quentin Lauer, 71–147. New York: Harper and Row, 1965. Originally published as *Philosophie als Strenge Wissenschaft*, *Logos* 1 (1910–11): 289–341.

———. *The Philosophy of Arithmetic*. Translated by Dallas Willard. Dordrecht: Kluwer, 2003. Originally published as *Philosophie der Arithmetik*. Vol. XII of *Husserliana*, edited by Lothar Eley (The Hague: Martinus Nijhoff, 1970).

———. "Rapport entre la phénoménologie et les sciences." *Les Etudes philosophiques* 4 (1949): 3–7.

———. *Shorter Works*. Edited by Peter McCormick and Frederick A. Elliston. Notre Dame, IN: University of Notre Dame Press, 1981.

Hyder, David J. "Foucault, Cavaillès, and Husserl on the Historical Epistemology of the Sciences." *Perspectives on Science* 11, no. 1 (2003): 107–29.

Hyder, David J., and Hans-Jörg Rheinberger, eds. *Science and the Life-World: Essays on Husserl's "Crisis of European Sciences."* Stanford, CA: Stanford University Press, 2010.

Ihde, Don. *Instrumental Realism: The Interface between Philosophy of Science and Philosophy of Technology*. Bloomington: Indiana University Press, 1991.
———. *Technics and Praxis*. Dordrecht: Reidel, 1979.
Janssen, Paul. "Die Problematik der Rede von der Lebenswelt als Fundament der Wissenschaft." In Ströker, *Lebenswelt und Wissenschaft in der Philosophie Edmund Husserls*, 56–67.
———. "Ontologie, Wissenschaftstheorie und Geschichte im Spätwerk Husserls." In Claesges and Held, *Perspektiven transzendental-phänomenologischer Forschung*, 145–63.
Juha, Himanka. "Husserl's Argumentation for the Pre-Copernican View of the Earth." *Review of Metaphysics* 58, no. 3 (2005): 621–44.
Kant, Immanuel. *Critique of Pure Reason*. Edited and translated by Paul Guyer and Allen W. Wood. Cambridge: Cambridge University Press, 1965.
Kattsoff, Louis O. "The Relation of Science to Philosophy in the Light of Husserl's Thought." In Farber, *Philosophical Essays in Memory of Edmund Husserl*, 203–18.
Kern, Iso. "Die Lebenswelt als Grundlagenproblem der objektiven Wissenschaften und als universales Wahrheits-und Seinsproblem." In Ströker, *Lebenswelt und Wissenschaft in der Philosophie Edmund Husserls*, 68–78.
Kerszberg, Pierre. "Of Exact and Inexact Essences in Modern Physical Science." In Hardy and Embree, *Phenomenology of Natural Science*, 93–118.
Kisiel, Theodore J. "Husserl on the History of Science." In Kockelmans and Kisiel, *Phenomenology and the Natural Sciences*, 68–90.
———. "On the Dimensions of a Phenomenology of Science in Husserl and the Young Dr. Heidegger." *Journal of the British Society for Phenomenology* 4 (October 1973): 217–34.
———. "Phenomenology as the Science of Science." In Kockelmans and Kisiel, *Phenomenology and the Natural Sciences*, 5–44.
Kjosavik, Frode. "Husserl's View of the Life-World and the World of Science." *Revue Internationale de Philosophie* 57 (2003): 193–202.
Klein, Jacob. "Phenomenology and the History of Science." In Farber, *Philosophical Essays in Memory of Edmund Husserl*, 143–63.
Klein, Ted. "'Essences and Experts': Husserl's View of the Foundations of the Sciences." In *Issues in Husserl's "Ideas II,"* edited by Thomas Nenon and Lester E. Embree, 60–87. Dordrecht: Kluwer, 1996.
Kochan, Jeff, and Hans Bernhard Schmid. "Philosophy of Science." In Luft and Overgaard, *The Routledge Companion to Phenomenology*, 461–72.
Kockelmans, Joseph J. "Gurwitsch's Phenomenological Theory of Natural Science." *Research in Phenomenology* 5 (1975): 29–35.
———. "Idealization and Projection in the Empirical Sciences: Husserl vs. Heidegger." *History of Philosophy Quarterly* 6, no. 4 (1989): 365–80.
———. "The Mathematization of Nature in Husserl's Last Publication, *Krisis*." In Kockelmans and Kisiel, *Phenomenology and the Natural Sciences*, 45–67.
———. *Phenomenology and Physical Science: An Introduction to the Philosophy of Physical Science*. Pittsburgh: Duquesne University Press, 1966.
———. "Phenomenology and the Critique of the Scientific Tradition." In Embree, *Essays in Memory of Aron Gurwitsch*, 423–42.

———. "Review of Aron Gurwitsch's *Phenomenology and the Theory of Science.*" *International Studies in Philosophy* 7 (1975): 207–8.
Kockelmans, Joseph J., and Theodore J. Kisiel, eds. *Phenomenology and the Natural Sciences.* Evanston, IL: Northwestern University Press, 1970.
Kosso, Peter. *Reading the Book of Nature: An Introduction to the Philosophy of Science.* Cambridge: Cambridge University Press, 1992.
Koyré, Alexandre. *From the Closed World to the Infinite Universe.* Baltimore: Johns Hopkins University Press, 1957.
———. "Galileo and Plato." *Journal of the History of Ideas* 4 (1943): 400–428.
———. *Galileo Studies.* Atlantic Highlands, NJ: Humanities Press, 1978.
——— *Metaphysics and Measurement: Essays in the Scientific Revolution.* Cambridge, MA: Harvard University Press, 1968.
———. *Newtonian Studies.* Chicago: University of Chicago Press, 1965.
Kuhn, Thomas S. "Koyré and the History of Science." *Encounter* 34 (1970): 67–69.
———. *The Structure of Scientific Revolutions.* Chicago: University of Chicago Press, 1970.
Kvasz, Ladislav. "Galilean Physics in Light of Husserlian Phenomenology." *Philosophia Naturalis* 39, no. 2 (2002): 209–33.
———. "The Mathematisation of Nature and Newtonian Physics." *Philosophia Naturalis* 42, no. 2 (2005): 183–211.
Ladrière, Jean. "Mathematics in a Philosophy of the Sciences." In Kockelmans and Kisiel, *Phenomenology and the Natural Sciences*, 443–65.
Laudan, Larry. "Ernst Mach's Opposition to Atomism." In *Science and Hypothesis*, 202–25. Dordrecht: Reidel, 1981.
———. *Progress and Its Problems: Towards a Theory of Scientific Growth.* Berkeley: University of California Press, 1977.
Lee, Edward N., and Maurice H. Mandelbaum, eds. *Phenomenology and Existentialism.* Baltimore: Johns Hopkins Press, 1967.
Leiss, William. "Husserl and the Mastery of Nature." *Telos* 5 (1970): 82–97.
Leplin, Jarrett, ed. *Scientific Realism.* Berkeley: University of California Press, 1984.
Levin, David Michael. "Husserl's Notion of Self-Evidence." In *Phenomenology and Philosophical Understanding*, edited by Edo Pivčević, 53–77. Cambridge: Cambridge University Press, 1975.
———. *Reason and Evidence in Husserl's Phenomenology.* Evanston, IL: Northwestern University Press, 1970.
Locke, John. *An Essay Concerning Human Understanding.* Oxford: Oxford University Press, 1975.
Luft, Sebastian. "From Being to Givenness and Back: Some Remarks on the Meaning of Transcendental Idealism in Kant and Husserl." *International Journal of Philosophical Studies* 15, no. 3 (2007): 367–94.
Luft, Sebastian, and Søren Overgaard, eds. *The Routledge Companion to Phenomenology.* London: Routledge, 2012.
Mach, Ernst. *The Analysis of Sensations: And the Relation of the Physical to the Psychical.* New York: Dover, 1959.
———. *Knowledge and Error: Sketches on the Psychology of Enquiry.* Dordrecht: Reidel, 1976.
———. *Popular Scientific Lectures.* La Salle: Open Court, 1943.

———. *The Science of Mechanics: A Critical and Historical Account of Its Development*. La Salle: Open Court, 1960.
Majer, Ulrich. "Geometry, Intuition and Experience: From Kant to Husserl." *Erkenntnis* 42, no. 2 (1995): 261–85.
Mall, Ram Adhar. "Phenomenology of Reason." In Claesges and Held, *Perspektiven transzendental-phänomenologischer Forschung*, 129–43.
Marcuse, Herbert. "On Science and Phenomenology." In Cohen and Wartofsky, *Boston Studies in the Philosophy of Science*, 2:279–90.
Margenau, Henry. "Phenomenology and Physics." *Philosophy and Phenomenological Research* 5 (1944): 269–80.
Maxwell, Grover. "The Ontological Status of Theoretical Entities." In *Scientific Explanation, Space, and Time*, edited by Herbert Feigl and Grover Maxwell, 3–27. Vol. 3 of *Minnesota Studies in the Philosophy of Science*. Minneapolis: University of Minnesota Press, 1962.
McCarthy, Thomas A. "Logic, Mathematics and Ontology in Husserl." *Journal of the British Society for Phenomenology* 3 (1972): 158–64.
McGill, V. J. "Evidence in Husserl's Phenomenology." In *Phenomenology: Continuation and Criticism; Essays in Memory of Dorion Cairns*, edited by Frederick Kersten and Richard Zaner, 145–66. The Hague: Martinus Nijhoff, 1973.
McGinn, Colin. "Mach and Husserl." *Journal of the British Society for Phenomenology* 3 (1972): 146–57.
McKenna, William R. *Husserl's "Introductions to Phenomenology": Interpretation and Critique*. The Hague: Martinus Nijhoff, 1982.
McMullin, Ernan. "A Case for Scientific Realism." In Leplin, *Scientific Realism*, 8–40.
———. "Compton on the Philosophy of Nature." *Review of Metaphysics* 33, no. 1 (September 1979): 29–38.
———. "The Conception of Science in Galileo's Work." In *New Perspectives on Galileo*, edited by Robert E. Butts and Joseph C. Pitt, 209–57. Dordrecht: Reidel, 1978.
———, ed. *Galileo: Man of Science*. New York: Basic Books, 1967.
McTighe, Thomas P. "Galileo's 'Platonism': A Reconsideration." In McMullin, *Galileo: Man of Science*, 365–87.
Milkov, Nikolay. "The Formal Theory of Everything: Exploration of Husserl's Theory of Manifolds." In *Analecta Husserliana* 88, edited by Anna-Teresa Tymieniecka, 119–35. Dordrecht: Springer, 2005.
Mohanty, Jitendramath N. *Edmund Husserl's Theory of Meaning*. The Hague: Martinus Nijhoff, 1976.
———. *Husserl and Frege*. Bloomington: University of Indiana Press, 1982.
———. *The Possibility of Transcendental Philosophy*. The Hague: Martinus Nijhoff, 1985.
Moran, Dermot. "Husserl and the Crisis of the European Sciences." In *The Proper Ambition of Science*, edited by M. W. F. Stone and Jonathan Wolff, 122–50. London: Routledge, 2000.
Mormann, Thomas. "Husserl's Philosophy of Science and the Semantic Approach." *Philosophy of Science* 58, no. 1 (1991): 61–83.
Morriston, Wesley. "Intentionality and the Phenomenological Method: A Critique of Husserl's Transcendental Idealism." *Journal of the British Society for Phenomenology* 7, no. 1 (1976): 33–43.

Motroshilova, Nelya. "The Phenomenology of Edmund Husserl and the Natural Sciences—Juxtaposition or Cooperation?" In *Analecta Husserliana* 34, edited by Anna-Teresa Tymieniecka, 139–49. Dordrecht: Kluwer, 1991.
Norris, Christopher. "Structure and Genesis in Scientific Theory: Husserl, Bachelard, Derrida." *British Journal for the History of Philosophy* 8, no. 1 (2000): 107–39.
———."Theory-Change and the Logic of Enquiry: New Bearings in Philosophy of Science." *Review of Metaphysics* 53 (1999): 21–68.
Null, Gilbert T. "The Role of the Perceptual World in the Husserlian Theory of the Sciences." *Journal of the British Society for Phenomenology* 7, no. 1 (1976): 56–59.
Olafson, Frederick A. "Husserl's Theory of Intentionality in Contemporary Perspective." *Noûs* 9 (1975): 73–83.
O'Neill, John. "Marcuse, Husserl and the Crisis of the Sciences." *Philosophy of the Social Sciences* 18 (1988): 327–42.
———. *Worlds Without Content: Against Formalism*. New York: Routledge, 1992.
Orth, Ernst W., ed. *Die Phänomenologie und die Wissenschaften*. Freiburg im Breisgau: Alber, 1976.
Patočka, Jan. "Edmund Husserl's Philosophy of the Crisis of Science and His Conception of a Phenomenology of the 'Life-World.'" *Husserl Studies* 2 (1985): 129–55.
Patzig, Günther. "Kritische Bemerkungen zu Husserl's Thesen über das Verhältnis von Wahrheit und Evidenz." *Neue Hefte Philosophie* 1 (1973): 12–32. Translated by Jitendranath N. Mohanty as "Husserl on Truth and Evidence." In *Readings on Edmund Husserl's "Logical Investigations,"* edited by Jitendranath N. Mohanty, 179–96 (The Hague: Martinus Nijhoff, 1977).
Philipse, Herman. "Transcendental Idealism." In *The Cambridge Companion to Husserl*, edited by Barry Smith and David Woodruff Smith, 239–322. New York: Cambridge University Press, 1995.
Pietersma, Henry. "Husserl's Views on the Evident and the True." In Elliston and McCormick, *Husserl: Expositions and Appraisals*, 38–53.
———. *Phenomenological Epistemology*. Oxford: Oxford University Press, 2000.
———. "The Problem of Knowledge and Phenomenology." *Philosophy and Phenomenological Research* 50 (1989): 27–47.
Plato. *The Republic*. Translated by G. M. A. Grube and C. D. C. Reeve. Indianapolis: Hackett, 1992.
Popper, Karl. *The Logic of Scientific Discovery*. New York: Harper and Row, 1959.
Prendergast, Christopher. "Phenomenology and the Problem of Foundations: A Critique of Edmund Husserl's Theory of Science." PhD diss., Southern Illinois University, 1979.
Psillos, Stathis. *Scientific Realism: How Science Tracks Truth*. London: Routledge, 1999.
Reeder, Harry P. "Husserl's Phenomenology and Contemporary Science." In *Husserl in Contemporary Context: Prospects and Projects for Phenomenology*, edited by Burt C. Hopkins, 211–34. Dordrecht: Kluwer, 1997.
Reid, Thomas. *An Inquiry into the Human Mind on the Principles of Common Sense*. Edited by Derek R. Brookes. University Park: Pennsylvania State University Press, 1997.
Rizzacasa, Aurelio. "The Epistemology of the Sciences of Nature in Relation to the Teleology of Research in the Thought of the Later Husserl." In Tymieniecka, *Analecta Husserliana* 9:73–84.

Rollinger, Robin D. "Brentano and Husserl." In *The Cambridge Companion to Brentano*, edited by Dale Jacquette, 255–76. Cambridge: Cambridge University Press, 2004.
Rouse, Joseph. "Husserlian Phenomenology and Scientific Realism." *Philosophy of Science* 54, no. 2 (1987): 222–32.
Ryckman, Thomas. *The Reign of Relativity: Philosophy in Physics, 19151925*. Oxford: Oxford University Press, 2005.
Sanchez, Halley D. "Critical Realism and the Scientific Realism Debate." In Hardy and Embree, *Phenomenology of Natural Science*, 157–71.
Sargent, Rose-Mary. "Husserl's *Logical Investigations* and Contemporary Issues in Philosophy of Science. *Journal of the British Society for Phenomenology* 19, no. 2 (1988): 155–64.
Schérer, René. "Sur la philosophie transcendentale et l'objectivité de la connaissance scientifique." *Revue de métaphysique et de morale* 62 (1957): 436–64.
Schlick, Moritz. "Positivism and Realism." In Boyd, Gasper, and Trout, *The Philosophy of Science*, 37–55.
Schuetz, Alfred. "Discussion: Die Phaenomenologie und die Fundamente der Wissenschaften (Ideas III by Edmund Husserl)." *Philosophy and Phenomenological Research* 13 (1953): 506–14.
Schuhmann, Karl. "Husserl and Twardowski." *Poznan Studies in the Philosophy of the Sciences and the Humanities* 28 (1993): 41–58.
———. *Husserl-Chronik: Denk- Und Lebensweg Edmund Husserls*. Vol. I of *Husserliana Dokumente*. The Hague: Martinus Nijhoff, 1977.
Seigfried, Hans. "Scientific Realism and Phenomenology." *Zeitschrift für philosophische Forschung* 34 (1980): 395–404.
Sellars, Wilfrid. *Science, Perception and Reality*. London: Routledge and Kegan Paul, 1963.
Shapere, Dudley. *Galileo: A Philosophical Study*. Chicago: University of Chicago Press, 1974.
Sinha, Debabrata. "The Crisis of Science and Husserl's Phenomenology." *Journal of the Indian Academy of Philosophy* 2 (1963): 29–38.
Sklar, Lawrence. *Theory and Truth: Philosophical Critique within Foundational Science*. Oxford: Oxford University Press, 2000.
Smart, J. J. C. "The Reality of Theoretical Entities." *Australasian Journal of Philosophy* 34, no. 1 (1956): 1–12.
Smith, Barry. "Logic and Formal Ontology." *Manuscrito* 23, no. 2 (2000): 275–323.
Smith, David Woodruff. *Husserl*. New York: Routledge, 2007.
Smith, David Woodruff, and Ronald McIntyre. *Husserl and Intentionality: A Study of Mind, Meaning, and Language*. Dordrecht: Reidel, 1982.
———. "Intentionality via Intensions." *Journal of Philosophy* 68 (September 1971): 541–61.
Soffer, Gail. "Phenomenology and Scientific Realism: Husserl's Critique of Galileo." *Review of Metaphysics* 44 (September 1990): 67–94.
Sokolowski, Robert. "Exact Science and the World in Which We Live." In Ströker, *Lebenswelt und Wissenschaft in der Philosophie Edmund Husserls*, 92–106.
———. "Husserl's Discovery of Philosophical Discourse." *Husserl Studies* 24, no. 3 (2008): 167–75.

———. "Review of Phenomenology and the Theory of Science by Aron Gurwitsch." *Man and World* 2, nos. 1–2 (1978): 207–11.
Son, B. H. *Science and Person: A Study on the Idea of "Philosophy as Rigorous Science" in Kant and Husserl.* Assen: Van Gorcum, 1972.
Sowa, Rochus. "Eidetics and Its Methodology.' In Luft and Overgaard, *The Routledge Companion to Phenomenology*, 254–65.
Stone, Abraham. "The Continental Origins of Verificationism: Natorp, Husserl and Carnap on the Object as Infinitely Determinable X." *Angelaki* 10, no. 1 (2005): 129–43.
Ströker, Elisabeth. "Einleitung zur Zweiten Auflage." In Husserl, *Die Krisis der europaischen Wissenschaften und die transzendentale Phänomenologie*. Hamburg: Meiner, 1982.
———. "Geschichte und Lebenswelt als Sinnesfundament der Wissenschaften in Husserls Spätwerk." In Ströker, *Lebenswelt und Wissenschaft in der Philosophie Edmund Husserls*, 107–23.
———. "Husserl and Philosophy of Science." *Journal of the British Society for Phenomenology* 19, no. 3 (1988): 221–34.
———. *The Husserlian Foundations of Science.* Edited by Lee Hardy. Lanham, MD: Center for Advanced Research in Phenomenology and University Press of America, 1987.
———. "Husserls Evidenzprinzip: Sinn und Grenzen einer Methodischen Norm der Phänomenologie als Wissenschaft." *Zeitschrift für philosophische Forschung* 32, no. 1 (1978): 23. English translation: "Husserl's Principle of Evidence: The Significance and Limitations of a Methodological Norm of Phenomenology as a Science," in Hardy, *The Husserlian Foundations of Science*, 31–53.
———. "Husserl's Idea of Phenomenology as the Foundational Theory of Science." In *Husserlian Foundations of Science*, 1–14.
———, ed. *Lebenswelt und Wissenschaft in der Philosophie Edmund Husserls.* Frankfurt am Main: Klostermann, 1979.
———. "Science and Lifeworld: A Problem of Cultural Change." *Human Studies* 20, no. 3 (1997): 303–14.
Suppe, Frederick. "The Search for Philosophic Understanding of Scientific Theories." In Suppe, *The Structure of Scientific Theories*, 3–241.
———, ed. *The Structure of Scientific Theories.* 2nd ed. Urbana: University of Illinois Press, 1977.
———."Theories and Phenomena." In *Developments in the Methodology of the Social Sciences*, edited by Werner Leinfellner and Eckehart Köhler, 45–91. Dordrecht: Reidel, 1974.
———. "What's Wrong with the Received View on the Structure of Scientific Theories?" *Philosophy of Science* 39, no. 1 (1972): 1–19.
Suppe, Frederick, and Peter D. Asquith, eds. *Current Research in Philosophy of Science.* East Lansing, MI: Philosophy of Science Association, 1979.
Tharakan, Koshy. "Husserl's Notion of Objectivity: A Phenomenological Analysis." *Indian Philosophical Quarterly* 25, no. 2 (1998): 215–25.
Tieszen, Richard. "Free Variation and the Intuition of Geometric Essences: Some Reflections on Phenomenology and Modern Geometry." *Philosophy and Phenomenological Research* 70, no. 1 (2005): 153–73.

———. *Phenomenology, Logic, and the Philosophy of Mathematics.* Cambridge: Cambridge University Press, 2005.
———. "Science as a Triumph of the Human Spirit and Science in Crisis: Husserl and the Fortunes of Reason." In Gutting, *Continental Philosophy of Science*, 93–112.
Toulmin, Stephen. *Foresight and Understanding: An Enquiry into the Aims of Science.* London: Hutchinson, 1961.
———. *The Philosophy of Science: An Introduction.* New York: Harper and Row, 1953.
Tugendhat, Ernst. *Der Wahrheitsbegriff bei Husserl und Heidegger.* Berlin: De Gruyter, 1967.
Tymieniecka, Anna-Teresa, ed. *Analecta Husserliana.* Vol. 2. Dordrecht: Reidel, 1972.
———, ed. *Analecta Husserliana.* Vol. 9. Dordrecht: Reidel, 1979.
Vajda, Mihály. "Lukács' and Husserl's Critique of Science." *Telos* 38 (1978–79): 104–18.
Vallor, Shannon. "The Pregnancy of the Real: A Phenomenological Defense of Experimental Realism." *Inquiry* 52, no. 1 (2009): 1–25.
Van Atten, Markus. "Why Husserl Should Have Been a Strong Revisionist in Mathematics." *Husserl Studies* 18, no. 1 (2002): 1–18.
Van de Pitte, M. M. "Husserl: The Idealist Malgré Lui." *Philosophy and Phenomenological Research* 37 (September 1976): 70–78.
Van Fraassen, Bas C. "On the Extension of Beth's Semantics of Physical Theories." *Philosophy of Science* 37 (1970): 325–39.
———. *The Scientific Image.* Oxford: Oxford University Press, 1980.
Van Peursen, Cornelis. "Creativity and the Method of the Sciences: A Problematic Issue in Husserl's Phenomenology." In *Analecta Husserliana* 14, edited by Anna-Teresa Tymieniecka, 375–85. Dordrecht: Reidel, 1983.
Velmans, Max. "How Experienced Phenomena Relate to Things Themselves: Kant, Husserl, Hoche, and Reflexive Monism." *Phenomenology and the Cognitive Sciences* 6, no. 3 (2007): 411–23.
Videla, Daniel. "On the Narratives of Science: The Critique of Modernity in Husserl and Heidegger." *Human Studies* 17, no. 2 (1994): 189–202.
Wagner, Hans. "Husserl's Ambiguous Philosophy of Science." *Southwestern Journal of Philosophy* 5, no. 2 (1974): 169–85.
Welton, Donn. *The New Husserl: A Critical Reader.* Bloomington: Indiana University Press, 2003.
———. *The Origins of Meaning: A Critical Study of the Thresholds of Husserlian Phenomenology.* The Hague: Martinus Nijhoff, 1983.
Weyl, Hermann. *Space-Time-Matter.* Translated by H. L. Browse. New York: Dover, 1952.
Willard, Dallas. *Logic and the Objectivity of Knowledge: A Study in Husserl's Early Philosophy.* Athens: Ohio University Press, 1984.
Zahavi, Dan. *Husserl's Phenomenology.* Stanford, CA: Stanford University Press, 2003.
Zilsel, Edgar. "Phenomenology and Natural Science." *Philosophy of Science* 8 (1941): 26–32.
Zucker, Francis J. "Phenomenological Evidence and the 'Idea' of Physics." In Bruzina and Wilshire, *Phenomenology: Dialogues and Bridges*, 269–90.

INDEX

abstraction, 3, 42, 132, 133, 153, 154, 160; ideating, 51, 149, 150
Ameriks, Karl, 167, 174
antirealism, 1, 4, 83, 130, 131, 154, 161
appearances, 119, 124, 131, 133, 134, 136–43, 148, 157, 160, 164, 165, 177, 178, 198, 202
approximation, 47, 130, 131, 151, 152, 153, 155, 198, 220nn10–11
Aristotle, 13, 15–17, 19, 22
Arnauld, Antoine, 72
attitude: eidetic, 147; natural, 61, 62, 64, 68, 80, 121, 188, 189, 192, 193, 200; phenomenological, 63, 67, 68, 117; propositional, 139; skeptical, 128

Ballard, Edward, 96, 164, 187, 188
Berkeley, George, 1, 26, 177, 178
Boyd, Richard, 6
Bunge, Mario, 162

Cairns, Dorion, 116
Carr, David, 159
Cartwright, Nancy, 153, 154, 157
Chisholm, Roderick, 184
clarification, 41–44, 51, 55, 61, 69, 70, 71, 72, 96, 180, 218n13
Compton, John, 1
consciousness, 21, 38, 39, 65, 66, 67, 72, 73, 80–84, 86, 90–96, 100, 101, 104–6, 109, 111–15, 117, 123, 137, 150, 160, 164–76, 178–81, 183, 185–93, 196, 199, 201–3, 205, 206, 208, 210n1, 227n14; perceptual, 81, 83, 145, 146, 165, 173, 189; propositional, 23, 24; pure, 63; scientific, 110; transcendental, 43, 67–71, 165, 177, 191

De Boer, Theodore, 43, 188, 189
Descartes, René, 15, 21, 40, 72, 97, 116, 118–20, 158, 182, 186
doubt, 22, 42, 64, 65, 98, 99, 107, 116, 119, 177, 186, 193
Dupré, Louis, 81, 82, 187

empiricism, 164
Enlightenment, 49
epistemology, 63, 64, 82; critical, 63–66, 70, 187; externalist, 215n12; foundationalist, 38; internalist, 85, 215n12
epoché, 45, 65, 176
essence, 51, 58–60, 86, 89, 93, 95, 96, 104, 138, 159, 160, 163, 166, 183, 189, 210n1; of consciousness, 172, 175; exact, 150, 151; inexact, 150; of intention, 89, 103; of knowledge, 65, 66; of material things, 147, 148, 151; of mathematics, 52; of nature, 159; of science, 19, 45, 46, 48, 225n49; of theory, 54, 55; of transcendental subjectivity, 165
evidence, 28, 36–38, 48, 49, 73, 79, 80–83, 85, 86, 89, 91–93, 95–100, 108–10, 112, 115, 117, 118, 123, 199, 215nn13–15, 216n24, 217n28; adequate, 37–39, 73, 94–96, 101, 105, 196; apodictic, 37, 95; empirical, 35; inadequate, 94, 96, 97, 101, 105, 211n13; monothetic, 85, 90; synthetic, 85–87, 89

experiments, 142, 156, 203, 204
explanation, 33, 39, 78; scientific, 31, 32

falsification, 28
Feyerabend, Paul, 31
Fink, Eugen, 71
foundationalism, 13–15, 19, 36–39, 43, 116, 117, 119, 122–24, 195, 196, 210n2
Frege, Gottlob, 45, 190

Galileo, 2, 5, 155–60, 177, 199
geometry, 20, 21, 146–51, 155, 224n22
Gurwitsch, Aron, 187
Gutting, Gary, 1, 121, 130, 198

Hanson, Norwood Russell, 31
Harvey, Charles, 4, 201–4
Heelan, Patrick, 1, 3, 207
Heidegger, Martin, 2
Hilbert, David, 15
Hopkins, Gerard Manley, 154
Hume, David, 26, 119, 182

idealism, 81, 82, 90, 98, 162, 168, 170, 177, 188, 192, 198, 199; metaphysical, 164, 170, 176, 226n3; phenomenological, 179; transcendental, 170, 176, 178, 188
idealization, 3, 4, 36, 37, 124, 130, 131, 133, 149, 150, 151, 153–57, 198, 199, 220n8, 224n34
ideation, 51, 95, 149, 150, 151
imagination, 84, 93, 95
indicative sign, 138, 143, 203, 206, 208
induction, 2, 34, 36, 39, 121, 196
instrumentalism, 1–7, 126, 129–31, 154, 161–64, 198, 202–6, 219nn3–4; provisional, 4, 201–6
intentionality, 38, 68, 69, 71, 83, 165, 176, 180, 184, 227n26
intuition, 14, 22–24, 28, 36, 43, 60, 83, 85, 86, 111, 124, 142, 148–50, 158, 167, 198, 210n3; categorial, 61; empirical, 147, 149; of essences, 20, 28, 36, 59; pure, 148; sensuous, 3, 137, 150

judgment, 14, 18, 19, 38, 44, 49, 50, 63, 67, 70, 71, 86, 89, 90, 92, 96, 110–12, 117, 124, 212n14; analytic, 50; categorical, 88; evident, 49, 88, 92, 215n13; immediate, 14, 18, 117; mediate, 14, 18; scientific, 38, 44, 117, 118
justification, 14, 18, 19, 31, 45, 49, 50, 60, 71, 73, 79, 82, 83, 90, 96, 97, 101, 102, 108, 117, 169–71, 174, 175, 179, 185, 186, 192, 199, 201, 210n3, 229n16

Kant, Immanuel, 161, 193
Kisiel, Theodore, 2
knowledge, 13, 21–26, 34–36, 43, 44, 49, 50, 61–65, 66, 68, 69, 72, 78, 84, 85, 99, 116, 120–22, 124, 126, 133, 152, 155, 158, 159, 207; apodictic, 116; approximate, 131, 152, 155; demonstrative, 16, 23–25; empirical, 161; essence of, 66; exact, 131, 152, 155; habitual, 24, 26; intuitive, 24–26, 42; mediate, 19, 116; objective, 69, 70, 155, 156, 197; philosophical, 116–18, 120, 159; positive, 66; predictive, 132, 158; probable, 26; scientific, 5, 8, 13–17, 19–21, 23, 25, 26, 35, 38, 39, 40, 43, 44, 46, 48, 50, 51, 56–58, 62, 63, 117, 130, 132, 157, 195, 211n4, 212n15; situational, 218n12; theoretical, 55
Kockelmans, Joseph, 70, 151, 199
Kosso, Peter, 6, 206
Koyré, Alexandre, 158–60
Kuhn, Thomas, 31

laws, 5, 7, 9, 29, 30, 32–35, 77, 125, 130, 132, 134, 153, 154, 160, 162, 163, 193, 225n39; empirical, 126, 155, 156; exact, 34, 161, 210n19, 221n13; ideal, 34; inexact, 34; mathematical, 2, 34, 159, 198, 207, 210n19; real, 34
lifeworld, 2, 44, 70, 124, 131–33, 149, 155, 157, 197, 213n6
Locke, John, 13, 21–27, 34, 141, 182
logic, 21, 29, 44, 46–48, 52, 56, 57, 59, 61; formal, 57, 58, 61; pure, 48, 49, 51, 54, 213n6

Mach, Ernst, 1, 156
mathematics, 3, 7, 35, 52–55, 72, 122, 124, 131, 150, 151, 154, 159
McIntyre, Ronald, 180, 185
McMullin, Ernan, 1, 199, 207
metaphysics, 3, 161, 225n48
models, 153, 154
Mohanty, Jitendramath, 190
Morriston, Wesley, 175

naturalism, 133
noema, 103, 104, 106, 185–87, 189, 190–92, 228n41
noesis, 103, 106

objectivity, 43, 70, 72, 135, 136, 155, 221n15, 222n17
objects: empirical, 161; external, 178, 183; geometrical, 146, 147; ideal, 2, 85, 130, 131, 133, 146, 148–50, 155–57, 160–63, 193, 198, 207; intentional, 181–85; internal, 182; mathematical, 160; perceived, 138, 145, 202, 222n18; physical, 131, 136, 143, 151, 172, 173, 177, 178, 201, 203; real, 131, 151, 156, 163, 166, 167, 187, 190, 192, 198, 221n14, 222n18; transcendent, 65, 66, 85, 93, 94, 95, 118, 177, 200
ontology: formal, 57, 58; of lifeworld, 45; material, 45, 59, 60, 147–49, 213n6; regional, 44, 45, 58, 59, 60, 61, 147, 148

Patzig, Günther, 79, 80, 82
perception, 22, 54, 80, 83–85, 91, 95, 139, 141, 142, 155, 163, 164, 166, 168, 169, 177, 182, 189, 191, 199, 200, 203, 205, 206; direct, 139, 140; indirect, 139, 140
Philipse, Herman, 1, 176–78, 186
philosophy, 13–15, 40–43, 54, 73, 103, 115, 116, 120, 150, 207, 213n6, 225n49; Anglo-American, 5, 7, 9, 13, 57, 129, 161; empiricist, 57; logical positivist, 152; modern, 158; natural, 26, 122; of science, 1–9, 13, 27–31, 38, 57, 60, 62, 64, 66, 68, 70, 72, 74, 89, 129, 161, 187, 195, 197, 198, 201, 206;

scientific, 72, 103, 116, 119–21, 133; *Weltanschauung*, 121
physics, 2, 44, 123, 130, 131, 134, 136, 137, 142, 145, 147–49, 152, 155, 158–62, 193, 202, 221nn13–14, 222n16, 222n19; Galilean, 2, 148, 157, 159, 160, 177; mathematical, 2, 3, 8, 124, 125, 135, 148, 149, 152, 155–60; modern, 2, 3, 125, 141, 148, 149, 155, 156, 158, 160, 161, 199
Pietersma, Henry, 82, 129
Plato, 21, 40, 45, 160
Popper, Karl, 28
positivism, 1, 2, 6, 7, 125, 152
possibility: ideal, 35, 90, 91, 92, 93, 108–10, 167, 191, 199, 204, 205; real 92, 93, 167, 191, 204
Prendergast, Christopher, 27, 28, 187, 195
Psillos, Stathis, 6, 77
psychologism, 45, 92

rationality, 8, 24, 57, 99, 102–4, 107–16, 118, 119, 121, 164, 192, 193, 200; finite, 218n10; phenomenological, 116, 117, 200; philosophical, 102, 115, 217n3; scientific, 116, 117, 120, 200, 210n24, 218n13
realism, 4, 6–9, 90, 129, 154, 167, 168, 170, 178, 179, 191; scientific, 77
reduction: eidetic, 149; epistemological, 65; phenomenological, 106, 169, 180, 191; transcendental, 43, 165, 185, 186, 188, 192, 227n13
Reid, Thomas, 99
Rizzacasa, Aurelio, 1
Rouse, Joseph, 1, 4
Rutherford, Ernest, 203

Schlick, Mortiz, 125
science: deductive, 41; descriptive, 33; eidetic, 21, 27, 30, 37–39, 59, 83, 146, 147, 149, 196; empirical, 13, 21, 26–32, 35–37, 39, 58, 59–62, 77, 78, 124, 129, 130, 146, 147, 196, 200, 213n6; exact, 131; mathematical, 151; natural, 34, 46, 123, 134, 148, 159; objective, 62; physical, 2, 3, 13, 60, 77,

science (cont'd.)
  130, 133–37, 139, 142–46, 148, 149,
  151, 152, 155, 156, 161, 164, 168, 191,
  193, 196–99, 201, 202; positive, 39,
  63, 69, 74, 121, 135, 179, 193, 213n6,
  213n10, 214n14; theoretical, 33, 78,
  100, 126, 168, 203, 208
secondary qualities, 136
Sellars, Wilfrid, 28
sensations, 137, 172, 177, 178, 180, 186,
  201, 215n11, 227n14
sense, 66, 71, 96, 97, 104, 111, 133, 137,
  172, 177, 178, 180, 184–86, 189–91,
  201
skepticism, 90, 97, 98, 99, 122
Smith, David Woodruff, 180, 185
Soffer, Gail, 4
Sokolowski, Robert, 151
space, 20, 44, 55, 59, 134, 136, 146–49,
  151, 160, 163, 164, 198
Ströker, Elisabeth, 36, 37, 95, 96, 196
Suppe, Frederick, 5, 6, 152

theoretical entities, 4, 8, 9, 78, 79, 82, 83,
  100, 101, 103, 129–31, 144, 161–68,
  186, 191, 193, 195, 199–201, 203–5,
  207, 210n19, 223n20, 229n16
theories, 5, 7, 9, 28–31, 39, 42, 46, 48,
  49–54, 61, 62, 69, 77, 80, 148, 161,
  164, 196; mathematical, 154, 157, 160;
  objective, 70; phenomenalistic, 178;
  scientific, 4–8, 27, 57, 58, 78, 83, 100,
  101, 126, 129, 130, 152–54, 162–66,
  168, 170, 186, 191–93, 195, 198, 202,
  207, 208, 210n24
thing: material, 147, 148, 151; perceived,
  137, 143, 146; physical, 63, 123, 133,
  134, 136–47, 163–68, 172, 182, 189,
  190, 193, 201–3, 221n14
Toulmin, Stephen, 130
transcendental ground, 44, 45, 62, 63, 69
transcendental subjectivity, 44, 45, 68,
  73, 74, 165, 180
truth, 23, 24, 34, 37, 44, 49–51, 61, 109,
  110, 197, 199, 216n17; absolute, 38; a
  priori, 58, 148; and being, 78, 79,
  87, 90; contingent, 21, 29; eidetic,
  59; and evidence, 82, 85, 89–101,
  216n24; evidence theory of, 8, 79–82,
  91, 100; and existence, 79, 81, 82,
  94; necessary, 15–17, 20, 28, 32, 59;
  self-evident, 16, 19
Tugendhat, Ernst, 92, 95

van Fraassen, Bas, 5, 206
van Peursen, Cornelius 27
verification, 2, 29, 30, 87, 89, 121, 165,
  175

Wagner, Hans, 126, 131, 197
Welton, Donn, 79, 80
Weyl, Hermann, 55
Willard, Dallas, 79, 92
wisdom, 116, 120

Zucker, Francis, 4

www.ingramcontent.com/pod-product-compliance
Lightning Source LLC
Chambersburg PA
CBHW031239290426
44109CB00012B/366